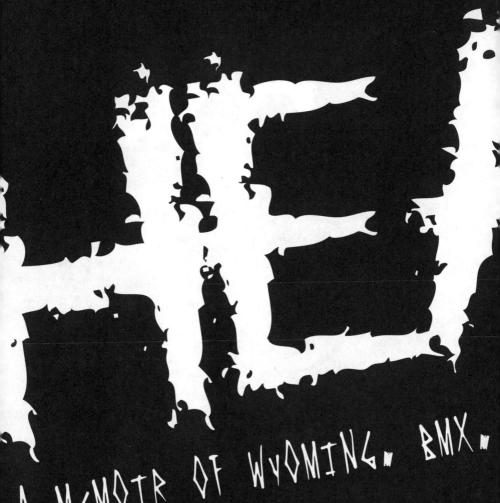

A MEMOIR OF WYOMING. BMX.

...S, AND HEAVY FUCKING MUSIC

J. J. ANSELMI

This and everything else I write is for my mom and sister.

I'VE BEEN GOING THROUGH a process of tattoo removal for the past eight years.

When I was eighteen, I got the signature guitar of Tony Iommi, the guitarist for Black Sabbath, tattooed on the inside of my left wrist, along with the song title and lyric, "Killing Yourself To Live," wrapped around my wrist. I got three more tattoos engraved onto my skin within the next six months: Pantera's emblem, CFH, on my right wrist; a large skull with sharp teeth and bats pushing through it that Metallica used on merch and posters during their *Master Of Puppets* tour, which covered my right forearm; and Black Sabbath's effeminate fallen angel on my right shoulder.

Two years later, I felt like I needed to erase my tattoos. But I also decided to keep the fallen angel.

Every six or seven months, a surgeon cuts elliptical strips of skin from my arms and sutures me back together, slowly cutting away the tattoos and leaving scars in their place. My Pantera tattoo is completely gone, and so is "Killing Yourself To Live." There's only a remnant of Tony Iommi's guitar on my left wrist—a long, crooked white scar cuts through the oddly shaped blob of black ink. An eight-inch-long strip of pearled scar tissue has replaced most of the skull on my right forearm.

*

SUBSIDENCE

I LAST VISITED ROCK SPRINGS, Wyoming during the summer of 2011, when I was twenty-five. A sign for the Outlaw Inn, my dead grandfather's motel, loomed over the interstate. Sandstone cliff faces yawned. After exiting off I-80 West, I passed a green sign with white lettering—Rock Springs; Population: 23,036. Since I'd moved away six years earlier, methane gas in Jonah Field and Pinedale Anticline, both about seventy miles north, motivated over five thousand people to move here.

Wind pushed against my truck, making me veer to the left. A Shell and Phillips 66 sat across the street from each other. Decrepit cars, trucks, and other mechanical equipment cluttered the fenced-in yards next to each building. These gas stations looked exactly the same as they did when I was a child. Even though I no longer lived in Rock Springs, the feeling that I'd never leave rose in my throat. Throughout junior high and high school, this feeling was unremitting.

Half a block down the street, the white outline of an eagle flew above rates for the Renegade Motel. Next door, a gold-painted statue of Buddha sat on a throne, welcoming people into the parking lot of the Sands Cafe, a Chinese-American diner. Passing the restaurant, I thought about the Rock Springs Massacre. In 1885, 150 white railroad workers slaughtered twenty-eight Chinese immigrants, wounded fifteen, and forced several hundred others out of town, because, in part, Chinese workers were willing to work for less than whites.

Driving through downtown, I looked at a white metal arch with red lettering: "Home of Rock Springs Coal." Built in 1929, the arch welcomed people who came into town by train. Later, it was dismantled and left in a field as scrap metal. During the early nineties, right around the time when hydraulic fracturing operations started in Jonah Field, my great uncle, John, decided that the sign should be refurbished and placed downtown.

An 1850 survey party discovered coal in the Rock Springs area. In his account of the expedition, Howard Stansbury recalls finding "a bed of bituminous coal cropping out of the north bluff of the valley, with every indication of it being quite abundant." The party also discovered a creek, later named Bitter Creek because of its foul taste.

Water in the desert and a surfeit of coal motivated Union Pacific to lay train tracks through this area in

1868. From 1875 to 1930, Rock Springs produced more coal than any other town connected to the Union Pacific Railroad. Even so, aside from a meager creek, coal, (and now) methane gas, Trona, and oil, Rock Springs doesn't offer much for humans, a fact made apparent by the types of vegetation that survive here: sagebrush, cedar trees, and prairie grass.

I turned onto a road leading toward Carson Street, where my family's old house sits. Driving up a hill, I watched Rock Springs sprawl behind guardrails, nestled between sandstone cliffs and hills covered with cedars and sagebrush. Buildings and houses glinted like broken glass.

ROCK SPRINGS IS A microcosm of Wyoming, where the per capita suicide rate is consistently one of the highest in the US. I had my first encounter with suicide when I was nine, and my dad's best friend, Freddy Martinez, shot himself with a twelve-gauge shotgun.

As a child, I didn't see beyond the happy-go-lucky character Freddy projected. Wide shoulders on a solid frame of fat and muscle, black hair past the middle of his back, and a thick beard—he seemed like a friendly ogre, which, I'm pretty sure, is exactly how he wanted to present himself.

One afternoon, while a few kindergarten friends and I threw water balloons at each other in my parents' front yard, Freddy pulled into our driveway on a new motorcycle, which he wanted to show my dad. Its black gas tank and mirror-finish chrome tubing shimmered

in the summer sun. I immediately wanted to bombard it
with water balloons.

"Hey, little J. J. Where's big J. J.?"

"Probably in the basement. Can we throw water
balloons at your motorcycle?"

Laughing as he walked toward the front door, Freddy
said, "Go for it, you little weasels."

Of course our water balloons didn't hurt the motorcycle. Still, letting my friends and me do this seemed to
complicate Freddy's desire to show off his powerful new
toy. To me, this memory illustrates something about his
personality that didn't quite fit other characters he inhabited: Freddy genuinely liked to make other people feel good.

He was also a man of extremes. In oil fields near Rock
Springs, Freddy would work for eight or nine months at a
time and then quit. Unemployed for two or three months,
he'd spend his money traveling and partying. Broke, he'd
go back to work for one of the oil companies again. As
long as my dad knew him—about fifteen years—Freddy
repeated this cycle.

Some anecdotes about Freddy from my dad, and
Freddy's first cousin, Thomas, who I worked with when
I was nineteen: drunk and tripping on LSD, Freddy
once broke into an elementary school in Green River,
Wyoming, a town ten miles west of Rock Springs. He ran
up and down the halls, turning lights off and on, until a
neighbor called the cops. While the police looked for him,
Freddy escaped from the school. He walked into a nearby
house and pissed in a coat closet.

Also tripping on LSD, Freddy drove his motorcycle through a gnarly Wyoming blizzard with Thomas, who was much smaller, riding on the back—looking, I imagine, like a drug-crazed baby koala hanging onto Freddy's shoulders—to Salt Lake City from Rock Springs, a 180-mile trip, to see a concert.

When I ask my dad about his favorite concerts, he usually talks about a Journey show he saw with Freddy in the seventies, which involved copious amounts of weed and booze.

Thinking about Freddy, I often picture his dingy yellow trailer, which sat in the corner of a weed-filled lot. One day, when I was seven or eight, Dad picked me up from baseball practice and then stopped at Freddy's place. He told me to wait in the truck, even though I wanted to go inside because Freddy always made me laugh. Pissed that I had to wait outside, I watched a cat hunt grasshoppers, turning to look when loud vehicles drove down the adjacent street. When Dad finally came outside, the right side of his upper lip curled up, and red lines reached from his blue irises. Similar instances happened routinely. I'd heard about weed from D.A.R.E., but I didn't think parents got high.

I remember going into the trailer a few times. Posters and pictures of famous sixties and seventies musicians— one of which, a black-and-white picture of Jimi Hendrix, now hangs in the main room of my rental house—hung on Freddy's walls. Replaying these memories, I think about how Freddy and Dad encouraged each other to inhabit a stoner's caricature.

My dad has smoked pot for over forty years; he started when he was fifteen. When I look at the faded picture of Jimi Hendrix on my wall, I think about getting twisted with Dad during my early twenties, listening to him pound a pair of bongos along with Carlos Santana, Neil Young, or The Rolling Stones while stoned out of his gourd. I think about watching my dad roll joints with one hand.

He often wore shirts from his favorite rock concerts, like Queen and Aerosmith. I can't count the amount of Cheech and Chong-esque stoner clichés I've heard Dad say: "Come on, man, I know you have some grass," overusing "killer" as an adjective, "Right on, man," "It's all good," "Let's catch a buzz," and several others. As a teenager, I reacted to these stoner idioms with anger. Dad's drug use disrupted my narrow view of reality. Now, when I hear him say these phrases, when I see red lines branching across his eyes like cracks in a windshield, I mainly feel worry.

A few years before he died, Freddy contributed to a bizarre rock album. I remember a song called "Kill the Holy Cow." Over a simple drum and bass line, maniacally high, pitch-altered voices sing, "We will kill the holy cow / then make friends with Chairman Mao." Freddy performed backup vocals and played drums for this song and a few others. As I try to remember these sounds (my dad lost the CD), I imagine Freddy and a few other guys getting really, really high, then, in characteristic stoner fashion, recording songs that, if only to themselves, sounded amazing.

Freddy often told my dad, "Jay, you have a beautiful wife and two beautiful kids. You're the luckiest guy I know." Really, I think he was saying, *I'm completely fucked-up, and I don't know how to build another life.* Freddy often augmented his two- and three-month benders with cocaine. Today, I see a man who surrendered to the idea that he was just a party animal.

Dad thinks that a fucked-up relationship Freddy had with a junkie was the main cause of his suicide. As I attempt to construct who I think Freddy was, this only seems like a small part of his hopelessness to me. I think he killed himself because he didn't think he could change.

I find myself wondering about his attraction to destruction, one I've shared. When you feel like you can't build a productive life, destruction can be a way to counter powerlessness. I think Freddy had a sense of the creative aspects of destruction when he decided to kill himself. Instead of examining his personality and trying to dismantle the fucked-up parts, though, he took physical destruction to an extreme.

I clearly remember Dad coming upstairs to my room on the day Freddy shot himself. I put down my Super Nintendo controller when I noticed tears in his eyes—one of only a few times I'd seen Dad cry.

"Freddy died," he said, opening his arms to give me a hug.

"What? How?"

"He shot himself."

Downstairs, I asked my mom why he would do something like that. She said, "Well, baby, I think he was just really unhappy."

At the time, I felt intensely confused.

THE FIRST HIGH SCHOOL in Rock Springs, built in 1916, which became East Junior High when the town built a new high school in the fifties, was demolished recently. I attended seventh, eighth, and ninth grade at East, and it was within the walls of this school that I began to see myself as a rebel.

In seventh and eighth grade I became a nu-metal fanatic, attracted to the anger in bands like Korn and Limp Bizkit. I played baseball and basketball through grade school but lost interest in organized sports during seventh grade. I was also beginning to realize that none of the hot girls thought I was cute.

Inspired by stoner kids, goths, and punks, I experimented with my look. Every day before school, I sculpted my hair into liberty spikes, spending at least an hour in front of my mom's bathroom mirror. I worked a viscous gob of Dep 8 Gel—the strongest hair gel I could find—into my dyed-red hair. I twisted chunks into vertical, three-by-three rows of symmetrical spikes, and then carefully blow-dried each spike. Guys at school often messed up my hair by roughly rubbing my head. Each time, a flurry of gel flakes settled on my black T-shirt, looking like really bad dandruff.

I took drum lessons, wanting to be David Silvera, Korn's drummer, whose tribal beats I loved. Drummers are rare compared to guitarists, especially in junior high. I wore JNCO jeans and black Korn and Limp Bizkit T-shirts my mom bought for me at Hot Topic. Over and over, I scrawled "Korn" on all of my notebooks, emulating the messy font the band uses on album covers and merchandise.

With a few other kids, I started a nu-metal band, Sterile. Each song sounded the same—the guitarist playing pick-rake-driven riffs over my sloppy interpretations of Dave Grohl's drumming on "Smells Like Teen Spirit." We played two or three shows, one of which was our school talent show.

After our one-song set, a group of stoner kids sang a karaoke version of Pink Floyd's "The Wall." During the second or third repetition of "All in all you're just another brick in the wall," the group beckoned kids in the audience to rush the stage, invoking an onstage mosh pit. I followed one of my bandmates through rows of seats. Seeing dismay on teachers' faces, I felt like a true rebel. Onstage, I jumped onto a heap of kids, somewhere under which was a microphone. We screamed along to the chorus. Teachers had a hard time getting this scene under control, ultimately resulting in no more talent shows at East.

A few months afterward, staying with a childhood friend, Tike, in Salt Lake, I decided to get drunk and high, both for the first time. For four or five hours, Tike's sister drove us and a few other kids around Salt Lake in her Honda Civic. Giggling, Tike and I watched two thirteen-year-olds fuck in the backseat, right next to us. Later, back at Tike's house, he told me that his older cousin, who lived in Rock Springs, got high with my dad all the time. I'd found one of Dad's pipes in our basement a few years earlier, but I tried not to think about it. Skateboarding to a donut shop with Tike the next morning, I decided that I'd never get stoned or drunk again.

A year or so after I got twisted for the first time, Dad got high with one of my classmates, Drew, on a hunting trip with Drew's older cousin, after which Drew told several other kids about my dad's drug use. The anger and embarrassment I felt when kids at school asked, "Does your dad really smoke weed?" motivated me, in eighth grade, to develop an identity based on sobriety— straight edge.

In the early eighties, Ian MacKaye, the singer for Minor Threat, coined the term "straight edge" to separate himself and his band from all the partying in punk rock. I identified as straight edge for similar reasons: it was a way to rebel, to be different from my dad, as well as all the kids in school who liked to get fucked-up. Because of similar motivations, I also began to define myself as a BMX rider in junior high.

BUILT ON TOP OF an old mine shaft, the foundation of East Junior High cracked when the shaft caved in. The only solution was to destroy the school, and start over.

Subsidence holes appear when mineshafts cave in, and they've been opening in Rock Springs since the early nineteen hundreds. During Sunday Mass at the downtown Catholic church in January of 1949, a massive patch of street suddenly caved in, creating a sixty-by-eighty-foot maw directly in front of the church. Before getting his followers out of the building, the priest finished his sermon. Several voids opened under a small neighborhood in 1968, severely damaging ten houses.

Rock Springs has been attempting to deal with subsidence since the early seventies, when workers poured massive amounts of sand and water into mines. But the water destroyed support beams in the mines, mostly just causing more subsidence holes. A much more effective method has since been developed. Grout is injected into several sections of a mine, which creates stabilizing columns. Wyoming has spent over 160 million dollars on these efforts within the past thirty years.

But subsidence is still an issue in Rock Springs. Throughout the eighteen and nineteen hundreds, mine owners often lied about the square footage of their mines because the taxes would increase along with the size of the mines, resulting in unreliable and incomplete coal mine maps that the town is still dealing with.

The problem of subsidence holes was worsened by another attempted fix—dynamic compaction. In 2007, twenty- and thirty-ton weights were smashed into the ground to cave in mines, and thus avoid unforeseen subsidence. But vibrations from this process damaged homes in the nearby Tree Street neighborhood. Mines that officials didn't know about opened under houses. Peoples' walls cracked. Floors and driveways sunk. Window and doorframes warped. A few people got carbon monoxide poisoning from gas that was trapped underground.

Despite the destruction stemming from this caricature, Rock Springs still proudly identifies itself as a mining boomtown.

ANOTHER CLOSE FRIEND OF my dad's, Joey Hay, shot himself in 2006. Joey and Dad had known each other for over thirty-five years.

Joey was a descendant of the Blair family. In 1868, Archibald and Duncan Blair opened the first coal mine in Rock Springs. One of the Blair's daughters married John Hay, eventually becoming Joey's grandmother. In 1907, John Hay became president of Rock Springs National Bank. John's son took over the bank in the late nineteen-forties, and Joey's older brother, Ben, inherited their father's business during the nineties. The Hay family is still one of the wealthiest in town.

Living in Denver in 2006, three months before I ended the two-year drug-and-booze binge that I'd begun just before graduating from high school, I talked on the phone with my mom. "What else has been going on?" I asked.

"Well... Joey shot himself a few days ago."

My Adam's apple became a lead weight, but I wasn't surprised. Joey loved to inject heroin, cocaine, and methamphetamine into his veins, and, since Freddy had killed himself, I'd learned a lot about hopelessness. I thought about Trevor, Joey's nephew.

Following my liberty spike years, I became obsessed with freestyle BMX, and I encapsulated myself in a close-knit group of friends. Until he moved to Utah for private school (I think his parents worried that Rock Springs would be a bad influence), Trevor was part of this group. One day, riding our bikes in front of Trevor's parents' house, Joey pulled up on his motorcycle and parked in the driveway, behind Trevor's mom's Lexus. The motorcycle engine rumbled my eardrums.

"What are you little shits up to?" Joey asked. Watching one of us do a trick, he said, "You little fuckers are getting pretty good at that shit." A maniacal chuckle tumbled out of his mouth. He had bucked, gapped teeth. "Trevor, your dad inside?"

"Yeah, I think he's upstairs."

As I examine this memory, Joey's leather jacket stands out. Like the knees of his slim-fit Wranglers, its elbows are brown and worn. His jacket contrasts with his brother's immaculate house, a large two-story with bay windows and a four-car garage, sitting on top of a hill that Rock Springs locals call Snob Hill.

This memory also makes me think about my dad. Like Joey, he never wanted to run his father's business. In the nineties, Dad let his older brother, Nick, take over the motel their father had built and ran. I picture Dad in front of Uncle Nick's house, a block down the street from Ben's. His stained T-shirt and sneakers, orange swimming trunks, which he always wore during summers (although he rarely swam), and his faded baseball cap seem out of place in front of Uncle Nick's house—an off-white, two-story house with navy blue window frames and shutters.

The house looks like it's been relocated from upper class New England.

Trevor mimicked Joey's chuckle after Joey went inside, making my friends and me laugh our asses off. Most of the times I've heard Trevor talk about Joey, he impersonated his laugh.

Another of my clearest memories of Joey involves him on a motorcycle. When I was eight or nine, I was staying at the family cabin in Bondurant, an hour south of Jackson Hole, with my mom, sister, and dad. Dad's grandpa had built the cabin in the nineteen-fifties. Sitting at a picnic table, I watched Dad inspect fishing equipment, preparing for us to fish the nearby Hoback River. Highway 91 lay perpendicular to the cabin's gravel drive.

The drone of a motorcycle spaced into stutters as Joey turned onto the drive. Sun reflected off his aviator sunglasses. With his leather jacket, tight jeans, and handlebar mustache, he looked like Dennis Hopper's character in *Easy Rider*. Dad set down a piece of fishing line, at the end of which he'd tied a gold spinner.

"Hey Joey, you motherfucker, what's up?"

After putting down his kickstand, Joey walked over to my dad, and they drew each other in for a one-armed hug. Joey and Dad's interactions always made them seem like brothers. They often didn't see each other for several months, but I never noticed any awkwardness between them. They both came from successful Rock Springs families and were surrounded by expectations—from family members as well as anyone who knew about the Anselmis or Hays.

"You want to go fishing here in a bit with me and my boy?" Dad asked.

"Shit, Jay, that sounds great. How you doing, little J. J.? But I need to get my ass back to Rock Springs here pretty quick." Joey sat down next to me, took off his leather jacket, and lit a cigarette. Smoke trailed from his nostrils. The leathery skin on his arms looked loose, but defined veins led from his forearms to his biceps. "You look just like your mom, little Jay," Joey said. "And you grow a foot every time I see you." While he and Dad talked, Joey's signature laugh burst from his throat every so often.

I stared at his motorcycle. Sun glimmered off the silver-outlined purple lettering that flowed across the white sparkle gas tank. The chrome tubing, foot pedestals, and handlebars looked like they were made of the same material as the villain from *Terminator 2*.

"What do you think, little Jay? You want to go for a short ride?" Joey said as he snubbed out his cigarette. He tossed the butt into the ashes beneath a nearby barbeque. "I don't have time to go fishing, but I could take you on a short ride." Joey and I looked at my dad.

"Yeah! Can I, Dad?"

After pausing for a few seconds, Dad said, "I don't think your mom would be too happy with me if I let you ride without a helmet."

"Shit. He'll be fine, Jay. We'll just go up the road and turn around."

Dad said that my mom would get pissed if she found out. Joey sighed and said, "Alright, alright." Looking back at Joey's quickly rising and diminishing excitement, I see a person who, like Freddy and Dad, loved to immerse himself and the people around him in ecstatic moments.

Dad has told me stories about going on skiing trips with Joey when they were teenagers. I can see them racing down mogul-pocked slopes, doing spread-eagles off huge jumps. Like my friends and me with BMX, they pushed each other with competitiveness and a genuine desire to see each other progress.

Joey, like my dad and me, flunked out of college during his freshman year. He worked for a natural gas company, Mountain Fuel, before working at FMC, a Trona mine outside Rock Springs. Dad worked for Pacific Power for twenty-five years—first as a warehouse worker and later as a meter reader—and he now has two herniated discs in his back. Trying to prove that they could build their own lives, Joey and my dad worked themselves to the bone.

In Rock Springs, expectations stemming from the Anselmis' success constantly fucked with my dad, mom, sister, and me. Coming from second-generation Italian immigrants, my grandpa, Don, and his brothers became some of the most lucrative businessmen the town had ever seen. Grandpa started out as a laborer. He soon got a job as a car salesman, eventually saving enough money to start his own dealership during the early sixties. In 1965, he sold the dealership and built the Outlaw Inn along with three partners. He was also the Democratic State

Chairman of Wyoming from 1973-1978. His brother Paul owned an apartment complex, two hotels, a laundromat, and a bank. Bill owned a few car dealerships. Among other business ventures, John was one of Grandpa Don's partners at the Outlaw.

But, in 1977, a *60 Minutes* episode, "High Noon in Cheyenne," solidified a bad reputation for the Anselmis. In the episode, Dan Rather accuses Grandpa Don of being connected to organized crime–related real estate and gun dealings, as well as political corruption. Around this same time, *The Denver Post, LA Times*, and a few other newspapers printed accusatory articles about Grandpa's involvement in a stolen guns case.

Throughout the episode, Dan Rather and a few people he interviews repeatedly mention Grandpa Don's connections to organized crime. Because we're Italian, these accusations led a lot of people in Rock Springs to believe that the Anselmis were in the mafia. During elementary school, junior high, and high school, people would routinely come up to me and say, "You're an Anselmi? You guys are in the mafia, right?" From an early age, I started to assume that most people in town saw my family and me through the lens of Dan Rather's accusations, and I think this led me to worry that I'd always be the person others thought I'd be.

I'm pretty sure similar feelings constantly weighed on Joey. Blairtown, a large park in Rock Springs, is named after the Blair brothers. As he drove past this park, as well as the Rock Springs Coal sign, I bet Joey always thought about his business-minded family members. I think Joey experienced the same sickly feeling I did when he thought about how his family's success shaped the way people saw him. He knew he couldn't control who everyone thought he was.

Dealing with looming family history and expectations, as well as hard-core drug use, I imagine that Joey grappled with the idea of free will for most of his life. In an environment that constantly tells you that you are powerless, deciding to kill yourself and making serious moves toward this act—feeling the tenuousness of life tingle your finger tips—is one way to grasp the extent to which humans are capable of shaping identity. At the same time, suicide, for anyone from Rock Springs, is an act of conforming—another name on the long list of people who've killed themselves there.

*

IN THE CENTER OF my brain, as well as my dad's, Freddy's, and Joey's, I imagine that there's a crumbling diorama of Rock Springs. Cracks slither across roads and sidewalks, and paint peels off decrepit houses. Dust, tumbleweeds, and bits of human detritus, blown by wind, flit through town. Rust and dirt cover the Rock Springs Coal arch.

BOY TRIPS

GRANDPA DON ORGANIZED AND paid for two fishing trips for the boys in our family, the first to Eureka, California and the second to British Columbia, during which I was eight and nine years old. My grandpa, dad, two uncles, and three cousins were super excited to fish in these amazing places. To me, fishing mostly consisted of tense waiting. Gutting fish—making a slit down the belly, pulling out the innards, and washing away the blood sack—canceled out the pleasure I got from catching them.

Looking back, I see that a lot of my anxiety about the trips stemmed from how closely connected fishing was to manliness in our family and also in Wyoming. I knew I should like fishing as much as my dad, grandpa, uncles, cousins, and the other boys at school, but I always felt like I was missing something about the ritual. During and after these trips, I often worried that I'd never fit the mold of an Anselmi man.

Grandpa took the helm of both fishing trips. When we went to Eureka, we stayed in rental cabins near a lake. After breakfast one morning, we gathered in Grandpa Don's room.

"Today we're going to take a break from fishing and drive through the Redwood Forest," Grandpa told us. He was stout, with a push-broom mustache, and his left eye was just a little higher than his right—a trait all of his sons, and their sons, including myself, inherited. Uncle Nick, Uncle Gabe, and my dad nodded as they sipped coffee. I pictured a metal pointer in Grandpa's hand, as if he was a high school geography teacher pointing to finite points on a map. Most days during both trips started in a similar way: gathering in Grandpa's room for instructions.

We piled into the rental van, which Grandpa Don drove. For me, tension was constant during both trips, and being cramped in a van with my male family members amplified this feeling. Sitting in the middle seat between Uncle Nick's two sons, I shivered, feeling the cold leather of the seat through my jeans.

When Grandpa turned the van's key, music blared from the speakers. The night before, Dad had driven the van to a nearby gas station to get beer. After turning off the radio, Grandpa said, "You'll blow out your goddamn eardrums listening to music that loud."

In most of Grandpa's words, I heard a congealed mass of gruffness and love. He had to wear hearing aids in both ears, so he knew how frustrating hearing loss was. He genuinely cared about his sons and grandsons, but he grew up during the Great Depression, when showing emotion was a sign of weakness. Grandpa Don's father died before I was born, but I imagine that, like his son, he also occluded his emotions with a net of gravel.

My cousins—Matthew, who was six years older than me, and Gerald, four years older—started teasing me after a few minutes of driving. The day before this drive, fishing with guides on a river, I'd caught more fish than both of them. Responding to one of Matthew's jabs, I reminded him of this.

"Yeah, because your dad reeled in every fish for you," Matthew said.

My dad was, and still is, an expert hunter and fisherman. In our house in Rock Springs, he filled a basement room with animal mounts—three deer, four antelope, one elk, several fish, and one badger, which he'd shot when it tried to attack our dog. A coyote hide sat in the middle of the floor, staring with yellow eyes.

A year before our trip to Eureka, Dad had caught a world-record mackinaw. I was sitting at home on a summer afternoon when I heard his truck pull into our driveway. I opened the front door when I heard him shouting.

"J. J.! Hey, Jojo Gun! I caught one today!" Muscles in his arms tightened as he held up a monstrosity of a fish. Sun glinted off his one-piece sunglasses. Barefoot, I walked to the boat, little pieces of gravel sticking to my feet. The fish was longer than me. I touched its stomach, which felt heavy, as if filled with concrete.

"It took me eight hours to reel this bad boy in." I usually didn't care about the fish my dad caught, but this one was obviously special. He gave me a high five, unintentionally stinging my hand.

He'd caught the forty-two-pound mackinaw on a six-pound test line—a freshwater world record for that line strength. Although it was expensive, he had to get it mounted. Dad worked long shifts in a power plant for a middle class income, priding himself on the fact that he didn't depend on Grandpa Don's money, unlike his two brothers. We weren't poor, but there were a lot of times when money was pretty tight—and when Dad caught this fish, I don't remember he and my mom arguing about whether or not he should pay a high-end taxidermist to mount it.

The Virginian, a nice motel in Jackson Hole, paid Dad a monthly fee to keep the mount in their lobby. Proud of his son, Grandpa Don also put the fish on display in the Outlaw for several months. When Dad finally brought the fish home, he and Mom disagreed about where it should go. Mom thought the fish belonged in the basement, with his other mounts. It ended up in our living room, on top of the entertainment center. Walking through the front door, this pillar of manliness was the first thing you'd notice.

A taxidermist had meticulously recreated the fish. It swam above rocks and driftwood in a glass case. White spots on its head melted into black-and-red dots along its back and tail. The fish dominated the room. When light came through the blinds, its greenish-yellow eyes glinted. Throughout grade school, junior high, and high school, the fish always seemed to watch me.

AFTER ABOUT AN HOUR and a half of driving in the cramped van, I told Dad or one of my uncles that I had to pee. "Don't be a pussy. Just tie a rubber band around your dick," Gerald said, laughing. "Just let someone know when it gets purple." Grandpa Don pulled over so I could pee after he told Gerald to stop messing with me.

Gerald had recently begun puberty. Ten or fifteen minutes later, he whispered, "Hey, check this shit out." Looking to make sure an adult didn't see, he quickly pulled down his pants, revealing a thicket of dark pubic hair.

Stressed out and curious, I wondered when I'd grow hair like that. When I did grow similar hair, I also wondered if I would become less self-conscious—unlike the shy kid, who, in the few locker rooms I'd been in, felt horribly embarrassed by and for the naked men around me—prompting me to show this hair to other males.

Not wanting to seem like a wuss, I didn't tell on Gerald, but I tried to make eye contact with an adult, hoping my dad, uncles, or grandpa could somehow alleviate my stress. In the front of the van, Grandpa and Uncle Nick talked. Dad snored in the backseat, his head propped against the window, on his Gore-Tex coat. Uncle Gabe, the youngest of Grandpa Don's sons, sat next to Dad. When I looked at Uncle Gabe, he stuck out his brown, tobacco-stained tongue, trying to make me laugh.

Gerald had also teased me during the flight from Rock Springs to Eureka. I can't remember what he did to piss me off, but I do remember punching him in the face. Executing the punch was awkward because Gerald sat to my left and I'm right handed, but I still planted a few knuckles on his chin. Red-faced, he got up and told his dad. Uncle Nick looked at me, then back to Gerald, yelling at him instead of me. I didn't punch Gerald after he showed me his pubic hair, but I wanted to. I tried to shift my focus outside the van, where silky fog curled around tree trunks.

We drove through a tunnel carved through a massive redwood, and Grandpa Don pulled over to take pictures. I stood in front of my dad, nestled against his pillowy belly fat, his arms on my shoulders. I noticed droplets of water on leaves, weeds, and other foliage. We huddled with my cousins and uncles.

"Okay," Grandpa said, holding up a camera. His voice boomed off the redwoods. "On the count of three, everyone say 'sex.'"

The word fumbled through my big, gapped teeth.

MY CLEAREST MEMORY FROM the trip to British Columbia is of eating in an upscale restaurant in Vancouver. I ordered French onion soup. Grandpa Don and my dad sat on either side of me.

A waitress placed the bowl of soup on my placemat. Gobs of gorgonzola drooped from the bowl's lip, and floating chunks of onion looked like they'd melt on my tongue. Trying to cool the soup, I blew on the entire bowl.

But the hot liquid burned my tongue when I tried to eat a spoonful.

"Didn't anybody ever teach you to eat soup the right way?" Grandpa asked. His voice seemed to echo through the restaurant. He took the spoon from my hand, dipped it into the soup, and blew on it. "See," he said, dragging the 'ee.' "You blow on it one spoonful at a time. You look like an idiot doing it the other way. Blowing on the whole bowl doesn't do anything." Like my uncles and cousins, Dad kept his head down.

This wasn't the first time Grandpa Don had scolded me for using bad manners. Now, Grandpa's enforcement of table etiquette makes me think about his concern for his image and reputation. I'm not sure how he got started in politics, but I imagine that his sharp intellect helped him become the Democratic State Chairman of Wyoming. Grandpa only had a high school diploma, so when he mingled with educated politicians, adhering to proper table etiquette was an important part of belonging.

I also think his words stemmed from a desire to see me succeed. He wanted me to know how to carry myself in upper class social situations because he hoped that I'd find my own place in this world one day. Although I felt otherwise at the time, I now see that he had this expectation for me because he thought I was a smart kid, that I had potential. But I also know about Grandpa Don's past in Rock Springs and how maddening it can be to feel like you can't control how people see you. Part of him wanted everyone in the Anselmi family to act a certain way because of how our actions reflected back onto him.

Grandpa was raised on the American ideal that you can be whoever you want with enough hard work. He achieved success with his laser-precise business intelligence, but his reputation in Rock Springs was beyond his control—a sculpture of himself that other people could mold. I think Grandpa Don sometimes focused the frustration he felt from not being able to control his reputation on his family.

In 1978, my dad got busted with two ounces of weed in Rock Springs and had to spend a night in jail. After Dad's arrest, which was covered by the local newspaper, Grandpa wrote him a letter saying that the arrest was the catalyst for his own political downfall. In reality, what destroyed Grandpa's political career was the *60 Minutes* episode, "High Noon in Cheyenne." Before it aired in 1977, I'm sure that gossip about how the Anselmi brothers became so successful flowed through Rock Springs, but people didn't have anything concrete to latch onto.

Grandpa Don wanted people to see him as a shrewd businessman who'd raised himself up by his own bootstraps. After growing up in the Great Depression, a time when he saw a can of Spam as a feast, he quickly climbed to the top tiers of society. But I think he had some help.

I recently watched "High Noon in Cheyenne" for the first time. As Dan Rather asks Grandpa Don if he attempted to cover up his partner's son's drug-related arrest, I can feel anger radiating from Grandpa. He smokes a cigarette, which is eerie considering that I watched him deteriorate from lung cancer twenty-five years after this interview.

"I have never—*never*—done anything of the kind," Grandpa Don tells Dan Rather. Emphasizing the second 'never,' his eyes widen, and his tar-soaked monotone becomes cutting. However, when Rather asks him about some specific real estate deals involving "mobsters," Grandpa falters before denying the allegation.

When I was growing up, everyone in my family told me that the *60 Minutes* episode and the rumors it spawned were bullshit. Watching it now, I'm not so sure.

The governor of Wyoming, Ed Herscheler, asked Grandpa to resign in 1978, afraid that bad press about his State Chairman would prevent him from getting reelected. Shortly afterward, Grandpa Don found a personal outlet for his anger toward Dan Rather and CBS in his letter to my dad. Dad doesn't like to talk about the letter—I found out about it from my mom. Dad dropped out of college two years before he got arrested. When he received the letter, he was twenty-one, living and working under his father's shadow in Rock Springs.

BMX KID

EHIND MY PARENTS' HOUSE in Rock Springs, motorcycle paths snaked through a sagebrush-pocked prairie. Back here, neighborhood kids built dirt jumps for their BMX bikes in a circular clearing that was littered with rocks and tumbleweeds. Like me, most of these boys wanted to ride motorcycles but either weren't old enough, or their parents wouldn't let them.

One summer day when I was eleven, I watched an older kid pedal his red Dyno toward the biggest jump in the clearing. I sat off to the side, on my Diamondback Viper. The kid's white tires zipped off the lip. Spokes in his front and back mag wheels looked like the blades of a slowing ceiling fan. I needed to know how he felt in the air.

I loved baseball during grade school. Tall and lanky, I was a sidearm pitcher. Randy Johnson, with his mean-ass glares and nasty slider, was my hero. I made the

Little League All-Star team when I was twelve, at the end of sixth grade. We drove for eight hours in the dry Wyoming heat to compete in the state tournament. Here, pressure from parents and coaches, as well as the coaches' nepotism—picking their own sons to start and taking other players out when their kids made errors—reached levels I hadn't experienced.

A few months later, a friend showed me an issue of *BMX Plus*. In it, an interview with Chase Gouin, a BMX icon, featured pictures of contorted flatland maneuvers alongside text with cusswords, both of which seemed really cool. Gouin wore baggy corduroy shorts and a striped shirt with holes in it. He didn't seem to give a shit about anything but riding his bike.

I decided to quit playing baseball.

MY BUDDING INTEREST IN girls during fifth and sixth grade became an obsession in junior high. Walking to classes in seventh grade, I stared at hot girls. But these girls weren't interested in me. I had scrawny arms, and large pustules had begun to bubble up on my face, neck, and back. I also had gapped teeth and a right eye that seemed bigger than my left. I wasn't confident enough to date the funky-looking girls who thought I was cute.

Junior high also marked a transition from the one-punch fights of grade school, of which I'd won a few, to bloody bouts in ditches and parks, which scared the shit out of me. As I walked to class, larger boys, whose alcoholic dads worked in the oil field, power plant, coal, or

Trona mines, often said things like, "What you looking at pussy?" or, "What, faggot?" when I looked at them.

I MET STEVE IN a seventh grade science class, during the spring of 1998. Like me, gnarly acne covered his cheeks, neck, and back. Steve told me about some dirt jumps on the north end of town, just past the Outlaw Inn, called Baker because they were in an empty lot behind Baker Oil Tools.

"You should come ride with us after school," he said.

My parents had recently bought me a Gary Fisher BMX bike, which I thought was badass. But Steve made fun of it when I met him after school.

"What are those—one-piece cranks? You're going to fuck those up really fast," he said, laughing. Steve's bike was custom-built. He'd ordered the frame and parts and put the bike together himself.

I had trouble keeping up with him as we rode north. Steve wore a Schwinn baseball cap and black shin pads, which extended from his ankles to the bottom of his plaid shorts. Coasting down a hill, zipping past houses, he pulled up on his handlebars and balanced on his back wheel—a wheelie without pedaling.

"Whoa! What the fuck was that?"

"A manual? Haven't you seen anyone manual before?" Steve manualled again. His front wheel hovering above the concrete.

It took about forty minutes to ride to Baker. Behind the Baker Oil warehouse, dirt lips and landings, ranging from two to six feet in height, sprouted from the ground, looking like dirt EKGs.

Steve pedaled toward a line of jumps. He flew off each lip, landed, and then, in less than a second, glided over the next set. His smooth athleticism reminded me of Doctor Jay, who I'd seen videos of on ESPN. Over the last jump, Steve's feet floated off the pedals, hanging in the air for a second before he brought them back.

A handful of other boys I knew from school also rode at Baker. Most of them flowed through the jumps, although not as gracefully as Steve. Someone had sloppily painted "Baker" on the corrugated wall of a nearby warehouse in lime-green house paint. Compared to the rigid structure of Little League, this world seemed like *Lord Of The Flies,* and I loved it.

Steve and the other riders egged each other on, as well as me. I rode up to the first jump of a rhythm section but veered off.

"Don't be a pansy, J. J." Steve said. "You can make it through that set."

I looked at the first jump again. The lip and landing were both steeper than the jumps behind my house. I watched Steve flow through the rhythm section again.

I pedaled hard at the first jump, gaining too much speed. I stiffened up in the air and overshot the landing. My feet slipped off the pedals, and I smashed my nuts on my seat. I turned away from the second jump.

"Damn, dude. You okay?" Steve asked, riding up to me.

Trying not to act hurt, I told Steve that I was fine, but a burning nausea constricted my stomach. After about fifteen minutes of feeling like I might cough up my testicles, I decided to try again. This time, I made it through the first two jumps. In the air, time slowed.

"See? You got that shit," Steve said.

Before meeting Steve, I'd been riding with my grade school friends, Trevor Hay, Jared Spann, and his younger brother, Bryan Spann. With Steve, we became a BMX crew. I replaced my Korn and Limp Bizkit T-shirts with BMX shirts. Like the pro riders we admired, my friends and I grew out our hair until it covered our ears. By eighth grade, our classmates and teachers knew us as the BMX kids.

With the exception of Trevor's, all of our dads got high or drunk every day, and most of our peers loved to get fucked-up. Like me, my friends' response was to identify as straight edge. We weren't preppy, we weren't jocks, we weren't rednecks, and we weren't fucked-up kids. We were straight edge BMXers.

ONE DAY IN EIGHTH grade, Steve and I sat in the school auditorium waiting for an assembly to start. Drew, who had bleached hair and silver hoops in both ears, sat in front of us. Dad had just gone elk hunting with Drew's older cousin, Shaun, who'd brought Drew along. In the auditorium, Drew told Steve, me, and a few other kids about the hunting trip.

"So I got back to the tent after getting some more wood for the fire," Drew said, "and there was your dad, taking a *huge* bong rip." After Drew promised that he wouldn't tell anyone, he got high with my dad and Shaun. Telling us the story, he laughed, strings of spit connecting his upper and lower brace brackets.

Discomfiture singed my cheeks. D.A.R.E. and thirty-second public service announcements on TV had taught me that parents weren't supposed to get high. Although I liked to tell myself that I was a rebel, I was bothered by my father's use of pot because it was was illegal. I also hated how my dad being a stoner affected the way people saw me.

"Shut the fuck up, Drew. You're full of shit," Steve said, although he knew that Drew wasn't lying—he'd seen my dad high more than a few times. Steve was at least a head taller than Drew.

After this assembly, kids started coming up to me and saying things like, "That's badass that your dad gets high. I wish my dad smoked pot." This continued throughout junior high and high school. I didn't know how to digest Dad's pot smoking, how to reconcile it with him as a father figure.

I hated how people assumed that I'd become a stoner, too. Around this time, I began to understand that most of the Anselmi family, in addition to people in Rock Springs who knew about Dad's drug use, expected that I'd become a fuck up. As this expectation became more clear to me, my straight edge identity became increasingly rigid.

BECAUSE RIDING WAS RARELY televised, my friends and I had to order BMX videos. These videos helped us study tricks and also connected us to a world of BMX that existed outside of Rock Springs.

When I was fourteen, I convinced my mom to let me order *Madd Matt*, an early Hoffman Bikes video. Mat Hoffman is basically the Tony Hawk of BMX, a rider who pioneered countless tricks and also started his own bike company. After a week of waiting, I found a cardboard box on our dining room table when I got home from school. Before playing the video, I closed the blinds in our living room so sun wouldn't gleam off the glass case of Dad's world-record mackinaw.

The video begins with a shot of Mat Hoffman sitting on the deck of a sixteen-foot vert ramp, which is four feet higher than a standard vert ramp. Hoffman has a small motor attached to his bike. He pulls a start-chord and looks into the camera while making the metal horns sign with his right hand. After dropping in, he soars ten feet above the coping on the other side of the ramp.

Later in the video, Hoffman gets towed by a motorcycle and rocketed toward a twenty-foot quarter pipe. He launches twenty feet into the air—a world record. Throughout this section, surgical footage of the inside of Hoffman's knee is mixed between clips of him riding. Threads and plates hold his ACL together, and I thought it was badass that he still rode after going through such gnarly injuries. He immediately became one of my idols after I watched the video, and I wished that I was as manly as him.

I also loved Taj Mihelich's section in *Madd Matt*. Taj, another BMX legend, rides dirt jumps, street, and ramps. His street riding seemed particularly rad. Jared, Bryan, Steve, and I had recently started grinding curbs, rails, and riding on walls. Seeing these objects through the eyes of a BMX rider presented new possibilities in Rock Springs.

During the fall, spring, and summer, when the wind wasn't blowing too hard, we'd ride all over town. Compared to an actual city, the street spots in Rock Springs were few and far between. Soon, we knew about every grindable ledge or rail in town, as well as every other rideable obstacle. Rock Springs had a small skate park we often rode, but it was more fun to ride things that weren't meant to be ridden.

We'd usually start our street sessions at East Junior High and slowly make our way downtown. Long, knee-high ledges with wax engrained into them lined one side of the track at East. I'd pedal at a ledge and bunny hop, grinding along the edge with metal pegs that extended from my wheel axles. The fingernails-on-the-chalkboard sound of metal scraping concrete was both abrasive and soothing. I wasn't as good as Jared, Steve, or Bryan, but that didn't matter as much as the power I felt while riding these ledges.

The small downtown area of Rock Springs often felt claustrophobic when I was a kid and teenager. Locally owned businesses lined a flat main street. Staring at each storefront eventually felt as familiar as staring into a mirror. The burger place, movie theatre, brewery, three bars, bike shop, pharmacy, hardware store, and bank—I passed these nondescript buildings every day, the same cars and trucks always parked in the lots. Most of the owners and employees of these businesses knew who I was.

From an early age, I remember feeling like Rock Springs was a dead end, like I'd never be able to build my own life here. But BMX helped me see this place as a playground. Ledges, stair sets, and rails in front of businesses and schools presented years' worth of riding opportunities. I loved that these things weren't designed for riding, and also that it was illegal to ride most of them. My friends and I frequently got kicked out of street spots or had to evade security guards.

After riding the ledges at East, we'd pedal a few blocks to city hall, which doubled as the police station. A few white signs that said "No Skateboarding. No Rollerblading. No Bike Riding" were posted next to stair sets and ledges around the squat brick building. During the day, we didn't ride here for very long because we could've gotten busted for destruction of property, but these signs also made it more fun to ride city hall.

A lot of our classmates that drank and got high thought we were preppy. Aside from Bryan, though, none of us really cared about our grades. Taking out chunks of concrete ledges with our pegs—even though this wasn't intentional, it was part of riding street—and leaving tire marks on walls was a way to prove that we weren't mindless, rule-abiding preps.

Riding BMX was also a way for me to subvert expectations attached to my last name. Although it was an exaggeration, I always felt like Grandpa Don and his brothers had built Rock Springs, especially the downtown. Like Grandpa Don, I hated that I couldn't control how people in town saw me. No matter what I did, I'd always be an Anselmi.

Part of this might've been in my head, but, everywhere I went, people in town seemed to convey disdain in the way they looked at me, a look that said, *We know who you're going to become.* This desire to see me fuck up stemmed partially from jealousy, as well as the collective contempt for my family that the *60 Minutes* episode bred. Most people in town thought that Grandpa and his brothers reached their success through shady business tactics, which led them to want Grandpa Don's progeny to fail.

Grinding ledges and jumping over stairs in front of city hall was a way to feel power over Rock Springs. I couldn't change the world around me, but I could control how I saw this world. No one expected that I'd become a straight edge BMX rider, and the playground of street riding that BMX opened was the result of my own decision-making. Everywhere I go, I still see rails, ledges, and other rideable obstacles through the eyes of a BMX rider.

From city hall, we'd usually make our way to the old Catholic church, where I'd often gone to Mass with my dad and grandparents. Low ledges bordered the manicured grass in front of the church. Metal spires and stained glass windows loomed above the wax-blackened, concrete ledges. From here, you could see the Rock Springs Coal Arch, which was only a few hundred yards away. The arch stood directly behind Rock Springs National Bank, the bank Joey Hay's older brother ran. Watching Jared, Bryan, and Steve ride, I'd often look from the ledges to the church, bank, or arch. Then, when I began pedaling toward a ledge, my brain blocked these things out, laser-focused on trying to grind the waxed concrete.

Navigating the grind successfully meant that I'd avoid wrecking. After a few hard wrecks, pushing past the fear of pain became an inescapable part of riding. But this pain was self-inflicted—no one forced me to ride. About to bunny hop onto a ledge in front of the Catholic church, my brain was momentarily consumed by Rock Springs, reducing my world to fear and overcoming that fear. Looking back, I think I was attracted to freestyle BMX because it taught me about the ledge of free will.

METALHEAD

MY FIRST CAR WAS a burgundy 1986 Chrysler New Yorker that my maternal grandma, Rose, gave me just before I turned sixteen. A year earlier, when I was in ninth grade, Grandma Rose went through chemotherapy in Salt Lake, where she lived. Mom traveled there about twice a month, often taking my friends and me along so we could ride the awesome skate parks in the area.

Most nights, Grandma Rose fell asleep listening to classical music on her Bose stereo—one of few extravagances she bought for herself, even though she made a decent living as a dietician. She had curly red hair and type 2 diabetes, and she'd grown up in a strict Mormon family in rural Utah. She didn't talk about her background often. If she did, she usually launched into rants about what assholes her brothers were.

When Grandma went to Weber State in Ogden, she discovered feminism—a school of thought that told her she was right to hate her oppressive upbringing. This is also where she met a tall basketball player named Leighton, who'd stopped believing in God after returning from his mission in Australia. Grandpa studied history at Weber State, eventually getting a graduate degree in Montana. Grandma got a BA in liberal studies, later completing her Master's in nutrition at a school in Seattle, where my mom was born. At some point, Grandma's disdain for Mormon culture branched out to include most of mainstream America, something that's still alive and kicking within me. I remember more than a few times when, watching the evening news, she said, about the president or some other politician, "That pig should be tried for treason."

Grandpa Leighton and Grandma Rose divorced in 1988, when I was three. Before they broke up, they'd started and run a high-end restaurant in Rock Springs. They moved here from Nebraska, correctly predicting that their gourmet dishes would be a hit in a place where, during the energy boom of the seventies, everyone had extra money to spend. One of my earliest memories is of scooting around Grandpa and Grandma's chaotic restaurant kitchen in a walker. My first word was 'hot.' I also remember listening to a caustic screaming match between them when I was three or four.

When Grandma Rose got sick, I began to realize that it's possible for good people to die, and die alone. Her hair thinned at a chilling rate, and she quickly lost weight. I'd stare at her powdery white scalp between wisps of her red hair and feel guilty, like I was looking at something I wasn't supposed to.

During summers throughout junior high, before she was diagnosed with cancer, she'd often let my friends and me stay at her house for weeks on end so we could ride our bikes in Salt Lake. Before we'd leave to ride a skate park, she usually said, "Jay, I wish you guys would wear helmets when you do those goddamn tricks. You're too smart for that shit."

When Grandma Rose was going through chemo, my mom took Jared and me with her to Salt Lake one weekend. Right after we got to the city, our truck's transmission shit the bed at a busy intersection, so Mom rented a tiny purple Hyundai and had the truck towed to an auto shop. After our truck got fixed, Jared, who only had a learner's permit, drove the Hyundai back to the rental office, following my mom in Grandma Rose's New Yorker. Mom hesitated at a yellow light, skidding to a stop at the last minute. Jared slammed into the New Yorker. The Hyundai's hood buckled. The New Yorker's rear bumper and electrical system both got fucked-up, but the car was still drivable. Grandma Rose bought a new car and gave me the New Yorker just before I turned sixteen.

Grandma always hated the New Yorker, and I'm not sure why she bought it in the first place. It was a boat car with faux-leather upholstery that always felt cold. Sitting in her driveway, it seemed immovable, like it was made of bricks. The car was a part of American culture that Grandma Rose hated—the culture of ostentation and bigger-equals-better—and I wonder if she bought it because she was tired of feeling like an outsider. She'd gotten the car after being divorced from Grandpa for ten years—ten years of living and working as a single woman in Utah. But she quickly regretted buying it. Sounding like someone trying to speak while inhaling, the New Yorker had an electronic voice that repeatedly and erroneously said, "Your washer fluid is low." Grandma Rose would routinely get irritated by the voice and say, "Oh, shut the fuck up."

Grandma's cancer went into remission when I was in tenth grade, but dementia began to consume her brain within the next few years.

A favorite BMX video of mine during this time, Little Devil clothing company's *Criminal Mischief*, depicts riders driving an eighties luxury sedan, which looks similar to a New Yorker, into handrails, a television set, and off a loading dock. In silver spray-paint, "Hell," "Little Devil," and "666" are scrawled across the slate-blue car. Within a month after Grandma Rose gave me the New Yorker, I spray-painted white hypnotism spirals on each of its rims, "Poop" on the faux-leather roof, and placed BMX stickers on both bumpers and every window. The New Yorker reminded me of Grandma's deteriorating health, and I wished that her sickness was something simple and tangible that I could destroy.

*

TOWARD THE END OF ninth grade, I became obsessed with old school heavy metal—a style of music that promoted the rebelliousness I inherited from Grandma Rose. My favorite BMX videos featured metal soundtracks, and this music became attached to the power I found through BMX. I remember watching Dave Young's section in *Nowhere Fast* over and over. As the frenzied riffs of Slayer's "Reign In Blood" play, Young hurls himself down twenty-stair rails, getting completely thrashed, but also pulling off some of the gnarliest shit I'd ever seen. I saw beauty in his willingness to destroy himself, and, for me, heavy metal perfectly captured the idea that destruction, anger, and negativity could produce something beautiful.

I came home one day during ninth grade to find a stack of CDs that Dad's friend, Dennis, had left for me: Iron Maiden's *Number Of The Beast*, Black Sabbath's *Master Of Reality*, Danzig's self-titled album, Megadeth's *Countdown To Extinction*, and Metallica's *Ride The Lightning*. I'd heard of each of these bands but had only listened to Sabbath and Metallica.

"Whose CDs are those on the table?" I asked Dad as he sat in our living room, reading the newspaper.

"Oh, Dennis left them for you. I know I can't take that heavy shit—too depressing." He shook his head and turned a page.

Dad has always listened to good music: Neil Young, Led Zeppelin, The Rolling Stones, Santana, Journey, Lynyrd Skynyrd, J. Guiles, Jimi Hendrix, and pretty much any other classic rock band. He also loves pop radio. In junior high, I began to realize that he mostly likes music that makes him feel happy.

Dennis was one of several of Dad's friends that Mom didn't like. He's super nice but always piss drunk. I'm not exaggerating when I say that I've never seen him sober. He still lives with his mom in Reliance, a tiny community just north of Rock Springs, and he has an absurd amount of DUIs—at least twenty. I don't think he'll ever be eligible to get a driver's license again. Instead of listening to music for escape, Dennis liked music that reflected life in a shit-hole town in Wyoming.

I immediately fell in love with all the albums he gave me. I tried to find out as much about each of these bands as I could, constantly reading about them in metal magazines and on the Internet. I also loved to look at pictures of these bands, and I quickly decided that I wanted to look like an old school metalhead. The guys in these bands had messy long hair, often wearing band patch-covered jean jackets and worn-out T-shirts and jeans. Whether it was through facial expressions or actually flipping the bird, they always seemed to be saying, "Fuck you." Looking at old pictures of Metallica, Slayer, and Black Sabbath, I understood that these guys used their appearance to express feelings of social alienation and discontent, deliberately separating themselves from the mainstream.

Soon, I sold most of my CDs that didn't fit a metalhead persona.

IT WAS ABOUT THIS time that I got the New Yorker and started driving it around with Mom or Dad riding along, given that I was still a month away from turning sixteen. On my birthday, I drove alone through Rock Springs, blasting a tape of Metallica's *Ride The Lightning*. When I tried to eject it, the tape got stuck. The car didn't have a CD player, so I set up a boom box with a tape player on the backseat floor.

Most mornings during my sophomore year of high school, I'd put a tape of Black Sabbath's *Sabbath Bloody Sabbath* in my boom box before leaving my parents' house. In "Killing Yourself To Live," one of my favorite songs on this album, Tony Iommi's ugly, distortion-laden guitar notes stretch over Bill Ward's heavy drumming and Geezer's slithering bass as Ozzy sings, "You work your life away and what do they give? / You're only killing yourself to live."

I loved Tony Iommi's downtuned guitar work for Sabbath. When he was seventeen, Iommi cut off the tip of his middle and ring finger in a factory accident. So he could work guitar frets with his damaged fingers, he made finger covers and downtuned his guitars because loose strings were easier for him to play. To me, Tony Iommi's sound mirrored the bleakness of life in a dead-end, blue-collar town, and I knew that his portrait of the hopelessness, anger, and alienation that industrial society breeds wouldn't have been as poignant if he hadn't lost his fingers in a sheet metal factory. In Rock Springs, most uneducated men end up working in a coal mine, power plant, or gas field, which still didn't motivate me to get good grades in school.

Middle class houses lined the streets leading to Rock Springs High. One pickup and one car were parked in most driveways. Sandstone cliffs and empty prairie loomed in the background. I often thought about the people living in these houses, many of whom I knew, wondering why you'd wake up every day to work a job you hated. When Dad came home after long shifts at the power plant, or, later, reading electric meters in backyards, he always seemed miserable. These monotonous jobs eroded his self-esteem like wind erodes sandstone, and his coworkers often fucked with him because he came from a successful Rock Springs family.

Goths, punks, and stoners smoked cigarettes just beyond school grounds. In the parking lot, I'd pull into a space next to a large pickup, Sabbath blasting from my boom box. I wanted any classmates within earshot to know that I listened to old school metal. Walking toward the front doors, I'd often see Dane, an overachieving student who played soccer, football, and ran track.

"Whoo! Ozzy! Yeah, metal!" Dane would say, mockingly holding up the metal horns.

"Fuck you, Dane. That new Eminem album you were listening to is *so tight*, bro."

"I still can't believe you spray-painted those spirals on the wheels of your car. It makes me sick every time I see you driving it."

In the school's glass front doors, I'd look at my hair and shake my head side to side, trying to make it look messier, like my metal heroes' hair. Inside, I'd walk past the trophy case, where most of the popular kids gathered. Gavin, a motocross rider with short, gelled hair, usually sat next to Rory, easily the hottest girl in school, who I had had a crush on since the first time I saw her. To Rory, Gavin would say something like, "Look at Anselmi's hair. He looks like a little queer."

DURING LUNCH ONE DAY, Steve and I left school to get fast-food. Before leaving the parking lot, I put Sabbath's *Paranoid* in my boom box. The New Yorker's electronic voice, which my friends and I'd named Leroy, said, "Your washer fluid is low," as we drove toward I-80.

"Fuck you, Leroy," Steve said, laughing.

At Taco Time, Steve and I both ordered a super taco and large Mountain Dew—the same lunch we always ate at Taco Time. Waiting for our food, we listened to "Iron Man." I loved Bill Ward's combination of jazz and caveman-style drumming in this song, and I mouthed the words along with Ozzy as he sang, "Nobody wants him / They just turn their heads."

Back at school, Dr. Wendling, the principal, was talking with three hot girls in the main hallway. His muscles bulged under a tight polo shirt, which had "Rock Springs Tigers Football" stitched above the breast pocket. When Steve and I passed him, he leaned toward one of the girls and said, "I wonder what *they* were doing outside." He held his fingers to his mouth, smoking an imaginary joint. Wendling placed his hand on the middle of the girl's back, laughing with her and her friends.

Our classmates often told Steve and me that we looked like stoners, which irritated me. But getting wrongfully labeled by the principal, whose athletic and popular sons loved to get fucked-up, really pissed me off.

Of course, we totally *did* look like stoners, albeit from a different era. But I rigidly defined myself as straight edge, even though I also wanted to look like a member of Black Sabbath circa 1972—a band with songs about the magical powers of weed and cocaine. Mainly, I was trying to separate myself from my family's reputation, with a focus on my dad's. So hearing Wendling say this reinforced the claustrophobic tightness that defined how I usually felt in Rock Springs, and my immediate reaction was to say, "Fuck off," if only in my own head.

I've come to realize that I remember Wendling in uncomplicated ways because I never really knew him. Like a stereotypical principal character in a cheesy eighties movie, he let athletes slide with absences and bad grades. The football team walked around school in new, personalized practice jerseys on game days while we read shabby copies of *The Catcher In The Rye* in my English class. But I'd eventually learn that Wendling was also a reliable father figure for several students.

When Dr. Wendling made the stoner comment about me and Steve, I think he was actually helping me. Seeing myself as a rebellious metalhead depended upon an oversimplified us versus them mentality. At the time, I didn't think about how I needed what Wendling represented to define myself. Nor did I think about how my strict adherence to a metalhead persona made me as much, if not more, of a conformist as the jocks and popular kids I hated. I know now that my binary views of reality promised a violent fall. Nevertheless, as I try to see the world in complex and three-dimensional ways, which requires constantly building and breaking down ideas, I also miss the clarity and simplicity with which I saw myself and others during high school.

Walking to class after Wendling made the comment, lyrics from "Iron Man" reverberated in my brain.

ONE AFTERNOON, DURING THE spring of my sophomore year, my friends and I loaded our bikes onto the New Yorker's trunk rack and drove to a cement embankment on the north side of town. We'd recently begun filming our own BMX video, and I wanted some clips of us doing tricks on the New Yorker.

The three-foot bank was in the parking lot of a Mexican restaurant directly across the street from the Outlaw. After Jared, Steve, Bryan, and I took our bikes off the rack, I backed the New Yorker up so we could jump from the bank onto the rear bumper, which sagged from the collision in Salt Lake.

My fucked-up, spray-painted, sticker-covered car stood out everywhere I went, but particularly so against the backdrop of the Outlaw, with its triangular roof, potted plants, and immaculate parking lot. During this time, Uncle Nick ran the motel. I put a cassette of Metallica's *Kill 'Em All* in my boom box and cranked the volume, leaving the back doors of the New Yorker open. Thrashing drums, guitars, and bass clamored in my backseat, getting diluted by the wind.

While Bryan, Jared's little brother and the best rider in our crew, filmed, I rode toward the bank, jumped, turned ninety degrees to my left, and slammed my rear peg onto the bumper, holding my front end in a wheelie position—an ice-pick stall. My peg left a fat dent on the car's bumper.

Later that night, I uploaded this clip onto my parents' computer and watched it, over and over. You could see the Outlaw in the background.

ATHEIST

GRANDPA DON AND GRANDMA Vera wanted everyone in the Anselmi family to be a good Catholic. Until my First Communion, church mostly seemed like something I had to do, like going to school. I'd sit in a pew with Grandpa and Grandma on one side and my dad, mom, and younger sister on the other. The priest droned on and on, stretching an hour like a piece of sun-baked rubber.

During one mass, I saw a few tears running down Grandpa Don's cheeks, past his neatly trimmed mustache. Sun coming through the stained-glass windows cast a warm glow over his face, and this was one of only a few times when I didn't feel intimidated by Grandpa Don. Kneeling on the foldout pedestal, I closed my eyes to pray, but saw and felt nothing.

When I was nine and learning about communion and confession in Sunday school, I started to think religion was strange and kind of scary. The idea of drinking blood and eating flesh made me queasy, and confession confused me. When priests and Sunday school teachers talked about cleansing yourself of your sins, I always felt like there should be something in my past that was way worse than anything I'd actually done.

Finally, after I'd memorized all the right prayers, I nervously told a priest that I'd been cussing, teasing my sister, and committing some other little-boy mischief. He told me what prayers to say as my penance.

Afterward, as I stood in the communion line behind an older man with a humongous ass, my parents and grandparents watched from a pew, imprinting this moment onto their memories. When I got to the front, a priest said, "The body of Christ," as he placed a flavorless wafer on my tongue. I pictured elderly priests in a decrepit tomb, slicing off pieces of Jesus's maggot-ridden skin with potato peelers, collecting the pieces in jars, and then shipping them around the world. I knew that I wasn't really eating pieces of Jesus, but that thought wouldn't go away. With bits of wafer stuck to the roof of my mouth, I drank my first sip of alcohol and almost retched.

Shortly afterward, I told Dad that I didn't believe in God. He and my grandparents were disappointed and worried, but Mom said that I didn't have to go to church anymore. It scared me to see so many adults in mass play a weird game of pretend without calling it a game of pretend.

MY GRANDPARENTS MOVED OUT of Rock Springs when Grandpa Don retired from managing the Outlaw. They spent summers in Jackson Hole and winters in Tucson. When they visited Rock Springs, we usually went to mass.

When my family visited them, Grandpa Don would cook amazing dinners. One of my favorite dishes of his was stewed rabbit with polenta and brown gravy. Stringy rabbit meat dripped from the bones and melted on my tongue. Grandpa always made sure that no one left his table hungry, which meant that I waddled away from dinner feeling like one more bite would make me explode. Nevertheless, ever since the trip to Vancouver, I felt a constricting sense of expectation when I was around Grandpa.

During grade school, when I'd stay at my grandparents' house in Jackson, which was filled with the aromas of cherrywood and leather furniture, Grandma Vera would let me drink as many Cokes as I wanted. In one of the guestrooms, I'd pound sodas and watch Comedy Central. At home, Mom wouldn't buy soda for my sister and me. She'd also canceled our cable so my sister and I would read and play outside more. So visiting my grandparents often felt like a vacation.

As I got older, I started to feel like something was off in their house. Grandma and Grandpa acted differently after dinner, and it didn't take me long to realize that they got drunk every night. With a cigarette in her mouth and martini in her hand, Grandma would sometimes pat my shoulder or give me a hug—a rare sign of love from someone who, it seemed, often felt awkward around her kids and grandkids. She'd also literally tell my sister and me, "Do as I say, not as I do."

She began telling me that she prayed for me when I was in junior high. In addition to my lack of faith, I didn't have sparkling report cards like my cousins, Uncle Nick's kids. I think she both dreaded and expected that I'd become my dad.

Although Dad worked a back-jarring job at a power plant for over seventeen years, which seems amazing to me now, this didn't align with the future my grandparents had envisioned for him. Using the tough-love parenting they'd been subjected to when they were kids, Grandpa Don and Grandma Vera often told Dad that he was a failure. "Your dad has just fried his brain doing drugs," Grandma once told me.

Now, I think Grandma, like Grandpa, genuinely cared about me. But, when I was a teenager and she told me that she prayed for me, I thought she was saying that I was doomed to be a fuck up, and I reacted with a perpetually raised, mental middle finger. I also felt like my grandparents only wanted me to succeed for the sake of their own reputations—a goddamn cynical assumption for a teenager to make, but one that wasn't completely unjustified.

Grandma Vera always wore stylish clothes—mostly Eddie Bauer, Gap, and Tommy Hilfiger—and jewelry. She'd also get expensive, trendy haircuts. Both of my grandparents loved driving new cars. Almost every time I visited, they'd traded one of their cars for a new one. I don't remember them keeping a vehicle for longer than a year. Grandpa liked to have the latest Suburban, and

Grandma always had a new Jaguar. The new car scent still makes me think of my grandparents.

The first Jackson Hole house of theirs that I remember was on a golf course—vaulted ceilings, new fixtures, a pool table in the basement, five or six guestrooms, and floor-to-ceiling windows that provided a picturesque view of the Tetons. The next house they owned in Jackson was huge, too. From an early age, I understood that they didn't need most of the things they bought. Grandpa Don's valuation of table manners, his frequent outbursts about people's jealousy for the Anselmis, and my grandparents' desire to show off their wealth all told me that they thought about their reputation a lot.

They rarely showed affection, and I eventually came to believe that they wanted me to do well not because they loved me, but just so they'd look good, which wasn't true. Grandma and Grandpa both knew what it was like not to have enough to eat, something I've never experienced. Even though they'd become wealthy, I don't think any amount of money could've made them feel completely secure about the future. The Great Depression had taught them that things could always go wrong. They wanted to make sure their kids and grandkids would always be safe and comfortable, but they also got caught up in ostentation.

When I was a teenager, instead of examining the tangled mass of emotions connected to my grandparents, I focused on the things about them that I didn't like: religion, drinking, and their obsession with money. I directed much of my anger toward these characteristics, not realizing that I was inflicting a type of violence on both my grandparents and myself. It was easier to try to hate them than it would've been to recognize that we all hurt people we love, whether or not we mean to. I also think dealing with my grandparents in this way played a part in keeping me from understanding myself.

*

I FIRST LISTENED TO Slayer's *Reign In Blood* in ninth grade, my favorite songs immediately becoming the title track and "Jesus Saves." To me, Slayer defined what it meant to be a true metal band. From their first studio album, 1983's *Show No Mercy*, to 2001's *God Hates Us All*—an album title that seemed particularly rad—Slayer's sound didn't really change. Their album covers depicted pentagrams, inverted crosses, and other anti-Christian imagery.

During my sophomore year, Uncle Nick gave me a maintenance job at the Outlaw. I saved enough money to buy a Slayer ticket after I found out they were playing in Salt Lake. When I told my classmates that I was going to miss a day of school to see Slayer, I loved to hear responses like, "Holy shit. Aren't their concerts really crazy?" Steve, Jared, and I drove to Salt Lake for the concert.

Standing in line outside the venue, I felt like I'd found where I belonged. Dudes with long hair and gnarly tattoos wore Slayer shirts featuring different versions of the Sigil of Baphomet pentagram, depictions of Jesus as a goat-like creature, as well as the words *God Hates Us All*. During fights with my dad in junior high and high school, fights originally about his drug use, I often told him that his religion was bullshit, not thinking about the ways in which my metal fandom might be a form of religion.

In high school, I used to walk up to Mormon kids and say, "You're Mormon? That's bullshit." I thought it was hilarious. At the Slayer show, I told two metalheads about doing this when I heard them talking about how much they hated religion.

"Ha, that's sick dude. My buddy here," a guy wearing camouflage pants said while pointing to his friend, who had brown hair that hung to the middle of his back, "likes to go up to people outside churches and tell them, 'God hates us all.'" The guy with long brown hair grinned.

Hatebreed opened the show. After their set, I watched roadies set up Slayer's gear, paying close attention to Paul Bostaph's drum kit, hoping that I could figure out how he executed such intense, double bass drumming by studying his set up. Although I focused more on BMX during this time, I still loved to play the drums. My stomach buzzed with excitement as I waited for Slayer to start playing.

The venue lights shut off as the intro track for *God Hates Us All* blasted from speakers next to the stage. The crowd coagulated, ready to experience transcendence through anger. Lights illuminated the band as they began playing "Disciple." To me, each member looked otherworldly.

Tom Araya, the lead singer and bassist, headbanged between shouts, his long hair swirling in front of his warlock bass. Kerry King played machine gun guitar riffs. Tribal tattoos crawled up his arms, onto his neck, and across his razor-shaved head. I couldn't wait until my hair would be as long as Tom Araya's, or until I'd be old enough to pay a tattoo artist to inject ink into my skin.

I thought about Grandpa Don and Grandma Vera as Tom Araya shouted, "Drones since the dawn of time / Not once has anyone seen / such a rise of pure hypocrisy."

Although I rabidly consumed biographical information about each member of Slayer, I somehow missed this fact: Tom Araya is a practicing Catholic. Kerry King writes most of the band's antireligious lyrics, but Araya still goes onstage night after night, shouting lyrics that seem to denounce his own beliefs.

I learned about Tom's faith two years ago. I still love a lot of Slayer's music, but no longer with the fervor of a fanatic. Learning about this fact still shocked me, though. I thought about the six or seven times I'd seen Slayer, and particularly this first time.

Initially, I didn't understand how Tom could live this double life. But then I realized that he's probably aware that Slayer fandom is a religion for many people. His congregation just goes to concert venues instead of churches, and he spreads messages through shouts and thrash metal instead of reading bible verses. I now think Slayer fanaticism and Catholicism are essentially the same, driven by similar motivations: Slayer's lyrics seek to instill guilt in people who believe in God.

A lot of their fans get Slayer tattoos, proudly showing them off at concerts. I'm sure Tom Araya, who's a smart guy, recognizes that people worship him, taking Slayer's lyrics as gospel. On the surface, the lyrics he shouts attack his own belief system, encouraging people—mostly angry young men—to hate Christianity. But Slayer's lyrics derive from a rigid sense of morality, which is one of the things I still hate about most forms of organized religion.

During and after my first Slayer concert, my hatred for religion and my grandparents seemed completely true and pure—the exact way I should be feeling.

A FEW MONTHS AFTER this concert, my family and I went to visit Grandpa Don, who was dying from lung cancer. At my grandparents' house in Jackson, I followed Dad into the master bedroom. The smells of leather furniture and cherrywood that permeated the rest of the house contrasted with the oily stench of decaying skin inside the bedroom.

During his healthier days, Grandpa had an ample gut and pudgy cheeks. Now, he was emaciated. Folds of transparent skin hung from his jaw and chest. Between his protruding ribs, the skin was so thin, it looked like you could poke through it with a pen. He sucked oxygen from a tank. When he saw me, which was the first time in several months, he said, "So you decided to grow out your hair, eh?" Distaste dripped from his words, and he didn't say anything else to me.

I didn't know how to respond. Before I saw him, I'd been hoping that he'd say something about being proud of me, or give me some kind of life advice. It was the last time I saw him alive. A gold crucifix hung from his neck. I focused my acidic anger onto this piece of his personality.

*

ONE OF MY EARLIEST memories of Grandpa Don is of staying with him at our family cabin. I played in the living room while Grandpa chopped vegetables in the kitchen, preparing one of his elaborate family dinners. I was three or four, and we were the only ones in the house. I don't remember what I did to make Grandpa Don mad, and I can't remember what he said, only that he yelled at me.

There was an enclosed porch on the other end of the cabin. I ran to the porch, grabbed a croquet mallet, and swung it into the glass door that led outside. The mallet glided through the pane of glass as if it was a thin layer of water.

Grandpa dropped his knife on the cutting board and ran to the porch. He was pissed, but I also remember him being surprised by the effect his words had on me. He apologized repeatedly for losing his temper.

DEER TAG

I DREW A DEER TAG when I was sixteen. In Wyoming, hunters put their names in a tag lottery every year, hoping to draw a permit in a good area. My tag allowed me to kill one buck north of Jackson Hole, a few miles outside the one thousand–person town of Dubois.

I'd killed two antelope before I went deer hunting. You can hunt in Wyoming after you turn twelve and pass a hunter's safety course. When I was twelve, I liked hunting rabbits and gophers but didn't want to kill deer, elk, or antelope, knowing that hunting big game involved a lot more driving and waiting. Dad loved big game hunting, though.

He'd grown up hunting with his grandpa, father, and brothers, and I think they felt closest to each other during hunting and fishing trips. Looking at pictures in Dad's hunting room of him holding up a dead deer, elk, or antelope with Grandpa Don, Uncle Gabe, or Uncle Nick, I saw toothy smiles instead of the smart-ass grin I more commonly saw on the faces of Anselmi men.

The hunter's safety course lasted six weeks. Although Dad had been telling me that I should, I didn't study for the final exam. I thought the test would be super easy, and part of me hoped that I wouldn't pass. Taking the exam in a community college classroom, Dad held his Scantron at an angle so I could see his answers when the instructor wasn't looking. Four or five months later, we were hunting antelope in an area just north of Rock Springs.

We left before the sun rose. By midafternoon, we'd chased a few herds of antelope, careening through sagebrush thickets in Dad's red Silverado, but hadn't come upon a good opportunity for a shot. Finally, after what felt like several days of searching, we found a midsized buck and a few does.

We quietly got out of the truck as the buck munched yellow prairie grass, keeping his head close to the ground. His thick black horns curled in at the tips, almost making the shape of a heart. With his high-power rifle, which he'd cleaned and sighted in a few days before, Dad lay down on his belly, not at all bothered by getting his shirt and pants dirty. He unlatched the legs from the barrel of the gun, propping them on a dirt mound, and then looked through the scope to make sure I'd have a good shot.

When I kneeled down next to him, he told me to take the rifle. I eased down into the dirt, holding the gun like Dad had taught me. It took me a few seconds to look through the scope properly—so I could see more than just black.

The crosshairs shakily danced across the antelope's white-and-brown body. I inhaled, closed my eyes, and pulled the trigger. The rifle kicked hard, sending the butt into my meatless shoulder. A metallic ring filled my ears. The antelope dropped but quickly got back up. He took a few wobbly steps and ran away.

"Shit," Dad said.

We got in the truck and chased him down. Dad plowed over sagebrush and steep embankments. My head bumped against the roof of the cab a few times, and hunting gear fell from the backseat onto the floor.

Within a mile or two, the antelope collapsed in a small clearing because he'd lost too much blood. A strained, high-pitched scream pierced my ears when I opened the door. I didn't know that antelope could scream. It sounded like metal scraping concrete, with hints of something distinctly human. I'd hit him near his hindquarters—probably in the liver, Dad guessed. He rolled around on the ground, engraining dirt into a dark wound above his right haunch.

"Put him out of his misery, son."

Dreading the rifle's kick, I got down on my stomach, aimed, and shot the antelope just below his neck. He collapsed, seeming to deflate.

Dad gutted the antelope while I stared at its black eyes. Wind made the surrounding sagebrush and prairie grass quiver. The film on the antelope's eyes had dried by the time Dad removed all of its entrails, scattering them in the dirt and sagebrush for coyotes. Specks of dirt clung to the antelope's eyes.

Although I didn't want to, I shot another antelope two years later, when I was fourteen, taking more care to execute a clean kill.

WHEN I WAS SIXTEEN and about to go deer hunting with Dad, our relationship was tense. I'd stopped trying to deny that he smoked pot every day—both to classmates and myself. At this point, I identified as straight edge with the moral rigidity of a zealot. Dad and I had screaming matches several times a week.

He'd often yell at me for not trying in school. Today, I realize that Dad didn't want to see me get swallowed by a life of blue-collar labor, and I wish that I hadn't reacted to his words with anger. At the time, I thought it was hypocritical for him to tell me to get better grades so I could get into a good school. He'd dropped out of college during his freshman year because he couldn't stop getting high, and he still smoked pot every day. Still, Dad always provided for my mom, sister, and me. He also could've been a junkie, like some of his friends, or an alcoholic, like most of the Anselmis.

Like every human, Dad had flaws, but he'd always been amazingly supportive, something I didn't appreciate nearly enough as a teenager. In grade school, I dreamt of becoming a professional sidearm pitcher. Dad would spend hours with me in our backyard during the summer, even after long shifts at the plant, gently coaching and encouraging me, saying things like, "Beautiful pitch, son. Right down the middle, baby."

When I decided that I wanted to play drums at the age of twelve, Dad didn't hesitate to buy me a five piece Ludwig kit that I'd keep until my mid twenties, or pay for two years of lessons. There were days when Dad came home from work irritable and exhausted and asked me to stop playing, which, for a long time, didn't sound much better than a toddler banging pots and pans with spoons. More often, he'd lay on the couch in our living room while I played, telling me, when I came upstairs from the basement, that I sounded good.

I've always had a fierce love for my dad. But this love often mutated into anger during my adolescence. When Dad told me to try harder in school, I'd tell him that I didn't give a shit about his life advice because he was a criminal. Now, it seems ridiculous that weed's illegality contributed to my resentment, especially considering how little respect I had for the law and authority. I was, after all, a metalhead BMX rider who regularly trespassed and destroyed public property. In retrospect, I think my resentment partially stemmed from how Dad's drug use showed me that no one is perfect, that life is endlessly unpredictable. I wanted things to be simple.

Dad hid his pot smoking from my sister, Arielle, and me for a long time. When I was fifteen, after I'd already learned about Dad's drug use from finding one of his pipes in our basement and hearing Drew talk about getting high with him, my parents had a talk with my sister and me, which basically amounted to telling us what we already knew. Even after this talk though, Dad's pot smoking wasn't out in the open, and it always felt like a secret.

When Dad came upstairs from his fishing room or returned home with bloodshot eyes, Mom wouldn't make eye contact with him. Looking at Arielle or me, she'd shake her head disapprovingly. When I was supposed to be asleep, I'd listen to my parents fight, usually hearing Dad deny that he was high.

I think Mom tried to set rules for Dad's drug use, rules he often violated. He wasn't supposed to get high when my sister or I were home, and he wasn't supposed to be stoned around us. I've pieced these rules together over the years. Throughout my adolescence, Mom rarely talked to Arielle or me about Dad's drug use directly.

Mom was nineteen and Dad was twenty-one when they got married. Everyone smoked pot in the seventies, Mom has often told me, so she didn't think it would ever be a big deal. She thought he'd eventually grow out of it.

Although she hated it, Mom also understood why Dad felt like he needed to get high every day. She knew that Grandpa Don and Grandma Vera had often told him that he wasn't worth much, something he'd come to believe himself. She also knew that living in Rock Springs—that panoptic house of mirrors—turned his self-hatred into a chasm.

Mom hated how Dad's pot smoking made him slow and forgetful—a self-fulfilling prophecy after people in town and his own family had been telling him that he was dumb for most of his life. But she pitied him too much to get a divorce, and I think she worried that he'd kill himself if she broke up with him. In addition to Freddy and a few of his other friends, two of Dad's uncles had killed themselves. The frequency of suicide in Rock Springs—I remember reading obituaries for people who'd committed suicide on at least a monthly basis—was a constant reminder that we can end our own pain.

At sixteen, I was beginning to see the complexity behind Dad's choice to get high regularly, but I resented this complexity, and I tried to deal with it in violently oversimplified ways. I also hated that Dad's pot smoking made Mom unhappy. After one of my screaming matches with Dad, or one of the many times when Mom knew that my sister or I had noticed his bloodshot eyes or smelled weed on him, I often caught her wiping tears from her eyes. When I asked her what was wrong, she usually said, "Nothing," or, "I was just cutting some onions."

People in restaurants, stores, and everywhere else in Rock Springs saw Dad as just another fucked-up Anselmi—communicated in derisive grins and jokes I wasn't supposed to hear—and it pissed me off to no end how these same people thought I'd end up just like him. I could also feel condescension in the way Grandpa Don, Grandma Vera, Uncle Gabe, and Uncle Nick interacted with Dad. I wanted him to tell everyone in Rock Springs and his family to fuck off.

Dad's reputation as a stoner made him a black sheep of the already disreputable Anselmi family. As my dad's son, I was born into a maddening box of expectations. As Don Anselmi's son, the expectations surrounding Dad must've been even more constricting.

DAD EXCITEDLY PREPARED FOR our trip to Dubois. He meticulously cleaned two of his best high-power rifles and tried to get me to go to the shooting range with him to sight them in. After several evenings of telling him that I wanted to ride my bike with my friends instead, he sighted in the rifles alone. He bought expensive thermal long johns and an orange, down-filled hunting vest for me, even though he preferred to buy clothes at Walmart or Kmart.

I now see how badly Dad wanted to bond with me, and I wish that I would've taken hunting with him more seriously, treating the ritual with reverence. At the time, I felt anxious about going on the trip because of the tension in our relationship, and also because hunting connected so deeply to expectations of manliness in Wyoming— expectations I didn't fulfill.

The opening week of hunting season was an unofficial holiday in school. Most guys would be off hunting with their dads, uncles, or friends, leaving only girls and a handful of boys—a mix of effeminate nerds and other outsiders—at school. The halls seemed empty, and we usually watched movies or did extra credit in class. Boys came back with stories about shooting bucks and getting shit-faced with their dads and uncles. The excitement I heard in their voices wasn't part of my big game hunting experiences, and I often wondered if there was something about hunting that I'd missed.

Because Dad was an expert hunter and fisherman, a lot of my classmates expected that I'd be good at these things, too. As far as I know, Dad was the only person in town that held a world record for fishing or hunting.

In high school, after I grew out my hair to look like a metalhead, I got used to hearing things like, "Long-haired faggot," and "He looks like a little girl," on a daily basis.

ON THE MORNING DAD and I drove to Dubois in his red Silverado, I just wanted to get the trip over with. Dad never pressured me to hunt, always reminding me that it was my choice. Still, after killing my first antelope, I felt like I couldn't tell him that I didn't want to hunt anymore.

We drove without talking for most of the four-hour drive. It was late October, and hoarfrost crept over the highway. I stared at empty stretches of prairie and the gray, predawn sky, not seeing a clear distinction between them. Dad knew I had a sweet tooth, so he'd put a bag of bite-sized Snickers in the truck's center console before we left. Knowing that it would aggravate him if I ate any Snickers so early in the morning, I became obsessed with the candy bars.

Dust lined the Silverado's vents, and musty air coming from the vents made my nose stuffy. Dad drank coffee, letting out little sighs after each sip. As I stared at green numbers on the dashboard clock, I kept thinking about the Snickers bars. The bag crinkled when I reached into it.

"Those will just make you sick," Dad said. "Why didn't you eat a good breakfast before we left home, like I told you to?" Dad weighed about 250 pounds and was 5'11. But he seemed much larger during this moment. Brown stubble sprouted from his cheeks, making his mustache less defined. A blue stocking cap sat atop his head, its bottom edges just above his ears. It always seemed strange to me that Dad could be so unself-conscious about his appearance.

After stuffing a candy bar into my mouth, I told him that I wasn't hungry when we left. The sounds of the candy bar being broken down by my teeth were like little earthquakes in my head, and I was sure that Dad could hear each nut crunch in my molars. I chewed slowly, both wanting and not wanting to irritate him. The Snickers bar exploded with flavor.

DAD'S BUDDY, SHAUN, HAD drawn a deer tag for the same area. We met up with him and Uncle Gabe in Dubois. I felt awkward around most of the Anselmi men, which was the case with Uncle Gabe. He was short, with a potbelly and trimmed beard. I could see patches of scalp through his thinning brown hair—the same balding pattern Grandpa Don went through. Uncle Gabe was usually nice to me, but I also knew that he could be sardonic, perhaps the biggest smart-ass out of all the smart-ass Anselmis. In most of my memories of him, he has a smirk on his face.

At this point, I knew that Uncle Gabe got high, although I can't remember how I found out. Unlike Dad, he'd graduated from college. He also ran a travel agency in Jackson Hole. On some level, I think I resented Uncle Gabe because my grandparents weren't as harsh with him as they were with Dad.

Uncle Gabe and I didn't know how to interact with each other. He'd seen me go through my nu-metal phase when I was thirteen. During a trip to Jackson Hole with my family, I came down to dinner after arranging my dyed-red hair into liberty spikes, which took at least forty minutes. This hairstyle was absurd, and it was especially absurd that I'd do my hair like this before a family dinner. Still, I got pissed when Uncle Gabe said, "So you decided to spike your hair, eh?"

Several pictures of Dad and Uncle Gabe hung on the walls of Dad's hunting room. In each one, they had an arm around the other's shoulder, and ecstatic smiles crawled across their faces. Dad and I both wanted to find a similar intimacy. Awkwardly shaking Uncle Gabe's hand on this cold morning in Dubois, I think I was jealous of the bond he and Dad had found through hunting. He gripped my hand firmly when we shook hands, and I felt like my grip wasn't strong enough.

Anger swelled in my chest when I saw Shaun. In his mid-to-late thirties, he had a permed blond mullet and exceptionally white teeth. The edges of his brown goatee seemed perfectly straight. Unlike Dad and Uncle Gabe, Shaun didn't have a thick gut. "What's up, little J. J.?" he said, grinning. "You ready to kill a deer, or what?"

"Yeah." I shivered as a gust of wind slithered through the top of my coat.

When I looked at Shaun, I saw Drew, his younger cousin. After Drew first got high with Dad and Shaun, he began smoking with them regularly, and he'd never stopped bragging about it at school.

I thought about having Drew in my sophomore welding class. Rock Springs High only included grades ten through twelve, so sophomore year was my first in high school. On the first day of school, about a month and a half before going deer hunting, I sat in a classroom that led into the welding shop, waiting for class to start. I heard Drew's voice in the hall and hoped that he wasn't in this class. He walked in and sat behind me.

"J. J., you should've seen it last week," Drew said. "Your dad came by Shaun's all fucked-up, blasting Ja Rule." A few other boys in the classroom overheard him and laughed. I tried to laugh with them, but embarrassment burned in my chest.

Really, it *was* funny that Dad, who's a mountain man at heart and in appearance, would blast Ja Rule in his dirt-caked pickup, driving through Rock Springs. But I knew that Drew and Shaun saw Dad as a clown. They might've genuinely cared about him, but I couldn't see it, and I hated that Dad willingly acted out this role.

Shaun used to leave mocking messages for Dad on our answering machine. He'd mimic Dad's deep monotone, saying, "Right on" and "Far out" over and over, which were some of Dad's favorite phrases. Shaun repeated himself in the messages, sometimes acting like he'd lost his train of thought.

I'd also mock Dad with Jared, Bryan, and Steve. Their dads got drunk every night, and we'd sarcastically repeat their hilarious catch phrases, too. When we made fun of each other's dads, or our own, however, it was complicated by our understanding that pain and hopelessness fueled their partying. Hearing Drew or Shaun mimic my dad, I always wanted to say, "Fuck you. You don't know him." Mainly, I wished that Dad would tell them to fuck off himself.

THE FIRST TWO HOURS of the day went by pretty quickly. As the sun rose above the Tetons' escarpments and into the cloudless sky, we drove on snowpacked dirt roads, looking for deer. Uncle Gabe, driving his white S-10 with Shaun in the passenger seat, followed Dad and me. Pine trees and quaking aspens surrounded us. I looked on either side of the road as the truck crawled along, hoping to see a buck dart out of the trees.

At about ten, Uncle Gabe signaled for Dad to pull over, telling Dad that he and Shaun were going to venture out on their own. Soon, time began to move like near-frozen molasses crawling downhill. As I searched between tree trunks for the gray body of a deer, I became skeptical that I'd see one. Dad stopped the truck every hundred yards or so to search a clearing with his spotting scope. When he slowed to a stop, snow creaked like stressed wood beneath the truck's tires. He had to roll down his window to look through the spotting scope, which attached to the top of his window. Icy air crept into the cab.

"Can we turn on the heater, Dad?"

"If you're cold, grab one of those blankets in the backseat. We'll just be wasting gas if we run the heater."

In the backseat, two rifles in padded cases sat on top of coats, blankets, snow boots, stocking caps, and several boxes of bullets. I thought about the scene from *Home Alone* when Kevin tries to pull something from his brother's jam-packed closet and everything falls on him. I grabbed a blanket, feeling like the stuff in the backseat was going to fall on me.

I ate a few more bite-sized Snickers, unwrapping each one slowly. I'd gotten braces two or three months earlier, and pieces of nuts had lodged themselves in my upper right bracket. I tried to pick them out, but the space was too tight. I ate three or four more candy bars, hoping to dislodge the nuts with new ones. But the new nuts just got stuck between my gums and bracket, too. Soon, the gums on the upper-right side of my mouth started to feel sore, and I tasted blood when I ran my tongue over that area.

Dust on the dash, floorboards, and coming from the vents tightened my sinuses. As my near-empty stomach digested chocolate instead of real food, I started to feel queasy. I told Dad that I wasn't feeling good, hoping he'd say we should just go home.

"No wonder you don't feel good, eating all that damn chocolate," he said, shaking his head and looking out the window.

WE MET UP WITH Shaun and Uncle Gabe just before lunch. When they pulled up, their eyes were bloodshot slits. Outside the shade, the snow-covered hills and meadows were blindingly bright, but the air was still frigid. I stayed in the truck while Dad got out and talked to them, cracking my window so I could hear.

"You guys see any big ones?" Shaun asked. As I looked at him and Uncle Gabe, I thought about Drew and his friends. In every class I had with Drew, he usually showed up stoned out of his gourd with one of his buddies. They'd sit in the back of the room with their heads down, glancing at each other and trying not to laugh.

"Not yet," Dad said, looking back at me. "We had to stop for a while because Jay wasn't feeling too good."

Uncle Gabe and Shaun looked at me. I felt like a museum exhibit behind Dad's windshield. They left again.

When Dad came back, he told me that he was going to make sandwiches for us. In the rearview mirror, I watched him open the camper shell and grab the food-filled cooler. He cut slices off a roll of Genoa salami, placing them on pieces of wheat bread. He put two squares of cheese and a few squirts of mustard on each sandwich.

"Here you go, Jojo," Dad said, handing me a sandwich when he got back in the cab. I loved it when Dad used this nickname. He was the only person who called me Jojo. Sometimes he'd add "Gun"—Jojo Gun—which I also loved. "Why don't you get something solid in your stomach. It'll make you feel better."

The warmth in Dad's voice made me feel like an asshole for trying to irritate him with the candy bars. Like I had many times before, I wished that I could find the thing in hunting that Dad loved so much, but hours of sitting in the cramped truck loomed.

Like Dad said it would, the sandwich eased my stomach. Pieces of nuts were still stuck in my braces, though. I couldn't wait to get home and brush my teeth. I imagined how I'd pick the nuts out of my foamy spit, holding them up in the mirror like little trophies.

We resumed the process of creeping along and stopping to check every clearing. I intermittently pictured a seven-point buck jumping out of the trees, imagining what it would feel like to kill a buck big enough for the Boone and Crockett record book. Dad had never killed a deer, elk, or antelope big enough for Boone and Crockett, although he'd been hunting for over thirty years. I thought about how funny it would be to nonchalantly tell Shaun, Uncle Gabe, and Drew about the massive buck I'd killed. But I mostly wished that I'd see any buck, big or small, so I could just shoot it and go home.

As midday morphed into afternoon, I picked at a hangnail on my right thumb. I can't remember when I started this habit, but I'd sometimes dig into the irritated skin between a hangnail and fingernail with a pen, coloring that area blue or black. I found a pen in the glove box and pushed the tip into my thumb, widening the small strip of pink flesh into a blackened groove.

"You don't like hunting too much, do you?" Dad said. I didn't know that he'd been watching me. Sun coming through the windshield danced in the blond hairs of his mostly-brown mustache.

"No, I do. I was just getting bored since we've been in the truck all day." I hated that I couldn't get myself to just tell him that I didn't want to go hunting anymore. Shortly after this trip, when I finally did tell Dad that I didn't want to put my name in for another deer tag or any other type of big game, he was disappointed, but not mad. I'd built the moment up into something terrifying in my head.

"We can go home if you want."

Although I'd been waiting to hear these words all day, I said, "That's alright. I'm good."

"I'm sure we'll see a buck around here soon. Just keep your eyes open." He patted my shoulder and then looked out the window with his binoculars. "If we don't get one today, we can always get a room in Dubois and try again tomorrow."

As the reddish-pink sun began to sink behind the white peaks of the Tetons, Dad spotted a few deer in a thicket of quaking aspens. He eased the truck to a stop and handed me his binoculars. Three does, one fawn, and a buck with small, twig-like horns munched yellow grass that sprouted from the snow.

"What do you think?" Dad asked, looking through his spotting scope. "He's pretty small, ain't he?

"Yeah, but I bet he'll be really good to eat."

"I guess the young ones are nice and tender."

Dad got out of the truck, quietly taking a rifle from the cluttered backseat. He took the gun out of its case and loaded four bullets into the chamber. The bullets were huge—about three inches long with pointed tips. I got out and tiptoed over to his side, snow creaking beneath my feet. Dad handed me the rifle, which felt heavier than I remembered. This was the gun I'd used to kill both of my antelope.

"We're not supposed to do this," Dad said, "but why don't you use the hood for a rest." He laid the padded rifle case across the Silverado's hood so neither the rifle stock or his truck would get scratched.

Resting my elbows on the red hood, I looked at the deer—one hundred or so yards away—through the scope. The black metal of the scope felt cold against my left eyebrow.

"Just take your time," Dad whispered.

For a second, I didn't think it was possible that I could kill this deer. The crosshairs erratically moved across the buck's body. I held my breath, feeling like I was about to jump into an icy lake. When I was ten, I'd gotten a black eye from shooting a high-power rifle. I didn't properly brace the butt against my shoulder, and the sharp edge of the scope had kicked back, hitting the flesh just below my eye. Looking at this small buck, I closed my eyes and pulled the trigger. Immediately following the gun's thunderclap, a metallic ringing filled my ears.

"Yeah! Jojo Gun! You dropped him!" Dad's high-pitched laugh echoed in the clearing.

I felt giddy as Dad and I plowed through snowdrifts, parking a few feet from the deer. Blood oozed from a wound above his front quarters, pooling in the snow. Looking at his small horns, each about five inches long,

I felt embarrassed, knowing that Shaun, Uncle Gabe, and Drew would think this buck was really small.

Dad grabbed his hunting knife from the backseat. His Grandpa John had given him this knife, and Dad often told me that it would be mine one day. He pulled the razor-sharp blade out of its leather scabbard, which had Dad's initials, my initials, neatly carved into it. "Do you want me to show you how to gut it?"

This was the part of hunting that I dreaded most. Dad had gutted both of my antelope, and I knew that I should gut my own deer. But the thought of touching the animal's guts freaked me out as I looked into its empty eyes.

"I'll gut it for you. Why don't you just wait in the truck."

I both resented and loved that Dad let me sit in the warm truck as he gutted the deer. Through my window, I watched him slit the animal's throat. Blood poured down the deer's chest and onto Dad's stained jeans. He cut off its testicles and threw them into some nearby sagebrush, not wanting the testosterone to spoil the meat.

Dad slid his knife along the deer's underside, making a precise cut down the center. He pulled out its lungs, stomach, intestines, kidneys, and gallbladder, tossing them in the snow. His hands and forearms were covered in blood, and I wondered how this didn't bother him. Milky tendrils of steam rose from the brown, gray, and red mass of organs.

*

ONE MONTH AFTER THIS trip, in November of my sophomore year, there was a fire drill at school. Students and teachers gathered in front of a house across the street from Rock Springs High. Wearing a T-shirt, I stood with my arms crossed, blowing warm air into my cupped hands. I saw Steve, who stood a head taller than most of the other students. He was talking to Drew.

"You little pussy, J. J.," Drew said when I walked over to them. "Shaun told me you just cried for your mom the whole time you were hunting, like a little bitch." I was a few inches taller than Drew and not much skinnier, but he seemed terrifying.

Two weeks earlier, I'd told Dad that I didn't want to go hunting anymore.

LIVING THROUGH PANTERA

ANXIETY CRAWLED AROUND IN my throat like an amphetamine-crazed lizard when Dad's truck pulled into the driveway. I was watching TV in the living room. He slammed the garage door, making glasses and plates in the china cabinet rattle. I knew that he had another shitty day of meter reading, a job he'd started after quitting the powerhouse. I waited for him to walk into the living room.

"Did you find a job today?" He shut off the TV.

"I was going to pick up a few applications," I said, "but I ended up riding at the skate park."

"Goddamnit, son. It's always the same shit. Every day. You need to find a job and start trying harder in school." His harshness reminded me of the way Grandpa Don talked to him and to me.

I told him that I didn't want another bullshit job like working maintenance at the Outlaw, a job I'd recently quit.

The motel evoked thoughts that I wanted to escape, and seeing how blue-collar labor inflicted misery upon Dad made me not want to get another job. But I didn't say any of this to him.

"What are you going to do for money?" His voice was louder.

"I'll just get a paper route or work at McDonald's or some shit."

"That's another thing. You need to clean up your language. I don't want to hear you cussing anymore. You need to have a better attitude, son." Hearing the amount of cuss words that came out of his mouth every day, it seemed silly that he'd tell me to stop cussing. Behind his words, I heard, "Do as I say, not as I do," which Grandma Vera had been saying to both of us for our entire lives. As with Grandpa Don, Dad wouldn't admit that his mom had serious flaws as a parent. I focused anger for my grandparents onto my dad.

"Fuck you, Dad."

Like every other time I'd said this to him, he just looked at me for a few seconds, eyes widened. Then we started screaming at each other.

"Why the fuck should I listen to you?" I yelled. "You're just a stoner that dropped out of school." Without waiting for his response, I grabbed the keys to my car and left, driving to the belt route, down past the high school, and over a bridge with a brown, litter-strewn creek flowing underneath. Gnarled sagebrush jutted over the banks.

Eroding sandstone cliff faces surrounded gas stations, bars, and trailers at the bottom of the hill. Thinking about living in Rock Springs with my dad for another three years, anger surged through my veins.

I needed to listen to Pantera.

In my New Yorker, I played *The Great Southern Trendkill*, turning my boom box up full blast during "Living Through Me." As Phil Anselmo screamed, "I broke your fucking mold / then threw away the cast" in his guttural voice, which was intensified by Vinnie Paul's driving double bass rhythms, the crunch of Dimebag's guitar, and the thick rumble of Rex Brown's bass, I felt like someone patted me on the shoulder, saying, "You fucking *should* hate your dad." I also thought Pantera would always be better than me at expressing my emotions.

After driving west across vacuous plains on I-80 for a half hour, I turned around, wishing that I had somewhere to go besides my parents' house. I drove home, still listening to Pantera. Inside, Dad and I didn't speak to each other.

Lying on my bed, I looked at a picture of Phil Anselmo that hung on my wall. Black tattoos on white skin; long hair; thick beard; and Phil's signature sneer. Looking at the mirror above my dresser and wondering when I'd be able to grow a beard (at sixteen, I could only grow a patchy goatee), I adjusted my hair to look more like Phil's—parted down the middle, with gnarled split ends on both sides. I pictured tattoos covering my bony arms.

I wished that Phil Anselmo was my dad. I didn't think about it in these terms, but, as I examine my obsession with Pantera's singer and the rest of the band during my high school years, it always comes back to that desire.

I had so many fights with Dad when I was sixteen, seventeen, and eighteen, they blur together in my memory. We had the same fight for three years.

I'D CHOSEN PHIL ANSELMO, and, to lesser extents, the other members of Pantera, to fulfill my need for a reliable father figure, partly because of the space in each member's image. Phil, Dime, Rex, and Vinnie—they seemed like two-dimensional characters, leaving room for me to shape them. I consumed Pantera media that spanned fifteen years, but I never saw any real change in these guys.

Scowling as he screams into a microphone, Phil looks pissed in most pictures. With a dyed-red goatee, camouflage shorts and maniacal grin, Dimebag Darrel rips solos on his signature guitar. Wearing a black bandana on his head, scraggly muttonchops sprouting out, Vinnie beats the shit out of his drums. Rex headbangs in most pictures, his long hair swirling in front of his bass.

I imparted each of these characters with the things I craved in a father figure.

PHIL ANSELMO MAY HAVE lived in a narcotic bubble, but he'd never get high with one of my classmates. If Phil were my dad, I wouldn't have to deal with kids at school constantly asking about Dad's pot smoking. Phil often got so wasted before Pantera shows that, onstage, he'd just lie down and mumble into the mic. Nevertheless, according to my absurd thought process at the time, I wouldn't have to deal with all the fucked-up emotions connected to my real father if (my version of) Phil Anselmo was my dad.

I wouldn't think about Grandpa Don calling Dad a failure because he'd dropped out of college and gotten arrested for possession; because he'd never be like his business-savvy older brother; because his mind worked in ways that Grandpa didn't understand. I wouldn't think about Grandma Vera telling Dad that he'd fried his brain with weed and LSD. For me, all these thoughts connected to Dad's need to encase himself in a padded haze, and I didn't want to deal with them.

There were a lot of other things about Dad that I didn't understand, like his weird hang-ups about throwing things away. When my mom, sister, or I threw away moldy cheese or foul-smelling deli meat, Dad often picked these things out of the trash and ate them. He hung deer, elk, and antelope hides from the rafters in our garage. He'd skinned the animals himself, missing little chunks of fat on each hide. During the summer, the stench of greasy rot hit you as soon as you walked into the garage, but Dad refused to get rid of the hides.

Once, Mom and I found a maggot-ridden raccoon carcass in a cooler in the garage. We'd later learn that Dad had found it on the side of a road and decided to bring it home, although he never told us why. The smell in the garage seemed particularly rank one summer day, seeping under the garage door and into the kitchen. Mom and I searched it, dry heaving when we found the cooler and opened it. We put the cooler in the back of Dad's truck, drove a few miles outside town, and left it on the side of the highway.

Dad would often quickly switch from a good mood, talking and laughing with my mom, sister, and me, to being highly irritable. The exasperating thing about these mood snaps was their unpredictability. I never knew what would set him off.

All of these things should've illuminated a need to examine Dad in more complex ways. Instead, I responded to him in the same way as his parents, but with more anger.

DURING THE SUMMER I turned seventeen, Superjoint Ritual, a band Phil Anselmo formed after Pantera split, was touring on Ozzfest. Pantera had already broken up when I became an obsessive fan of the band, so seeing the members' post-Pantera bands would be the only way I'd get to see them in concert. The idea of seeing Phil in a live setting seemed incredible. Unlike Dime and Vinnie, I loved all of Phil's music after Pantera. He still knew exactly how I felt. Steve and I bought tickets and drove six hours to see the show in Denver.

After a long morning of metalcore bands, cigarette and weed smoke, stinky dudes and scantily clad women, I found out that Superjoint Ritual was doing a meet-and-greet. All I had to do to get a pass to meet them was buy one of their CDs or DVDs.

Holding Superjoint's *A Lethal Dose Of American Hatred* and trying to decide which part of the CD booklet

I wanted the band to sign, I waited in line, talking with my fellow Pantera fanatics. Talking to devout fans, you don't hear "Dimebag Darrell Abbott," "Vinnie Paul Abbott," "Rex Brown," or "Philip Anselmo" when they reference band members. You hear "Dime," "Vinnie," "Rex," and "Phil." We talked about the members of Pantera as if they were family.

Some fans had "CFH" etched into their skin, usually in black ink. In a circular shape, the CFH logo had become Pantera's emblem. It stands for *Cowboys From Hell*, which is the first album the band recorded with Phil. The tattoo is a rite of passage for hard core fans. At other metal concerts, I'd also met several people with CFH tattoos. Two years after this show, I'd pay a tattoo artist to engrave Pantera's logo into my skin. As the needle shot burning jolts through my wristbones, regret lodged in my throat, which I smothered by thinking about how people would react to my tattoo. Anyone who saw it would immediately know who I was.

I needed to prove my lifelong loyalty to the band by branding myself with their logo, ensuring my membership in the cult of true Pantera fans. I needed an absolute to counter my unstable relationship with my dad. Although a lot of rock and metal fans are outspokenly antireligious—I was a glaring example of this—they seek acceptance into groups that serve the same purposes as organized religion.

Like The Grateful Dead, Slipknot, Led Zeppelin, Slayer, Insane Clown Posse, and The Beatles, a lot of Pantera fans exhibit a cultish rabidness. As a devout fan, you can find an instant sense of community with other fanatics. Like myself, people who gravitate toward obsessive fandom are often social outcasts. To counter isolation, it makes sense that people would want to join a group whose members always feel connected, even if they've never met. But this fandom and the community that comes with it also fucks people up. Trying to fill the void of isolation with fictional relationships and superficial self-perception can destroy your ability to digest complexity.

Like any art form, music can be a direct confession. Combined with biographical information about artists, this intimacy often creates the illusion of one-on-one interaction. But there's an important difference between artistic communication and direct communication that I didn't think about as a Pantera fanatic. This differentiation separates obsessive fans from people who know that art only illustrates a portion of an artist's personality.

My favorite musicians occupied an elevated realm in my head, and I know this sounds strange, given how imperfect they all were. I think this idea of their perfection only made me more intolerant of my dad's imperfections. Instead of trying to understand my relationship with him, I wanted to believe that there are people who aren't bubbling masses of contradictions. But I didn't see any holes in my logic while enveloped in this culture. Waiting in line to meet Phil, I was just excited to meet people I immediately felt connected to.

Superjoint Ritual also consisted of Jimmy Bower from Eyehategod, a band I was just getting into, and Hank

Williams III, but Phil was my reason for waiting. An aura
surrounded him, like an original painting you've only seen
in prints. I wasn't nervous because I felt like I'd already
met him. Shaking his hand, I said, "Everything you do is
fucking genius, man."

He held his fist in the air as if we were fighting for the
same political cause and said, "Thank you, brother."

Later that evening, Steve and I snuck past security
guards to get into the VIP section, just a few feet from
the stage. During their set, Phil Anselmo and the other
members of Superjoint looked unreal, like cartoon
characters. Waves of music tickled my spine.

*

MY DAD IS FUCKED-UP, and I think it's fair to say that
he's crazy. But we're all fucked-up and crazy. I still catch
myself latching onto the idea that Dad's past can fully
explain what it's like to be around him. Never examining
his parents' flaws has been damaging for him in a lot of
ways. In his mind, they had good reasons for verbally
abusing him—an idea that's welded worthlessness into his
self-perception.

While these things do explain some aspects of Dad's
personality, a gap remains between my explanations and
actually being around him. A large part of reaching toward
an understanding of my dad has been admitting that I
might never understand him. Trying to deal with some of
his flaws in person—his mood snaps, how pissed he gets

when I criticize his parents, and his perpetually cloudy eyes—is always going to be hard. But I still have to attempt to understand him. I think I had to stop worshipping other artists to reconcile myself to these truths.

I now see that Dad destroyed his body through physical labor for my mom, sister, and me. It's taken me too long to realize that, during the screaming matches Dad and I had when I was in high school, his underlying message was always, *I want you to have a better life than me.*

During the summer I went to Ozzfest, however, I was years from seeing these things. Throughout the rest of high school, Dad and I got into a gnarly fight at least once a week. I remember standing a few feet away from him in our dining room and knowing that we both wanted to punch each other. Dad never would've hit me, and I'd never have hit him. But we refused to believe that we couldn't change each other. Our frustration collected in our chests like tight balls of electrified twine, constantly pushing us to the edge of the place where emotion becomes action.

ENTERING THE MOMENT

I HEARD THE RUMBLE OF Steve's Bronco when he pulled up to my parents' house. Two months earlier, I'd started my junior year of high school.

"Okay, mom, I'm going out to Jared and Bryan's to ride."

"Alright, baby," she said, looking up from her Anne Rice novel. Mom didn't care if I came home super late from Jared and Bryan's house or, oftentimes, not until the next day. When I was with my friends, she knew I'd be okay. Our obsessive focus on BMX kept Jared, Bryan, Steve, and me from fucking around with drugs or booze.

"I'll call if I stay."

Jared and Bryan lived seven miles outside of Rock Springs, in a small community called Arrowhead Springs. Kenny and Tammy, Jared and Bryan's parents, let my friends and me build ramps in their large garage. Within two years, we'd turned it into our own skate park. They also let Steve and me stay at their house too many times to count, basically adopting us into their family.

The fact that Dad had worked for Pacific Power for over twenty years seemed like a feat of manliness to me. In high school, my male classmates constantly talked about customizing their trucks and working tough jobs. I tried to follow their conversations, pretending that I knew what it was like to endure long shifts of backbreaking labor involving machinery that could eat you alive. But this world always scared the shit out of me. Building ramps with Jared, Bryan, and Steve helped me feel like a man in a town where I often didn't.

Over the years, my friends taught me some basics of construction. Although he'd worked in a power plant, Dad was a mountain man, and he'd never been mechanically savvy. I hated the only woodshop class I'd ever taken because I constantly worried that the teacher and other boys thought I was a pansy. But, in Jared and Bryan's garage, I loved to cut plywood and two-by-fours with an electric saw while listening to old school metal. My friends were patient when they taught me about ramp building, and their jabs about my lack of mechanical sense were mostly playful.

A gust of wind blew hair into my mouth when I walked outside. The October nights had become frigid, and the first snow of the year coated the sidewalks. Seven months of harsh Wyoming winter loomed. My breath snaked into the air, getting sucked from my throat by the wind. I looked at the plywood quarter pipe on the edge of my parents' driveway, its bottom corners curling up from being left outside.

During the previous summer, I'd bought the ramp from a rollerblader. With my friends' help, I hauled it to my parents' house in my truck, which Dad had given me right before Ozzfest. A year or so earlier, Dad had traded in his Silverado and bought a white 1998 Tacoma. Then, seven or eight months later, a mechanic told me that the New Yorker was likely to burst into flames on the road. Whatever was wrong would've cost more to fix than the car was worth. We gave the New Yorker away, and Dad gave me the white Tacoma after buying a newer, gold-colored one for himself. I immediately placed Black Sabbath, Pantera, Metallica, Slayer, and BMX stickers on the windows, trying to make the truck my own.

When we got the quarter pipe to my house, my friends and I set it up on the left side of the driveway. A few days later, I spray-painted "Six Six Six," "Destroy," and "Hate" on the ramp. I didn't believe in God or the devil. I was just an asshole metalhead, and I loved to piss people off. Dad had spray-painted black boxes over my tags, but I could still see my words beneath thin coats of paint. He hated the tags for the same reason I thought they were badass: anyone who drove by our house could see them.

Pantera's *The Great Southern Trendkill* pulsated my eardrums when I opened the back door of Steve's Bronco. I lifted my bike in, careful not to scratch my Metal Bikes frame. We drove uphill, passing Uncle Nick and Ben Hay's large houses.

On Highway 430, wind pushed against Steve's Bronco, making it more difficult to pick up speed. Icy snow danced across the cracked asphalt. Steve and I didn't try to talk over the music. "Suicide Note Pt. 1"—an acoustic ballad on an album that mostly consists of Southern rock-infused thrash—drifted from Steve's speakers. Phil Anselmo crooned, "Would you look at me now? / Can you tell I'm a man?"

We passed SF Phosphates, a chemical plant that marked the turnoff to Arrowhead Springs. Large concrete and metal cylinders emitted sickly white smoke into the air. The chemical plant, with its flickering green and red lights, looked like a tiny, diseased city.

A cottontail suddenly darted across the road. The rabbit sounded like a plywood plank slapping against the Bronco's wheel well when Steve hit it. "Those little fuckers," he said. "It's like they're on a death mission." We usually ran over at least one rabbit during the nights we drove to Jared and Bryan's house.

After we parked in the driveway and got out of the Bronco, I heard plywood and two-by-fours slap against concrete, punctuated by a *tink* of coping. Light seeped under the tall garage door, which Steve lifted up for us to walk under. Metallica's *Kill 'Em All* echoed off the insulated walls in the garage.

"Get the fuck out of here, you fucking peter-eaters!" Bryan yelled. We'd started calling each other "peter-eater" after Jared and Bryan's dad drunkenly mumbled it at Jared one night.

Bryan pedaled at a quarter pipe on the far end of the garage. A three-foot wooden ledge sat on the deck of the ramp. Bryan jumped from the quarter pipe and stuffed his shoe between his fork and front tire, stalling on his front wheel on top of the ledge. With seeming effortlessness, he jumped back into the quarter pipe, landing an inch or two below the coping. Above the next ramp, Bryan planted his left foot on the wall while holding his bike above him. His back wheel spun, freewheel ticking like a manic clock, before he dove back into the transition. Throughout the rest of his run, Bryan performed similarly difficult tricks with the precision of a mathematician.

When Bryan finished his run, Steve shot out from his spot next to me. After airing a quarter pipe, he made a sharp turn and rode up the adjacent vert wall—a super steep ramp we'd pushed against Kenny's tool room. Coming down, Steve pushed his tires into the transition to gain speed. He launched over the nearby hip and tilted his bike past ninety degrees, executing a perfect tabletop. Steve zipped around the garage, turning and spinning his bike the opposite direction without a hint of awkwardness.

Steve's smooth riding contrasted with his chaotic home life. His parents were divorced, and he switched between staying at each of their houses. Once, during a fight, Steve hit his step-dad in the kneecap with a hammer. Scared of getting his ass kicked, he rode to his dad's trailer across town. Watching their big-screen, chain smoking, and blasting Mötley Crüe, Steve's dad and step-mom got drunk every night. A pack of children with popsicle-smudged faces always seemed to be running around the trailer.

Like my dad, Steve's dad—who Jared, Bryan, and I called Old Steve—was super supportive. He used to ride BMX himself, and, every once in a while, he'd hop on his old Haro and ride with us. He'd also tell us stories about riding with his friends back in the day. They'd sharpen their pegs and do kick-outs into the doors of cop cars, which I thought was rad.

I can't count how many times Old Steve fixed my car or truck. He was an amazing mechanic, and he knew most of the auto shops in town would rip me off. He never called me a pansy or dumbass because I didn't know how to work on cars. Even though he spent forty-plus hours a week working in an auto shop, he never seemed to mind helping me out.

Of course, like all of us, Old Steve had his shortcomings. He and Steve's mom hadn't planned on having Steve. They were only kids themselves—both around seventeen or eighteen—and Old Steve didn't want to force himself into a monotonous adult life. Although he loved his son intensely, I think he wanted to be Steve's buddy instead of his parent. Steve only mentioned it to me a few times, but he and his dad had also gotten into a few fistfights, and I think this violence loomed over their relationship. When Old Steve teased his son as if he was his drinking buddy, Steve usually looked like he was trying too hard to smile. Riding fast and pumping each transition for momentum in the garage, Steve's mind entered a place where only the present moment existed.

Starting my run, I ice-picked the ledge above the quarter pipe. Unlike Bryan, Steve, and Jared, I didn't rotate mine the opposite direction during my runs. It felt awkward, and I didn't have enough patience with myself to learn. At this point, I felt too embarrassed to go back and learn the foundational tricks my friends had all picked up in junior high.

I rode straight up a different quarter pipe, slamming my back wheel into the adjacent wall while squeezing my brake lever. I stalled in an over-vertical position for a fraction of a second, my front wheel hanging over my head. I hopped into the transition backwards, back-pedaling and then quickly flipping around. I loved the sensation of going down a ramp the wrong way. Most of my tricks consisted of variations on these two maneuvers—a fakie wall ride and an ice-pick stall—whereas my friends' riding was much more varied.

"Yeah, J. J.," Jared said. He, Steve, and Bryan clapped, although they'd all seen me land this trick several times before.

Jared pedaled toward the quarter pipe furthest from where we sat. Launching off the ramp, he spun a 180 and landed on the three-foot ledge. His sprocket dug into the wooden edge, and his front wheel hovered just above the quarter pipe's coping. Jared used to tell me that this trick, called a disaster, is about overcoming the mental picture of flipping over your bars on the way back in and smashing your face on the ground. He hopped back onto the ramp, tires adhering to the transition as if magnetized.

Riding, each of us pushed beyond fear. Momentarily floating in this space, we disconnected from thoughts about our fathers' flaws and how much we hated Rock Springs. Even though I mostly did variations on the same tricks, overcoming fear was always part of the equation. You can't ride without getting injured, and riders often get hurt doing routine tricks.

BMX constantly fucked all of us up. My injury list: separated shoulder; two broken feet; broken leg; countless gashes—one on top of my head that had to be closed with staples—scrapes, and bruises; fluid buildup behind both kneecaps—my right knee used to swell to twice its normal size after bumping it, even lightly; and one concussion. And my BMX injuries were minor compared to a lot of other riders'. I remember getting around school on crutches after I broke my foot or leg. Most kids and teachers knew how I'd hurt myself, and I felt like a badass as I crutched through the halls.

We rode for about an hour and a half before going upstairs. Jared and Bryan's mom had bought KFC for us and set it out on the counter.

"Hi guys," Tammy said. "J. J. and Steve, have some dinner." Steve and I'd long gotten past the point of politely refusing food from Tammy, knowing she'd just tell us to eat anyway. On her way upstairs, she exhaled and stopped. To Jared and Bryan, she said, "Your dad won't be home until late." We all knew what this meant: Kenny was going to get shit-faced and drive home.

Bryan had recently ordered a new BMX video, *Manmade Chapter 2*. He put it in the DVD player while Jared, Steve, and I piled greasy chicken onto our plates and sat down in the living room. Filthy, tar-soaked riffs of Floor's "Assassin" play during Dave King's section, both of which made me feel giddy. Dave flies over huge dirt jumps, doing picture-perfect tabletops and turndowns—classic, style-oriented tricks. There's a tough, manly beauty in his riding. He and his bike become one entity, and I wished that I could ride like him. A rider usually needs a background in racing to attain this level of smoothness, and I'd never raced. As Dave rides, Floor's Steve Brooks, one of the few openly gay metal musicians I know of, sings "Crazy for the boy" in a weirdly soothing, off-kilter melody. This song perfectly fits Dave King's stripped-down riding.

An energetic From Autumn to Ashes song plays during Chase Hawk's section in *Chapter 2*, which follows Dave King's. Chase floats in the air, whipping his back end to the side over steep dirt jumps as if his bike is an extension of his body. He doesn't do circus tricks like double backflips, but, to me, his effortless flow was much more beautiful than the riding you'd see in contests like the X Games. You can hear the *zip* of his tires as he flies off the lip of a dirt jump, the *whoosh* of wind as he zooms past the camera. Over each jump, he performs an acrobatic dance that exists somewhere beyond human emotion. As

I did with Dave King, I wished I could ride like Chase. About two years after this night, I'd hang out with Chase and Dave in Austin, discovering their bisexuality, which seemed terrifying at the time but now makes perfect sense.

We heard Kenny pull into the upper garage in his vintage Jaguar, a car he'd rebuilt himself. Like most nights, he'd driven home after getting hammered at a bar in downtown Rock Springs. During his early twenties, Kenny, driving drunk with two female passengers, had gotten into a gnarly accident. One woman died and the other would never walk again. About fifteen years later, Kenny flipped a four-wheeler onto himself, breaking his neck and back. Now, to turn his head, he had to turn his entire body, and he usually wore a neck brace.

Kenny shuffled in from the garage. He grabbed a plastic bowl of salad from the fridge, eating lettuce and vegetables with his bare hands. My friends and I laughed hysterically. I waited for Jared or Bryan to fuck with him.

"Dad," Jared said. "You're a fucking weasel peter-eater." This phrase sent all of us into hysterics.

Kenny chewed a piece of lettuce, smacking his lips. Between incoherent mumbling, he said, "No, *you're* a fucking weasel peter-eater."

Laughing at Kenny, we told ourselves that we would never be like our fathers, even though we'd all inherited our penchant for recklessness from them. Although I laughed, I also knew that Kenny's drinking was a yawning pain for Jared, Bryan, their older brother Jesse, and Tammy. We never said this, but my friends and I all wished Kenny wouldn't drink anymore.

He was one of the nicest guys I've ever met. With short brown hair and a trimmed beard, he was perpetually hunched over from his back injuries, and his lips always curled up in a smart-ass grin. Like a stereotypical Irishman, his cheeks were deeply ruddy. I still can't believe that he let us fill his workspace with ramps.

Instead of telling us to be careful when he watched us ride, Kenny would try to get us to do crazier shit, often yelling, "Do a three-sixty!" When Steve and I came over, he never made us feel like mooches, even though we routinely raided his fridge and slept on his couches. He always told us to think of his expensive tools as our own, and his tool room became the go-to place when we needed to fix our bikes. Almost every time I saw Kenny, he asked me how my parents were doing. He and my dad had known each other for a long time, having a mutual friend in Joey Hay.

It was this mix of deep-hearted kindness and selfishness that made our dads so perplexing. Beneath our anger and sometimes-sarcastic view of our dads, I think we worried that they were constantly on the verge of killing themselves.

DURING HIGH SCHOOL, STEVE, Jared, Bryan, and I became friends with Josh, a Rock Springs BMX hero who was seven years older than us. When Josh moved to Salt Lake, he offered us an open invitation to sleep on his floor. He lived with Mike Aitken, a legendary BMX pro. Like us, Josh was straight edge.

When he visited Rock Springs, he usually rode our garage ramps. One weekend, we were listening to the Ramones' self-titled album as Josh walked his bike into the garage.

"Fuck this pussy shit," he said. He grabbed a Pantera CD from his truck and put it in the garage stereo. Phil Anselmo's anger on *Vulgar Display Of Power* sent ecstatic pulses through my veins. I'd listened to Pantera a few times, but this was the moment when I fell in love with the band's dirty Southern thrash.

Josh's lips curled into a tight frown while he rode. He went faster than any of us, and I always thought of the term "balls out" when I watched him ride. He launched at a wall above a quarter pipe, planting his rear tire at least three feet above the highest point any of us had reached. He glided back into the transition, his freewheel roaring like a table saw.

Between Josh's runs, I stared at his tattoos—tire treads on his right bicep, and a bike company logo on his left wrist, both in black ink. Sweat glistened on his closely-shaven head.

Around Josh, I often felt embarrassed and frustrated by my riding. Still, after I landed a trick, he usually said, "Yeah," or whistled.

DURING THE SUMMER BEFORE senior year, my friends and I finished our BMX video, which we'd been working on for the past two and a half years. Bryan and I edited the video on my parents' computer, teaching ourselves about editing as we went along. I loved feeling like I could control tiny snippets of reality.

Just a few weeks away from starting school, we watched our video at my parents' house one afternoon. I wished my section had more trick variety, but I also felt like it captured my personality. Megadeth plays while I ride full pipes, street spots, and skate parks in Wyoming, Utah, Colorado, California, Idaho, and Oregon. I was proud of my editing in the video, especially in this section. During the intro to my part, snippets of me riding, wrecking, and the tags on my quarter pipe flash, on beat with Megadeth's high-energy death rock in "Skin O' My Teeth."

One of my favorite clips was of me riding a metal cylinder that Steve and I'd found earlier in the summer. Driving along a highway just outside Rock Springs, one of us noticed rows of huge metal pipes, all lying on their sides in an industrial yard. "I wonder if we could ride those things," Steve said.

The gate was open, so I just drove in, passing three or four "No Trespassing" signs. Barbed-wire-topped fencing lined the perimeter of the yard, and immense work equipment surrounded us. I stared at metal teeth, intricate piping, and humongous tires.

With some maneuvering, we were able to get our bikes through a small opening in one of the cylinders. Rust coated the inside of the pipe, and it took a minute or so for our eyes to adjust. The cylinder was hard to ride. Unlike a half-pipe built for riding and skateboarding, there was no flat bottom, which would've made it a lot easier to accumulate speed.

I positioned myself at the bottom of one transition, then, pushing off, quickly rotated a bit less than 180 degrees on the other side. I spun on each side, then put pressure on my handlebars, pressing my front wheel into the transition's curve to gain speed.

The pipe amplified sound. A metallic roar replaced the usual zip of my tires.

Steve and I filmed some clips of each other. In the clip of me riding the cylinder in our video, rust rises from the pipe's surface, swirling around me as my tires touch the point where the transition curls over itself. Watching this clip now, I remember how rust particles floated into my nose and mouth, sticking to my teeth. I also remember how powerful I felt during those moments. The pipe weighed thousands of pounds, but it shifted, slightly, against my weight and momentum.

Breathing in rust became too much to handle after twenty or thirty minutes. The cylinder also magnified the dry Wyoming heat. A large work truck pulled up right after we got our bikes out. The driver, a middle-aged woman with short hair, said, "You guys should get out of here. I just called the sheriff's department."

Whenever I'd drive past the yard after riding the cylinder, I remembered the weightless feeling I experienced as I carved the pipe. I never found out why these cylinders had originally been built, and I didn't care. In Rock Springs, I usually felt alienated by the industrial machinery surrounding me. After riding one of these cylinders, they seemed like they were made of something softer and more malleable than industrial-strength steel.

MY FRIENDS AND I finished watching the video and then decided to ride the ramps in front of my house. We'd put our bikes in the garage, where the rancid air made us all gag. Fishing poles, reels, nets, coolers, boat oars, spare tires, rope, disorganized tools, and other random shit cluttered the garage floor. Bryan, Steve, and Jared covered their noses with their shirt collars as we picked up our bikes and went outside.

"Jesus Christ," Bryan said as we sat on our bikes on the walkway that cut through the front yard. "What's that smell again?"

"I think it's those hides on the rafters. I don't know why the fuck my dad still keeps them."

We rode the quarter pipe for fifteen or twenty minutes, mostly just messing around. Although we often rode seriously, we also spent a lot of time doing joke tricks that were either out of style or just plain ridiculous.

Dad pulled up in his truck, parking on the sloped curb next to our house. He grabbed a fishing rod and cooler from his flatbed. "Honest question," he said, walking toward us. "Which one of you guys can do the baddest trick?" He set down his cooler and took off his one-piece sunglasses. His eyes were red slivers. In his deep monotone, Dad said, "Let's see a möbius flip," referring to an old school skiing trick. During the seventies and early eighties, Dad used to ski off twenty-foot boulders, extending his legs into huge spread-eagles, of which I've seen a few pictures.

After each of our tricks, Dad said, "Hell yeah" or "Right on." He watched us for a few minutes, cracking us up with filthy jokes. Suddenly, he said, "Seriously though, you guys don't ride this thing much, do you?" His tone became gravelly. "You know you're going to have to get rid of it soon. I don't want this bullshit in my driveway anymore."

An awkward silence momentarily hung between my friends and me after Dad went inside. Jared pedaled across the walkway, toward the ramp. As he rode up the quarter pipe, I yelled, "Do a mobius flip you fucking peter-eater!" Laughing, he steered off the side of the ramp so he wouldn't eat shit. Steve and Bryan's high-pitched laughter echoed off the retaining wall behind the quarter pipe.

A MONTH OR SO later, Steve and I drove to Denver to see a Metallica concert, which I'd constantly been thinking about since buying my ticket. Black Sabbath, Slayer, Pantera, and Metallica—I felt like I could depend on these bands in the same way as each of my friends.

Driving through Wyoming in my Tacoma, we passed towns that seemed like smaller and larger versions of Rock Springs—middle class neighborhoods, gas stations, fast-food restaurants, and motels, all divided by large, empty lots and surrounded by sagebrush-covered hills. We listened to *Master Of Puppets*, *...And Justice For All*, *Ride The Lightning*, and *Kill 'Em All*.

To me, everything Metallica recorded after their self-titled LP—more popularly known as *The Black Album*—was bullshit. I liked *The Black Album* itself—the record featuring "Enter Sandman" that sent the band into super-stardom—but it didn't come close to capturing the same energy in the first four albums. Together, Lars's crazy double bass drumming and James and Kirk's gnarly guitar riffs form an aural assault.

I also loved the songs that move from delicate acoustic sections into crushing walls of heaviness—songs like "Fade to Black," "Battery," and "One." The movements in these songs reminded me of classical music, sans pretension. Listening to early Metallica, I felt deeply connected with the young, death-obsessed, and socially alienated brains of Lars Ulrich, James Hetfield, Cliff Burton, and Kirk Hammet. James, who, like me, had gnarly acne during his adolescence, sung lyrics about death as the only true escape from hopelessness.

Steve and I left a day before the concert to ride skate parks and street spots in and near Denver. On Sunday evening, we drove to a southern suburb, Aurora, trying to find a cement spillway called The Hook that some local riders had told us about. As we drove on I-225, Steve spotted the structure, which sat on the edge of a golf course.

I parked at a nearby apartment complex. An empty drive led into the golf course. Steve and I walked our bikes under a chain with a "No Trespassing" sign attached to it. We looked around the chain-link fence-enclosed golf course to make sure no one saw us. After Steve climbed the fence, I lifted each of our bikes over the top and into his reaching hands. When I jumped off the top of the fence, my shoes sunk into marshy ground beneath waist-high reeds and grass.

Painted dark green, The Hook looked intimidating—fifteen feet tall and about a hundred feet wide. Imagine a full pipe cut lengthwise, down the middle. The concrete monolith loomed above the grass of the golf course.

A dust-and-gravel-covered runway led to the massive transition. Before I even thought about mustering the balls to ride this thing, Steve pedaled at The Hook. His tires crunched on gravel, then zipped when they hit the smooth cement of the transition. He reached the point where the transition curled, becoming over-vertical.

A pool of black muck sat about twenty feet away from The Hook. Horseflies, dragonflies, mosquitoes, and gnats buzzed above plastic bags, beer cans, and other trash in the sewage. Immediately after gliding down the transition, Steve skidded to avoid this sludgy mess. The drone of nearby traffic echoed off the concrete wave.

I thought about Metallica's "Seek And Destroy" to get myself psyched. Steve, Jared, Bryan, and I, like other BMX riders, often referred to riding as destroying. To me, destruction was an act of creating beauty.

"Seek And Destroy" features raw, punk-infused guitar riffs, pushed by Lars's drumming and Cliff Burton's manic bass playing. During the middle of the song, the band pushes boundaries of control with tempo. These sounds echoed in my brain as I pedaled toward The Hook.

Climbing the transition, my tires zipped. At the height of my ascent, my right arm grazed cement that curved beyond ninety degrees.

After I carved it, The Hook didn't scare me as much. It was a humongous, unmoving cement structure, but I'd found my own way to use it.

BADASS

INDSAY AND I HAD French class together during our sophomore and junior years, but we didn't really talk. From the back of the room, I'd often stare at the creamy skin between her jeans and T-shirt. She was beautifully curvy, but she usually wore baggy band T-shirts and jeans. Her dyed, burgundy hair barely covered her ears, and she was about a head shorter than me.

We had a sculpture class together during senior year, and Lindsay wore a black AC/DC shirt to school one day.

"That's a badass shirt," I said to her.

"Fuck yeah, it is. What's your favorite AC/DC album?"

"*Back In Black*. Yours?"

Lindsay and I started talking about AC/DC, Guns N' Roses, Black Sabbath and Led Zeppelin in class. With an arrogance stemming from a lack of self-awareness, we loved to talk shit on the music our classmates listened to. To us, most kids in school were dipshits and assholes.

After a few weeks, I worked up the courage to ask her out. I constantly wanted to hit on girls at school, but I couldn't get myself to do it. Even so, asking Lindsay out didn't feel at all awkward. As we washed clay from between our fingers after sculpture one day, I said, "Do you want to rock out sometime?"

"Yeah, that sounds badass, J. J." She wrote her number on the back of my right hand in black marker. Throughout the rest of the day, I kept wanting to show my classmates that a cute girl had written her number on my hand.

Later in the week, I drove to Lindsay's mom's house. She lived in the same neighborhood as Grandpa Leighton, which mostly consisted of plain, middle class houses. Driving down the hill from my parents' house, I listened to the syrupy Southern riffs on Down's *Nola*, my heart matching Jimmy Bower's busy kick drum. I parked next to the sidewalk in front of Lindsay's house.

When I rang the doorbell, Lindsay yelled, "Come in! We're upstairs." Her voice always seemed playful. Lindsay and her mom, Linda, sat on a couch in the living room, watching *Seinfeld*, my favorite show.

"Hi, J. J.," Linda said. "It's good to see you again." I'd met her a few months before, when I broke my foot. She worked for the doctor who'd set my foot and gave me a plastic boot to walk around in. When I went to the doctor's office, I was wearing a black T-shirt that said "Listen to Slayer" in big white letters.

"Slayer's a band?" Linda asked after telling me to sit on a padded table in an examining room.

"Yeah, it's this crazy metal band."

"My daughter has been waiting and waiting for the new Perfect Circle CD to come out. Do you know them?" Not knowing that Lindsay was her daughter, I thought, *No, but I want to know your daughter.* The next day at school, Lindsay told me that her mom had asked about me.

On the first night we hung out, I talked with Lindsay and Linda in their living room, immediately feeling comfortable in their house. The smells of garlic, homemade marinara, and vanilla wafted from the kitchen. A few cats sauntered around the living room, skeptically eyeing me.

"So what do you want to do, J. J.?" Lindsay asked.

"Whatever you want."

"Let's drive around for a while."

Tool, Pearl Jam, and Led Zeppelin stickers covered the trunk and rear bumper of Lindsay's old, black Honda Civic. I'd seen her car hundreds of times, parked in the same spot in front of the high school every day, but I always wanted to see it from the inside. Empty Mountain Dew bottles littered the floor, and the clean upholstery smelled like Lindsay. I'd never sat in a car belonging to a girl I liked.

Lindsay backed out of her driveway after putting Tool's *Ænima* in her CD player. She'd burned me this CD a few weeks earlier. I had a hard time getting into Tool at first, but their industrial prog-rock quickly started to seem strangely fascinating. Danny Carey's drumming reminded me of Neil Peart's from Rush, only weirder. Carey constantly emphasizes the offbeat, placing crashes, fills, and snare hits in awkward and unexpected places. At the same time, he also knows when to groove, supporting the rest of the band during the heavy and melodic parts. Tool's odd timings, atypical song structures, and simultaneously discordant and soothing chord progressions made me feel like I was trying to fit my brain into a space it wasn't designed for, but I liked this feeling. When I play this album now, I can still smell the tangy lotion Lindsay used to wear.

I examined Lindsay's CD case, occasionally glancing at her. Several studs adorned both of her ears, and I really wanted to make out with her. Like me, Lindsay had organized her CD case into a list of her favorite bands and albums. Toward the back, I found *Sabbath Bloody Sabbath*.

She drove east from Rock Springs. We passed the apartment complex and two motels that my great uncle Paul had built and owned. I usually saw most things in Rock Springs through a gray scrim. When I was with Lindsay, this shit-hole town didn't seem quite as bad. She turned south on a highway leading to Flaming Gorge, the reservoir where Dad had caught his world record.

We saw another pair of headlights every once in a while, but, for the most part, we seemed to be the only two people around. I kept hoping that Lindsay would pull onto one of the dirt roads stemming from the highway and park her car. As we got further from Rock Springs, waist-high sagebrush dotting the hills on the sides of the highway morphed into four and five-foot cedars.

"You don't drink, do you J. J.?" Lindsay asked.

"Fuck no. I'm straight edge."

"That's good, J. J. That's really good." I could feel a playful warmth in her voice, and I wanted to wear that warmth.

We listened to a few Tool songs before she spoke again. "My dad is a really bad alcoholic." Sadness shook her voice, but she also spoke with a sense of forgiveness rather than resentment. Lindsay told me about the many times she and her sister had carried their dad, Randy, to bed after he fell down the stairs.

Two years earlier, Linda had given Randy an ultimatum: stop drinking or leave. He moved into a trailer in Point of Rocks—a town comprised of a bar, gas station, and cluster of trailers thirty miles east of Rock Springs. The tiny community, which looked like a shantytown against the backdrop of barren sandstone cliffs, had been built near the Pacific Power plant for workers who didn't want to commute from Rock Springs.

We realized that our dads had both worked at the plant. When I told my dad who I was dating a week or so later, he said, "Oh yeah, I know Randy. He's a good old boy. Always been nice to me." Dad's character judgment lapsed sometimes, but he also had an amazing ability to read people. When he called someone a good old boy, he was saying that the person was genuinely kindhearted.

On our second date, driving from Lindsay's house in my truck, she examined my CD case. We drove on a highway leading north of town. As she thumbed through Black Sabbath albums, then Pantera, then Slayer, then Metallica, Lindsay understood that my CD case was my identity. She'd pause every so often, talking about how she loved a song on a certain album.

During most of our dates, we drove around Rock Springs and its surrounding areas, listening to music and talking about our dads. When I was with my friends, I rarely talked about Dad's pot smoking directly. We'd often talk shit about our peers for getting drunk and high, our words laced with anger for our fathers. With Lindsay, I actually began to sift through some of the complicated and confusing emotions connected to Dad's drug use.

Lindsay and I both knew that we couldn't control our dads. Instead, we routinely constructed lists of our favorite bands and albums and organized our CD cases accordingly.

"Don't avoid the question, J. J. You hate Pearl Jam, don't you?"

Lindsay and I had been dating for a little over a month. A week earlier, on December twenty-third, she'd celebrated Eddie Vedder's birthday by inviting her friends and me over to eat a cake that she'd gotten personalized for Vedder.

"I just don't like Eddie Vedder. The rest of the band is decent though." I was leaning against a wall in my parents' basement, twisting the phone chord around my index finger. She'd asked me this question a few other times. To me, Pearl Jam represented the mainstream nineties rock that Phil Anselmo attacks on *The Great Southern Trendkill.*

Linda, who overheard Lindsay talking on the phone, said, "What if your soul mate doesn't like Pearl Jam, Lindsay?"

"My soul mate will like Pearl Jam," Lindsay told her mom.

I thought, *But I am your soul mate.*

I bought Lindsay an AC/DC T-shirt, a rose, and a box of Mike and Ike's, her favorite candy, for Valentine's Day. She bought me a king-sized Reese's, my favorite candy, and a Black Sabbath DVD.

We watched TV at her mom's house on the night of Valentine's. During a commercial, Linda asked, "So, what are your intentions with my daughter, J. J.?" Teasing me, she smiled slightly, but she also seemed serious.

"Uh…" I cleared my throat. "I don't know. I just think she's really badass." I wanted to say that I could see myself marrying Lindsay.

Linda watched TV with us for a little while before going to bed. Lindsay then went into her room and came back wearing a red camisole. She usually wore large T-shirts or sweatshirts, so seeing her cleavage made me feel like one of those cartoon dogs whose eyes bulge from their skulls when they see a beautiful woman. She sat next to me.

Although we'd officially been together for about two months, we hadn't done anything. I'd only kissed one girl, and I worried that I'd repel Lindsay with my awkwardness. I stared at the TV, trying to plan exactly how to make my move. During previous dates, Lindsay had said that I'd have to make the first move. Time stretched unbearably while also moving too quickly.

When infomercials replaced *Mad TV*, Lindsay said, "I think I'm going to go to sleep soon, J. J." She sat down on top of the stairs, giving me one more chance. I sat next to her. The idea of making a move was a rubber band ball of anxiety in my head. *She wants to kiss you, you fucking dipshit*, I thought. *Quit being a pansy.*

"Okay, J. J., I really have to go to bed now." Tired exasperation replaced the usual playfulness in her voice.

We got up, and I hugged her, holding my ass out.

Driving home, I yelled at myself for being such a dumbass. "She just wanted to kiss you, you fucking moron. She was *waiting* for you to kiss her." As I pulled into my parents' driveway, I knew that I had to go back.

Parking next to the sidewalk in front of Lindsay's house, the analytical part of my brain tried to take over again. BMX had taught me that you sometimes had to push yourself past the fear of consequence in order to live. Before I could scare myself into inaction again, I got out, walked to Lindsay's front door and rang the doorbell.

She opened the door, still wearing her red camisole. "Hi, J. J. I didn't think you'd come back."

Without hesitating, I took a step forward, put my hands on her hips, and kissed her. Her tongue darted between my teeth as she ran her fingers through my hair, and I moved my hands along her lower back.

Before driving home, I put At the Drive-In's *Relationship Of Command* in my CD player. Ethereal guitar notes, rising noise, and Cedric's punctuated breathing slither over a pounding tom groove in "Arcarsenal." A mass of lust writhed in my chest. The streets, houses, and trees of Lindsay's neighborhood seemed internally illuminated—a view of the world that I'd later come to associate with psychedelics. After At the Drive-In launches into frenetic post-punk, Cedric sings, "Have you ever tasted skin?"

LINDSAY BROKE UP WITH me shortly after our first kiss. I'd gotten accepted into film school in Aurora, Colorado, and she was going to study art at UW in Laramie. She was an amazing artist, one of the many things that made me fall in love with her. I think she wanted me to move to Laramie, but she never said this. I wanted to stay together, but she didn't want a long-distance relationship—Laramie is about three hours away from Aurora—and I'd been wanting to leave Wyoming since grade school. As with most towns in the state, Laramie seemed almost identical to Rock Springs—a few dusty drags with vacuous prairie looming in the background.

ALTHOUGH WE BOTH TRIED, we couldn't control how we felt about each other, and we'd end up getting together and breaking up a few more times before we moved.

During the summer after we graduated, Lindsay and I drove to Ogden, Utah to see Blue Öyster Cult, a band both of our dads loved, too. For us, seventies rock was both ironically and genuinely cool. We were aware of the many clichés in classic rock, but we also loved the straightforwardness of bands like Blue Öyster Cult, AC/DC, and early Aerosmith.

The concert was also a biker rally. We got to Ogden in the late afternoon, just as the sherbet sun was beginning to sink. It was Sunday, so the Mormon town seemed abandoned aside from the fact that the downtown streets, sidewalks, and buildings were spotless.

The concert was at a large park, and the bands played under a pavilion. Men and women with faded tattoos and frazzled hair sat on blankets and lawn chairs in the grass surrounding the pavilion, sipping beers, taking pulls of whiskey, rum, and vodka, and passing joints. Lindsay and I sat in the grass.

After the opening act, a wiry guy with sun-bleached hair and deeply tanned skin pointed to the tattoo I'd recently gotten. "What's your tattoo?" He asked.

"It's Tony Iommi's SG," I said, showing him the black guitar that covered most of my left wrist.

"Fuckin' A, brother. I got this B.O.C. tattoo when I was about your age, in 'seventy-eight." He turned his right shoulder to me and lifted up his sleeve. A small hook-and-cross was etched into his skin. It's an alchemical symbol for lead, the heaviest metal, which Blue Öyster Cult had appropriated. The black ink on the guy's shoulder had faded into a bluish green.

"That's badass," Lindsay said.

"What's your names?" the guy asked, holding out his hand for me to shake. "I'm J. J." I told him that we had the same name. Chuckling, he lit a cigarette. "I only met a few other J. J.s in my life, and they've all been cool as hell." He reminded me of my dad's friends—amazingly nice guys who seemed to have never left the seventies.

As roadies set up Blue Öyster Cult's equipment, Lindsay and I talked and looked at the other concertgoers. Right after we'd graduated, Lindsay decided to shave her head—just for the fuck of it, she said. At this point, my hair hung past my shoulders. People stared at us wherever we went, especially when we were together. We used these stares as excuses to rant about what assholes most people were.

Sitting a few feet away, a large guy with slicked-back hair and a goatee laughed at us, nudging his wife. "Which one's which?" he whispered, loud enough for me to hear.

"Fuck you," I said, standing up and staring into his eyes. He chuckled, not at all taking me, a scrawny, acne-ridden little asshole, seriously. I held my middle finger about six inches from his face. "Go fuck yourself, you old piece of shit."

The guy could've crushed me like an empty soda can. He stared at me, his eyes widening and cheeks turning red. My anger for the world, which was mostly anger for my inability to understand the world, was a tightly coiled mousetrap, often snapping for little or no real reason.

Luckily for me, the man's wife told him to let it go. Convinced that I'd done the right thing, I was surprised when Lindsay said, "J. J., who cares what that guy thinks? He's just some old jerk-off." She touched my back lightly.

By the time Blue Öyster Cult played, it was completely dark outside. Unlike most reunited seventies bands, they sounded crisp, like they do on their albums. The drummer was a short, fat guy with shaggy black hair combed over to cover a large bald spot. Wearing fingerless leather gloves and aviator sunglasses, he played a few songs with a cigarette dangling from his mouth. His chops were amazing. He reminded me of Bill Ward, one of my all-time favorite drummers.

Of course they closed with "Don't Fear the Reaper." The song sounded perfect. Metronomic cowbell hits pulsed from the speakers, and, at first, Lindsay and I thought it was a recording because we couldn't see who was playing it.

"Oh shit," Lindsay said, speaking into my ear and laughing. "Look at that guy behind the speakers." She pointed to a roadie standing behind the guitar cabinets. He banged out rock-solid quarter notes on a cowbell, not playing any other instrument. Wearing a leather vest, he had frizzy, shoulder-length gray hair.

Lindsay slept on the way home. During long stretches when I didn't see another vehicle on the interstate, I flicked on my brights. I kept looking away from the road to watch Lindsay breathe. Once, I looked at her for too long and had to swerve to miss a concrete barrier. I tried to concentrate on driving afterward, but I quickly found myself staring at her again.

REBEL

OVER ONE WEEKEND DURING my junior year, Mrs. Jasper, the only black teacher at our school, had our English class finish *The Catcher In The Rye*—one of the few assigned books I actually read in high school. On Monday, she said, "Some people best comprehend a text through visual interpretation. So I want you to draw a scene from the book that stood out to you."

I drew a stick figure version of James Castle jumping out of his dorm window. In the book, the boy commits suicide after getting tormented by his classmates. When Holden thinks about killing himself in New York, he remembers seeing James's splattered gore at Elkton Hills and decides not to jump out of a hotel room window.

Reading this section in *The Catcher In The Rye*, I thought about Erik Allen. During my sophomore year, Erik, a senior, and one of Jared and Bryan's older brother's best friends, killed himself with a .22 pistol. Erik's little brother found him in their room with a pillow covering his head.

FOR INITIATION AT OUR school, sophomores had to spray-paint seniors' names on a sandstone cliff face near the skate park. Jared and Bryan's older brother, Jesse, and his friends made Jared, Steve, and me paint their names. As Jesse drove us from Rock Springs High to the cliff, I thought about how the names we painted would just erode with the sandstone.

Erik didn't come to our initiation, probably because of some extracurricular activity, but Jesse still told me to paint Erik's name. I climbed the steep hill leading up to the cliff face, rocks and dirt tumbling under my feet, and sloppily wrote 'Erik A' with silver spray-paint. But I accidentally put the A too close to Erik: ErikA.

I thought Erik would be pissed. After he saw my tag, he came up to me at school and grabbed my shoulder. I was getting books from my locker, and I shuddered when I felt the weight of his hand. Erik was a bit shorter than me but much more muscular. His brown hair was coated in gel, and he wore a silver necklace. "Erika?" he said, tightly squeezing my scrawny bicep. "Why'd you write Erika?"

"Sorry, I didn't mean to," I said quickly.

"I'm just fucking with you, J. J." Erik laughed. "I actually thought it was pretty funny."

About seven months after initiation, Dr. Wendling busted Erik for drinking at the senior prom. A lot of kids were shit-faced at prom, including Wendling's own sons.

Afterward, Erik got kicked out of the National Honor Society, which required a 4.0 average and adherence to a rigid set of rules. He shot himself a week or two later.

At the time, I, along with several other kids I talked to, thought Wendling had singled Erik out for personal reasons. I played baseball and basketball with Erik and Wendling's sons throughout grade school. Like a lot of sports dads, Wendling wanted his sons to be the best at everything. Erik was an amazing athlete, often overshadowing the Wendling boys. He was also smarter than them, effortlessly acing every class. When I heard about Wendling busting Erik, I was sure that he'd done it to tarnish the reputation of a kid who often outperformed his own.

Today, I try not to let myself think the situation was so simple. Maybe Wendling wanted to make an example out of a popular athlete to stop so many kids from getting wasted at prom; or maybe Erik was more obviously drunk than everyone else. Still, even though I try to recognize other possibilities, I lean toward the idea that Wendling busted Erik out of spite. But I think getting in trouble for drinking was just one of many factors in Erik's decision to kill himself.

Erik's dad, Rick, always pushed him hard in sports. Despite his intensity with his sons, though, Rick was a super nice guy. He never made me feel like he saw me through my family's reputation, unlike most of the other sports dads in Rock Springs. He often gave me pitching or batting tips, making me feel like he genuinely wanted to see me do well.

But he was tough on his three sons, especially Erik, the oldest. When Erik stood at home plate in Little League, I could see anxiety constricting his body. Veins in his arms and neck pulsed as he nervously wiggled his bat. Unlike other boys at his skill level, Erik never seemed cocky. If he struck out or made a fielding error, Rick usually yelled at him. When Erik lost a game throughout grade school, junior high, and high school—he played baseball, basketball, tennis, soccer, and also ran track—tears often streamed down his reddened cheeks. There always seemed to be a lot at stake in sports for Erik. At some point, I think he internalized his dad's expectations, making them his own and becoming harder on himself than his dad ever was.

One week after Erik shot himself, Wendling interrupted our morning classes. Speaking over the intercom, he said, "I'd like to have a minute of silence for Erik Allen, who will be dearly missed."

Listening to Wendling's voice, I fully believed that he was a main cause of Erik's death, and I hated him. Really, I think my anger and frustration stemmed from knowing, deep down, that I'd never completely understand why Erik decided to die.

Perhaps Erik simply knew that pursuing a life of unrealistic achievement was doomed to make him miserable. Maybe he saw life as being inevitably pointless. I'm still frustrated and a little scared by the fact that I'll never know.

I TOOK ANOTHER CLASS with Mrs. Jasper during my senior year. One day, as she and the other AP students talked about *One Hundred Years Of Solitude*, I stared at a purple Jimi Hendrix poster taped onto her file cabinet, finding patterns in Jimi's afro.

Dr. Wendling knocked on the door and came in. "Sorry to interrupt," he said, smiling at my classmates and me. "I don't think Mrs. Jasper will mind, though. Teachers can't get their paychecks soon enough, right Mrs. Jasper?" Smirking, he handed her an envelope. "Well, I'd better get going." Watching him walk through the door, I hoped he would trip.

Mrs. Jasper looked at us and rolled her eyes. "I don't even want to get started on how inappropriate *that* was," she said.

I don't remember Mrs. Jasper ever hiding her dislike for Wendling. During my junior year, handing out dingy, tattered copies of *The Catcher In The Rye*, she said, "I'm really sorry about these books. It's ridiculous. They say the school doesn't have enough money for books when the football team gets brand-new game *and* practice jerseys." A few football players and cheerleaders shifted in their seats. "Anyway, I won't talk about that right now." I'm sure word got around about Mrs. Jasper hating Wendling, which must've pissed him off.

Later, in my senior English class, which consisted of five socially awkward kids, Mrs. Jasper said, also talking about poor book quality, "Well, this is what happens when a muscle-head football coach runs your school." When Wendling gave Mrs. Jasper her paycheck in class, I felt completely justified in my hatred for him. I knew that the state pays teachers, so handing her a paycheck during class seemed like a way for Wendling to make himself feel dominant. Although I try not to let myself think it was so cut-and-dry, I also know that Wendling really was an asshole.

WHEN I WAS SIXTEEN, Jared, Steve, and I went to see Integrity, a straight edge hardcore band, in Salt Lake with our older BMX friend, Josh.

Intricate graffiti decorated the low-ceilinged venue's walls. A local band was playing when we walked inside. Athletic boys wildly spun their arms and performed acrobatic jump-kicks in front of the stage. I'd never seen hardcore dancing before. These guys fought imaginary enemies, only occasionally making contact with each other. The violence and beauty in their movements both scared and excited me. Many of them moved with quick precision, as if they'd been trained in martial arts. Between kicks and punches, they shouted lyrics along with the band's vocalist.

In the early eighties, people used Ian MacKaye's lyrics in the Minor Threat song "Straight Edge" as an ideological foundation for a new subculture, although MacKaye has repeatedly said that straight edge was never meant to be a movement. You couldn't get high, drunk, or have promiscuous sex if you wanted to identify as straight edge. Throughout the eighties and nineties, a lot of edge groups became militant, often beating the shit out of people that were drunk or stoned. The violent version of straight edge spread like a virus in Salt Lake, a place where counter-cultures are often extreme. Raised amidst towering

Mormon temples, kids in Utah don't fuck around when it comes to rebellion.

Before this Integrity show, I'd heard about violence connected to straight edge in Salt Lake. In addition to countless beatings, there'd been a few straight edge–related murders in the city, leading local police to classify the group as a gang. Although this violence seemed scary and moronic, it also fascinated me. This Integrity show was my first direct encounter with the Salt Lake straight edge scene.

Standing in line and watching the opening bands, I stared at boys and girls with full tattoo sleeves—many of whom looked younger than eighteen—and large Xs drawn onto the backs of their hands with black marker, which signifies straight edge. I loved being around people who defined themselves according to rigid definitions of sobriety—a contrast to every metal show I'd attended. Steve, Jared, and I had shaggy hair, but we didn't look too out of place at this show, aside from the fact that we weren't wearing tight jeans and scout caps. Josh, with his tattoos, shaved head, and designer jeans, looked like he belonged here, which helped my friends and me seem in tune with this scene.

When Integrity started playing, I watched a guy with shaggy red hair, large metal hoops stretching his ear lobes, and "Straight Edge" tattooed above his Adam's apple spin his arms and perform ninja kicks in front of the stage. The whites of his eyes were illuminated with certainty and absolutism. Throughout the set, Integrity's vocalist repeatedly jumped from the foot-high stage into the crowd, holding out the microphone for others to scream into.

At this show, I felt reaffirmed in my idea that I was meant to be straight edge.

NEAR THE END OF our senior year, about two years after seeing Integrity, Steve and I went to a Bleeding Through concert in Salt Lake instead of our senior prom. Right before this show, Steve had gotten drunk during a trip to Vegas with Josh.

Jared and Bryan also went on this Vegas trip. On the Monday morning after getting back, they told me about Steve's drunken antics. Josh, who'd been straight edge for as long as I knew him, also got wasted on this trip.

A confusing mix of disappointment, worry, and desire spun in my stomach. It sounded like Steve and Josh had a lot of fun on the trip, which made me remember how much I enjoyed the only time I'd ever gotten stoned and drunk—the night in Salt Lake when I was thirteen. I also thought about Phil Anselmo, Dimebag Darrel, Kerry King, Jeff Hanneman, Jimmy Bower, Randy Blythe, and my other metal heroes who proudly identified themselves as alcoholics. For the first time in five years, I considered getting drunk. But I also tried to dismiss this thought by reminding myself that I was supposed to be straight edge.

At first, Steve seemed embarrassed about getting wasted. Soon though, he talked about how hilarious it was. Driving to Salt Lake with him to see Bleeding Through, a week or so after his Vegas road trip, Steve told me about dragging another guy's bike through mud when he was shit-faced. We laughed like hyenas.

Hardcore kids stood in line outside of the venue in Salt Lake. Most of them had black Xs on the backs of their hands, and all the guys had shaved heads or short hair. Several boys and girls had full tattoo sleeves. As Steve and I walked to the back of the line, people glared at us.

At this point, I hadn't gotten a haircut in two years. My Fabio-esque blond hair hung past my shoulder blades, and Steve's curly brown hair, square-framed glasses, and acne made him look like a nerdy, teenage version of Slash. I wore a black Pantera shirt; Steve wore a black Slayer shirt; and we were both wearing baggy jeans—at least, baggy in comparison to the skinny jeans most of the kids in line were wearing. We looked like old school metalheads.

A muscle-bound guy just ahead of us stared at Steve and me. "Stoner pieces of shit," he said. I was pissed but too scared to say anything. I put my hands in my pockets and looked at the gum-dotted sidewalk.

Inside the venue, a dude handed out pamphlets promoting the straight edge lifestyle. I saw an idiotic rigidity in his eyes, and I thought about how straight edge culture seemed like a cult. At the same time, this rigidity is what led me to identity myself as straight edge in the first place, and I was still attracted to it. Rigidity seemed to promise stability.

Throughout the opening band's sets, straight edge kids kept staring at Steve and me. I felt like I often did in school, where boys frequently threatened to beat my ass. Steve and I leaned against one of the walls, trying not to stare back. I wanted to yell, "I've probably been straight

edge for longer than most of you assholes." Waiting for
Bleeding Through to play, I thought about getting drunk
again, now as a way to separate myself from *this* scene.

For as long as I can remember, I've had a tendency to
rebel. I can't pinpoint exactly where this came from, but I
think part of it stemmed from seeing my dad's imperfection
at an early age and not knowing how to deal with it. But my
rebelliousness also stemmed from valuing what Dad had to
teach me. I was raised to see cops and laws as things to be
avoided and broken, and I'm grateful that Dad encouraged
me to question these types of authority. Whenever we
saw a cop in Rock Springs, he'd usually say something
sarcastic like, "Better watch out for Johnny Law." Riding
BMX solidified the rebel in me. But my tendency to resist
authority has often latched onto my attempts to establish
order in my own life. Sometimes I still unravel and fight
against what I know to be best for myself.

The crowd surged toward the stage as Bleeding
Through launched into a barrage of thrashing riffs and
chugging breakdowns. The lead singer, with tattoo sleeves,
tight clothes, and a short mohawk ran around, holding
his mic out when he saw someone shouting the lyrics.
Both guitarists swung their guitars in the air like battle-
axes, coming close to hitting a few fans. Straight edge kids
performed spin kicks in a tight circle in front of the stage.
Weaving through bodies as we moved toward the back of
the room, Steve and I had to dodge a few kicks.

From the back, I watched a small guy, who wore a
hoodie with "Straight Edge For Life" screen-printed on

it, barrel roll kick a girl in her stomach, knocking her to the ground. The guy and his friends laughed as the girl's boyfriend picked her up and took her outside.

AFTER LUNCH DURING THE following week, Steve and I sat on the floor in a corridor at school.

"I can't believe what dipshits those straight edge kids were," I said. "It makes me not want to be straight edge anymore."

"I know," Steve said, adjusting his glasses. "Those kids are fucking dumbasses." He took a drink of Mountain Dew and stuffed a Reese's in his mouth.

"Let's do it, dude. I want to get wasted."

"Alright, I'll get fucked-up with you," Steve said. "I had a lot of fun in Vegas."

For the past six months, I'd been playing drums in a pop punk band called Yesterday's Heroes. I wanted to play in a heavy band, but there weren't many metal musicians in Rock Springs, so I settled with pop punk, a genre for which I still have a soft spot. Our first show was on the upcoming Friday, in an old train depot downtown. Aside from me, each member of the band drank and got high. I decided that our show would be a perfect time to get drunk.

During the days before the show, I worked to justify my decision to myself. Grandma Vera and Grandpa Don immediately came to mind. I told myself that getting drunk wouldn't make me like them because my grandparents were defined by conformity, and I'd always be an antiauthoritarian metalhead. Most of my favorite musicians were drunks, so it made sense that I should drink, too. I'd realized that the straight edge scene was just another form of organized religion. Somehow, I didn't make this connection to metal culture, didn't think about what a conformist I truly was.

I also wonder if my decision to start drinking was a way of surrendering to peoples' expectations of me in Rock Springs. A lot of people expected that I'd become a fuck up, and, no matter what I did, I knew they'd see me this way. By deciding to get drunk, I was living up to those expectations. But I'd also decided to push drinking to an extreme, past what was socially acceptable, unlike most of the Anselmis, which was how I saw it as a form of rebellion.

I also knew that drinking would open new social doors for me. In high school, I wasn't nearly as neurotic as I am now, but I still spent a lot of time in my own head, overanalyzing. This mainly happened with girls. I was still a virgin, and I knew that drinking with girls would hugely increase my chances of getting laid. Riding freestyle BMX fulfilled the need to disconnect my frontal lobes. When I wasn't riding, or editing videos of my friends and me riding, I sat in my room, listening to metal, playing video games, and/or reading *The Lord Of The Rings* books. In a nutshell, I was a nerd. At this point, although I wanted to be with Lindsay, she and I had broken up.

After school on Friday, my bandmates and I carried our equipment upstairs from my parents' basement, loading it into my truck. I found a fifth of Jim Beam and an old flask in the liquor cabinet. The flask originally belonged to my great uncle John, who'd given it to my dad. J. A.—Uncle John's, Dad's, and my initials—was engraved into the polished silver. I poured whiskey into the flask.

At the old train depot, I set up my drums on a small plywood stage. Trying to show off, I played simple beats and fills while my bandmates, Mike, Shaun, Chris, and Josh, set up their amps and cabinets.

Mike and Shaun's girlfriends stood in front of the stage. They were sisters, and both of them were super cute. Watching Mike and Shaun nonchalantly put their hands on their girlfriends' shoulders and make out with them, I wished that I was less awkward around girls.

Just before our set, my bandmates and I huddled together and took pulls from my flask. Mike, our singer, said, "This will be our preshow ritual fellas," after taking a gulp.

Chris screamed backup vocals and swung his bass around his head throughout our set. A few people in the small crowd headbanged along with our generic songs. We were sloppy, but I still felt jolts of energy coursing through my body.

Chris slammed his bass on the ground during our last song, taking a big chunk from its body. He grabbed his microphone from the stand and screamed into it, his vocal chords cracking. This set showed me that playing live music could simultaneously be about creation and destruction, and I've been addicted ever since.

I hadn't played a concert since my junior high talent show. After our set, a few cute punk girls told me that I was a badass drummer. I woke up the next day with new numbers in my phone.

I downed the contents of my flask before the next band started playing. One of my buddies also let me drink some of his vodka, which he'd brought in a Big Gulp cup. I hadn't yet puked from drinking, so I could effortlessly down the burning liquid. I was stumbling around the train depot within twenty minutes. Steve also got shit-faced super fast.

Staring at girls, effortlessly talking to them, and laughing with Steve and my bandmates, I felt like I'd discovered an integral piece of my personality. *Metalheads were meant to get drunk*, I thought.

Outside, I saw a group of Mormon kids and walked over to them. "You guys are Mormon, right?" I said. "That's bullshit." I'd said this to these same kids before, but I wanted to show off in front of my friends. Then I waterfall-puked onto the sidewalk.

STEVE AND I RODE our bikes at the skate park the next day. Laughing, we tried to piece together some of the ridiculous shit we'd done the night before.

"Fuck it, dude. Let's just become alcoholics," I said.

"I'm down."

Even though I was going to film school in the fall, I didn't really know what I wanted to do with my life, and neither did Steve. Listening to classmates talk about what schools had accepted them, what they were majoring in, and what jobs they'd get after college—conversations on constant repeat during senior year—I both hated and envied the naive certainty that supported their words. Steve and I gravitated toward the predictability of becoming drunks. It was expected of us, and we knew where this decision would lead.

We started drinking every chance we got. When I drank, thoughts about my dad, Joey Hay, Freddy Martinez, my grandparents, and Jared, Bryan, Steve, and Lindsay's dads were always just below the surface.

SHORTLY AFTER THE TRAIN depot show, I drove to Salt Lake, alone, to get my first tattoo. A year or so earlier, I'd decided to get Tony Iommi's signature Gibson SG tattooed on my left wrist, along with "Killing Yourself to Live" wrapping around my wrist, and connecting to the guitar's body on either side.

Since I was sixteen, I'd been telling my mom that I was going to cover my arms with tattoos. I wanted to look like Phil Anselmo, Kerry King, Ozzy, James Hetfield, and my older friend Josh. Mom usually said, "Wait until you're twenty-five. What if your tastes change?"

I'd just tell her that my tastes would never change. I knew that I'd always love metal, and being a metalhead would always be part of my identity. What I didn't understand is that identity is fluid, and change is constant. Although I've tried to convince myself otherwise during the past few years, I knew who I was, and I'm still that person in a lot of ways.

Driving through Wyoming on my way to Salt Lake, I passed semis, stretches of sagebrush, rolling hills, and badlands. *You're about to get something permanently written on your body*, I thought. Like a pill going down the wrong tube, uncertainty lodged in my throat. But I told myself that, if I was a true metalhead, I *had* to get this tattoo.

For the sixth or seventh time during this trip, I played "Killing Yourself To Live." Leading the band into the chorus, Iommi changes from an up-tempo chord progression into heavy, grooving rock. Geezer's bass coils around the foundation of Bill Ward's grooves, forming a bulldozer of rhythm. This song seemed like a direct current of truth.

In Salt Lake, I stopped at the first tattoo parlor on State Street that didn't look like a complete shit-hole. "What's up, man?" asked a skinny guy with tattoos covering his arms and neck when I walked inside.

"I want a tattoo of this guitar on my left wrist," I said, handing him a picture of Iommi's SG. "And I also want two lines wrapping around my wrist, with 'Killing Yourself To Live' inside." I thought the artist would react by saying something like, "Holy shit, dude. This is going to be awesome," but he seemed aloof as he sketched the guitar and song title onto wax paper.

Sitting in the artist's chair, a burning sting shot through my lower carpals as he injected black ink into my skin. I stared at the water-stained ceiling, becoming delirious after the first hour. "Killing Yourself to Live" reverberated in my brain for the rest of the four-hour session.

When I got back to Rock Springs, I showed my mom and dad the tattoo. They were sitting at the dining room table, underneath a chandelier made of elk horns that

Grandpa Don had given us. "Killing Yourself to Live?" Dad said. "I don't get it." He seemed frustrated but not as mad as I thought he'd be.

"What does it mean to you, baby?" Mom asked.

"It means that I'll never change who I am to fit into this bullshit society."

"Shit," Mom said. "I know it's hard for you to see now, but I think your tastes will change."

In our upstairs bathroom, I looked back and forth from my hair to my new tattoo, holding my wrist in front of the mirror and feeling like a badass.

JUST BEFORE GRADUATION, STEVE and I decided that we had to fuck with Wendling somehow. In addition to everything else that made me hate him, Wendling and an art teacher, Mrs. Meeks, had barred Steve from entering his work into a state contest because they thought his drawings and paintings were obscene. Steve refused to turn in art they deemed acceptable, so he also failed his senior art class. He drew and painted skulls, swords, and daggers, but he didn't depict gore in his pictures. Steve was just a young metalhead who had a fascination with death. Failing the class destroyed Steve's chances of getting an art scholarship, which was the only way he could've afforded college.

As with my other reasons for hating Wendling, I probably oversimplified this situation. Maybe the skulls and death-related imagery in Steve's work genuinely worried Wendling and Mrs. Meeks. Back then, I was sure they'd singled Steve out because they didn't like him.

But Steve had several confrontations with Mrs. Meeks throughout high school—he even flipped her off once or twice—and maybe she really did think he was violent. Perhaps Wendling and Meeks were earnestly trying to curb the violence that dominates American culture. Steve and I hated Wendling with a certainty and simplicity that now scares me. Even so, I think we were partly right to hate him.

We considered taking shits on the hood of Wendling's car, egging his house, placing rotten food in his mailbox, and pouring sugar into his gas tank. Steve came up with the idea of flipping him off at our graduation ceremony. It seemed beautiful: our diplomas in hand, Wendling couldn't do shit to us.

Driving to Rock Springs High on graduation day, I listened to Pantera's *The Great Southern Trendkill*. Phil Anselmo screams "Fuck you all" after a spoken word rant about rock journalists who've ripped him apart, and I extended this sentiment to Wendling. Like the writers who didn't see Phil's obvious genius, I was sure that Wendling could never understand who Steve and I were.

Hundreds of folding chairs were set up in the middle of the football field. Steve and I sat in our assigned seats, a few rows apart. Teachers sat in the front, next to a stage where the administrators stood.

After giving the typical speech about our graduating class being the future, Wendling stood in the grass next to the stairs leading offstage. He shook each boy's hand and hugged each girl. Families and friends of students sat in the bleachers behind us, clapping and cheering.

Steve was called up before me. After getting his diploma, he shook hands with each administrator. Wendling held out his hand as Steve walked down the stairs. Steve quickly moved to the side, flipping him off. Furious, but also not sure what to do, Wendling just stood there as Steve walked back to his seat. A thick vein appeared on Wendling's bald head. To my surprise, none of my classmates sitting near me seemed to notice, and neither did the crowd.

"Holy shit, dude," I said to a kid sitting next to me. "Did you see that?"

"What?"

"Steve just flipped off Dr. Wendling." A few classmates heard me. Listening to their responses—"What the fuck?" "Holy shit," and "Why?"—I laughed, also feeling anxiety rise in my throat. *Fuck*, I thought, *now I have to do it.*

"J. J. Anselmi" drifted through the speakers. Walking to the stage, wind blew strands of hair into my mouth while I held my cap in place. After coming down the stairs, I dodged Wendling's outstretched hand, holding my middle finger inches from his face. People in the bleachers hushed, and Wendling's eyes widened. I'll never forget the rush of power I felt during this moment.

As the remaining students got their diplomas, Wendling tried to act like he wasn't pissed, but his face was completely red.

A FEW HOURS AFTERWARD, at a graduation party at my parents' house, I talked about what an asshole Wendling was with my grandpa Leighton and step-grandma, Sarah, who was a junior high music teacher. She and Grandpa Leighton were some of only a handful of people in Rock Springs with graduate degrees. They knew several high school teachers who hated Wendling, and they both told me that I'd done the right thing. "That motherfucker deserved it," my mom said.

Later, Steve and I went to a classmate's graduation party with a few of our new drinking buddies. When we got to the house, Steve lifted up an old garage door, and I followed him inside. Athletes, cheerleaders, and other popular kids in the garage stopped talking when they saw us. Most of them were huddled around two kegs in the middle of the concrete floor. I heard someone mutter, "Fucking faggots," and I could feel hateful glares as I filled a plastic cup with beer.

Soon, Brittany, a hot girl, walked down the steps leading from the inside of the house to the garage. "You guys are fucking assholes," she said.

Steve and I looked at each other and laughed.

"No, seriously. Fuck you guys." She had tears in her eyes. "Wendling is like a father to me. He's helped me through so much shit. You don't even know. You guys need to get the fuck out of here before someone kicks your asses."

In my buddy Tyler's van, we drove to the Senior All Night Party, a school-sanctioned event at the community college. We passed around a bottle of Captain Morgan, and Tyler put The Datsun's self-titled album in his CD player, blasting "Motherfucker From Hell." Over barreling rock riffs, the singer screams, "Like a motherfucker from hell!" We all shouted this line along with him.

Silence hung in the air as Steve and I walked into the atrium at the community college. I heard a few people say things like "Those dicks" and "They should've picked a different time to pull that shit." I loved that people thought we'd ruined graduation. On top of fucking with Wendling, I'd gotten back at some of the classmates I'd always hated.

Mark, a tall guy with large, rectangular glasses and thick arms, came up to Steve and me. "You little faggots," he said. "I should fuck both of you up." He shoved me hard, sending me into a brick wall.

"Fuck off, Mark," Steve said, shoving him back, although Mark was a lot bigger. Mark also had a reputation for being tough as hell—he'd beaten the shit out of more than a few other boys. I stood behind Steve, hoping that Mark wouldn't kick my ass.

His face inches away from Steve's, Mark yelled, "Wendling is like a goddamn *dad* to me. You fucking assholes ruined graduation."

Mark and Steve yelled at each other for a minute or so before an adult broke them up. Afterward, Steve and I mocked Mark and Brittany. We refused to consider how Wendling could be anything *but* an asshole. Mark was part of the group that my friends and I kindly called the redneck kids, who were also outsiders. Wendling must've helped Mark and Brittany get through school, and I'm sure they weren't the only ones. Nonetheless, if I could go back, I'd still flip him off.

Two weeks later, Steve and I each got a letter from Wendling. My letter:

June 3, 2004
Mr. J. J. Anselmi
1828 Carson Street
Rock Springs, WY 82901

Dear Mr. Anselmi:

Because of your recent actions on school grounds, during the graduation ceremony, you are not to be on the Rock Springs High School campus anytime—daytime or evening. **Violation of this will result in the Rock Springs Police Department being called and trespassing charges being filed.**

Should you have any questions concerning this matter, feel free to contact me at the high school.

Sincerely,
Dr. Randy Wendling
Principal

cc: Rock Springs Police Dept.

When I got the letter, it made me feel great, like a true rebel. For the past three years I'd felt powerless against Wendling. Now, Steve and I'd flipped the dynamic of power, and this was the best Wendling could do.

THE APARTMENT

WITH STEVE, I DROVE to Garrett and Tyler's apartment, Pantera's *Reinventing The Steel* playing in my truck's stereo. As Phil Anselmo screamed "Your trust is in whiskey...and Black Sabbath" in the song "Goddamn Electric," I felt a shiver of euphoria. I parked next to a Halliburton work truck with black-tinged dirt encrusted on its wheel wells. Before getting out of my truck, I looked at myself in the rearview mirror and adjusted my backwards trucker hat.

"Motherfuckin' J. J. and Steve," Garrett said, sitting on a cigarette-burned couch positioned a few feet from the TV. His rectangular-framed glasses sat just beneath his eyes, and his mouth curled into the half-grin that always appeared when he'd caught a buzz. Garrett had recently gotten a Spiderman tattoo on his right bicep. The tattoo was partially covered by the sleeve of an old button-down shirt, upon which he wrote band names in black marker. We sat next to him, watching him play Xbox and listening to the Misfits' *Plan Nine*. In my mind, Garrett was a true punk.

Tyler walked out of his bedroom and into the small kitchen area. "There's still some Captain in the fridge from last night," he said, making a drink for himself.

I poured rum and Coke—mostly rum—into a tall plastic glass.

"Yeah," Tyler said, "that's what I like to see—a J. J. mix." With shaggy brown hair and tattoos—a detailed heart on his right arm, and a statue from Nirvana's *In Utero* album on his left—that protruded from underneath the sleeves of his tight-fitting Strokes T-shirt, Tyler looked like a seventies rocker.

I downed my drink and made another.

Steve and I had decided to become alcoholics about one month before this night. Garrett and Tyler, both twenty years old, guided us in our drinking.

After a short while, Nate, Tyler's younger brother, came over. Tyler wrote songs and played guitar for his band, The Scissorhands, in which Nate played drums and Garrett played bass. Although Nate's hair only covered a quarter of his ears, I still saw him as a rocker. He didn't seem to give a shit about anything, and he loved all the classics. Wearing an AC/DC *Back In Black* T-shirt, Nate took nips from a pint of Black Velvet. Like most nights, he asked, "Any of you guys want some of this B. V.?" We all turned him down. Black Velvet was Nate's drink.

"Fuck it. More for me." He walked onto the balcony to smoke a cigarette.

Steve and I got drunk quickly. Warmth flowed through my cheeks. A few more of our drinking buddies came over, one of whom we only hung out with because he was old enough to buy booze. He'd brought a thirty-pack of Keystone and a handle of Canadian Mist. Soon, I was laughing at anything anyone said.

"Look at J. J.," Tyler said to Garrett. "He's such a badass. Let me see your tattoo again, J. J."

He got up from the couch and sat next to me on the carpet. I showed him my left wrist. The guitar reached from the bottom of my left hand to an inch or two below my mid-arm crease. Tyler traced the neck with his fingertips.

I tasted vomit sliding up into my mouth, and I tottered down the hall. After projectile puking in the bathroom, I looked at myself in the mirror. Bits of orange and yellow vomit clung to my hair, and I wondered how a true metalhead like myself could've stayed sober through junior high and most of high school. I thought about how the members of my favorite metal bands would love the way I drank.

Back in the living room, I said, "Let's listen to Eyehategod." Since I'd discovered the Southern metal band a year or two earlier, I liked saying their name as much as listening to their tar-soaked, Sabbath-worshipping riffs.

"There's a band called I Hate God?" Nate said, providing the exact reaction I wanted. "Holy shit."

After getting the CD from my truck, I put *Take as Needed For Pain* in Tyler's stereo, turning the volume up full-blast. Neighbors had called the cops multiple times for noise coming from the apartment. The walls were thin; you could almost hear people in surrounding units breathe. But I didn't give a fuck, and neither did Tyler or Garrett, even though the landlord had threatened to evict them several times. Everyone in the apartment watched while I swirled my hair, helicopter headbanging on beat with the filthy sounds coming from the stereo. I lost balance and fell into a wall behind the TV, laughing hysterically.

"Fuck yeah," Garrett said, also laughing. Drunk, his voice became high and maniacal.

I rolled around on the carpet next to the kitchen.

Over the music, Nate talked to Tyler. "When you guys first brought J. J. over, I said, 'I don't know about this guy. He just gets wasted and rolls around on the ground.' Now I know he's a true badass, though."

I passed out.

When I woke up a few hours later, everyone had either fallen asleep or left. I stumbled as I walked downstairs. During the first times I got drunk at the apartment, I'd tried to leave and drive to my parents' house while Steve and my drinking buddies were still awake, but someone always stopped me. In my truck, I scanned my CD case for a few minutes before deciding on Sabbath's *Master Of Reality*.

I carefully drove through the surrounding neighborhood. A sign for the Outlaw hovered over houses.

I pulled onto a main street. Instead of driving through town to get to my parents' house, which only took about ten minutes, I decided to take the freeway. I skipped the

CD forward to "Into The Void." Tony Iommi's downtuned riffs, propelled by Geezer and Bill Ward's tight-as-fuck rhythm section, electrified my body, making me headbang. I saw a flash of metal guardrail and swerved, but I overcompensated. In the left lane, my tires rolled over cement grooves. I hit a plastic reflector pole—a loud *slap* against my door. Regaining control, I drove back into the right lane.

A few minutes after I woke up the next morning, I remembered hitting the reflector pole and nearly smashing into the guardrail. When Dad came home after a day of reading electric meters in people's backyards, he asked me about the large scrape and dent on my driver's-side door. "It wasn't because you were driving drunk, was it?"

"No, I was driving on a dirt road with Steve, and I had to dodge this huge hole. But I didn't see a reflector pole that was off to the side, and I accidentally hit it."

"Goddamnit, son. You need to pay attention to what you're doing and be more careful." He knew I'd been driving drunk but probably thought, correctly, that he couldn't talk about it without pissing me off. I was still telling him and myself that I didn't give a shit about how he wanted me to live my life.

A week or two later, my buddies and I left Garrett and Tyler's apartment for a party in the same building, after we'd already gotten fucked-up. I followed Steve through the door and saw Drew sitting on a couch. I immediately wanted to leave.

After the girl who rented the apartment greeted us, Drew said, "Look at you, J. J. Remember when you used to be all anti, always bitching to your dad about him getting fucked-up? Now you're just doing the same shit as him."

Trying to think of something to say, I wished I was inside the walls of Garrett and Tyler's apartment.

IN THE MIDDLE OF June, I went on a road trip with Steve, Jared, Bryan, Josh, and Josh's friend, Bruce, to ride in Jackson Hole. I'd never seen Jared or Bryan touch alcohol before this trip, and afterward, they only drank once in a while. When they departed from straight edge, they didn't latch onto another extreme, unlike Steve and me. We stayed at the cabin Grandpa Don's father had built in Bondurant.

Riding at an indoor skate park, I felt animated by Jared, Bryan, Steve, Josh, and Bruce, a feeling that was becoming increasingly faint in my BMX experiences. Immediately after the three-hour session, though, all I wanted to do was get wasted.

Josh and Bruce bought some booze and we drove back to the cabin. Bryan and I got completely shit-faced within forty-five minutes. Bryan, Jared, and I had known each other since grade school. Having spent so much time together, we'd developed an elaborate system of inside jokes, all of which seemed way funnier on this night. In the midst of hysterical laughter, Bryan suddenly said, "Fuck you," looking at me.

Unsettled, I laughed. We always messed with each other, but now, his words had an edge.

"Fuck you," he said again.

Bryan and Jared worked their asses off in school and at their menial jobs, trying to save for college. To them, my decision to become an alcoholic was stupid. Neither of them had said anything about it before this night, but even then I could tell that "Fuck you" was Bryan's way of saying, *You're being a coward. You have better chances in life than most people.*

We sat around a fire pit behind the cabin. After telling everyone to move, I rode an old mountain bike directly through the fire. The rear tire jumped up when I hit a log, and the seat smashed my nuts. Everyone burst into high-pitched laughter.

About two hours later, after drinking myself into a stupor, I stumbled toward the cabin from the fire pit, just wanting to go to bed. As I walked, Bruce scribbled on my face with black marker while Josh filmed the scene with my parents' camcorder, which we'd been using to film our riding.

"Yeah! Ozzy! Say how much you love Ozzy," Bruce said, scrawling "Ozzy" on my forehead. I tried to bat his hands away, but my arms felt like two wet ropes. With Tony Iommi's guitar tattooed on my wrist, strands of hair stuck in my mouth, and wearing a Black Sabbath shirt, I felt like some kind of dumbass clown.

I slept for a while, but was woken up by Josh and Bruce spraying something on my face. I remember looking at Jared and Steve, who both laughed with them, before passing out again.

When I woke up a few hours later, everyone had gone to bed. Flashes of Josh and Bruce laughing and spraying something on me played in my head. Somehow, I became convinced that they'd pissed on me, although my shirt smelled like WD-40, not piss.

I had to get back at them. I went to the enclosed porch where we'd put our bikes. Josh and Bruce's bikes were finely tuned machines, both equipped with the best components you could buy. Josh's clear-coat frame shone in the moonlight. I knew how much work and money they'd both put into their bikes, which were customized to fit their riding styles. Each bike was probably worth over two grand. I knew that, to Josh and Bruce, their bikes were part of who they were.

Still drunk, I took the bikes to the log fence that lined the cabin's yard. As I walked through wet grass, the bikes' freewheels clicked loudly, like baseball cards ticking against spokes. A few feet from the fence, I let Bruce's bike fall, picking up Josh's and holding it over my head. Using the handlebars for leverage, I hurled it at the fence. The frame smashed into the top log with a dull, metallic thud. I picked it up and threw it into the fence a few more times before giving Bruce's bike the same treatment.

Josh and Bruce were sleeping in the bunkhouse, next to the main cabin. A light on the bunkhouse porch came on, and, when they saw what I was doing, they ran toward me. I'd badly dented both of their frames. Josh put me in a headlock and took me back to the main cabin. He kept yelling, "What the fuck are you doing? That's a brand-new frame."

Inside, he pinned me down on a couch and started choking me. A laser of concentrated hate shot from his eyes, and his fingers tightened around my throat, but I didn't struggle. I remember thinking, *I'm not afraid to die, motherfucker,* as I stared into his eyes.

When Josh finally let go, I started ranting about him and Bruce pissing on me, about how Jared and Steve were pieces of shit for letting this happen. "No one pissed on you, J. J.," Steve kept saying. "It was just WD-40."

"Fuck you assholes," I said. "I'm done with all of you." I went back into the bedroom, locked the door, and passed out.

When I woke up the next morning, Steve, Jared, Josh, and Bruce all told me, again and again, that no one had pissed on me. Finally realizing that they weren't fucking with me, I thought about all the hateful things I'd said to Jared and Steve, and I cried, worrying that I'd permanently fucked up our friendships. The night before, Bryan had locked himself in the bathroom so no one could mess with him. He stood in a doorway on this morning, his shaggy brown hair mussed, wiping sleep from his eyes and looking confused.

I remember thinking that none of this would've happened if we'd been drinking at Garrett and Tyler's apartment.

HANGING OUT AT THE apartment a few weeks later, I found some of Tyler's lyrics, scrawled on a piece of notebook paper. I remember something like, "Grayness / I drink to kill the pain." I laughed, thinking, *That's some cheesy-ass bullshit.* At the same time, I also believed that true rockers experience pain more intensely than most people, which is why they often stay drunk and stoned. I wanted everyone at the apartment to believe a similar story about me, so I never made fun of Tyler for writing the lyrics.

One day, I showed up at the apartment in the midafternoon. After waking up drunk, Garrett had immediately started drinking again. His pupils seemed to have swallowed his irises, and incoherent speech spewed from his mouth.

"Jesus," I said to Tyler. "He's just been drinking since this morning?"

"I guess he ran into Jenny yesterday at the store." Tyler said, talking about Garrett's first girlfriend.

To Garrett I said, "You really don't give a fuck, do you?"

"No, dude. Not at all." I loved Garrett's I-don't-give-a-shit-about-anything attitude, but it also scared me.

During another night, we went to a party in Green River, a town ten miles west of Rock Springs. Tyler walked into the double-wide trailer and, after a minute or two, went back outside. When Garrett and I came out to talk to him, Tyler said, "Did you fucking see who's in there? I can't deal with seeing Serena right now."

Back at the apartment, Tyler drank alone in his room, not letting anyone in. To me, his reasoning for acting like a child made complete sense. Serena had profoundly wounded him. Like Garrett, he told me that his first love had completely fucked him over.

When Lindsay first broke up with me in February, I attacked her with the most scathing words I could think of, which happened while I still defined myself as straight edge, so I couldn't blame my outburst on alcohol. I told Tyler and Garrett that my first girlfriend—who I fully believed was my true love, which they also implied when they talked about their ex-girlfriends—had broken up with me for no reason. But I didn't talk about my relationship with Lindsay in detail, which helped me avoid questioning the bullshit I told myself.

Alone, I listened to Down's "Stone the Crow" over and over. In his tar-pit croon, Phil Anselmo sings, "A bout of deep depression / Can't seem to move it forward / No one to share this hurt that is mine, mine / Mine." I often listened to this song on my way to the apartment, or before going in, parked in the complex lot. I constantly told myself that Lindsay was the only girl that could ever make me happy.

Although Garrett, Tyler, and I exaggerated our pain to justify getting fucked-up every night, our hurt was also genuine. Falling in love, especially for the first time, is intense and chaotic. I didn't know how to handle the fact that I was still completely in love with Lindsay. In addition to "Stone the Crow," I listened to Bleeding Through's "Revenge I Seek" on repeat. During the chugging, pinch-harmonic-laden breakdown, the singer screams, "I'll fucking hate you for the rest of my life / Why the fuck did I let you into my heart?" This song, and others like it, helped me believe that I was a victim, even though Lindsay's decision was perfectly logical.

The reality of the situation makes it hard for me to believe that I could've been so delusional. Despite my verbal attacks, Lindsay always said that she wanted to remain close friends, making constant efforts toward this end. She called just to talk and often invited me to hang out at her mom's house, although it might've been easier to just break off contact. Like so many other things in my life, there was gray area in this situation, but I wanted to see it in black-and-white.

ONE WEEKEND IN JULY, I drove to Salt Lake with Lindsay and her mom. I'd been planning to get Pantera's CFH logo tattooed on the inside of my right wrist for a while, and I decided this trip was a good time. They dropped me off at a tattoo parlor and then went shopping at a nearby mall. While the needle buzzed my wristbones, the idea that I'd always be a metalhead electrified my veins.

Driving back to Rock Springs, Lindsay asked me to take off the bandage so she could see the tattoo. She softly traced the swollen logo with her fingertips.

"What do you think?" I asked.

"I like it, J. J. I just think it's the same as your other tattoo."

When I showed my mom the CFH tattoo, she said something similar. "What if you don't like Pantera anymore when you're twenty-five?" she asked.

That night in the apartment, I showed Garrett, Tyler, Steve, and Nate my new tattoo.

"That's fucking badass," Steve said.

"Fuck yeah, J. J." Tyler said. "You're hard-core, dude."

AURORA

EY MAN, YOU WANT some green?" said a small black guy as Dad and I passed him, carrying my mattress into my new apartment building. It was a late August afternoon, and Dad and Mom had just driven a U-Haul from Rock Springs to Aurora, a three-hundred-fifty-mile trip, with me following in my truck. The guy wore a wifebeater and had short braids. He and two of his buddies were smoking cigarettes on the building's stoop.

"No thanks," I said, glancing at him and looking away.

"I'm just down the hall if you need some."

Dad talked to him while I carried in another load. I didn't smoke pot at the time, but, after a few months, I'd regularly buy weed from this guy.

With my mom, I went to a nearby 7-11 to get a money order because the landlord wouldn't accept a check for my deposit. Two skinny men, probably in their mid-to-late thirties, argued in the convenience store parking lot. One man shoved the other, and the guy who'd gotten pushed nearly fell. When they yelled at each other, I noticed that they both had crack-abraded teeth.

As we walked inside, Mom tapped my shoulder and shook her head, not wanting me to stare.

A LITTLE MORE THAN three hundred African American people lived in Rock Springs when I was a teenager. Only nine or ten black students attended Rock Springs High when I went there, and three of the five black boys I knew lived in an apartment complex at the bottom of a large hill.

My apartment was located in northeastern Aurora, on the edge of Denver. In 2004, housing in this area mainly consisted of cheap apartments and small, one-level houses. I only remember seeing a few other white people in my apartment complex. Most tenants were black or Latino, but there were also Indians, Ethiopians, Arabs, Haitians, and several other people from all over the world.

Driving through southwestern Aurora, I'd see pseudo-mansions and, almost exclusively, white people. Like most American cities, Denver and Aurora have a history of racist real-estate covenants, blockbusting, and redlining. Of course I noticed the racial disparity and segregation around me, but I didn't think about why these things existed, and I didn't try to find out.

MY HAIR, WHICH I'D been growing out for two and a half years, hung to the middle of my back, and I wore my band patch–covered jean jacket as if it was a protective shell.

I decorated my apartment before unpacking my dinnerware. Along with pictures of Tom Araya, Tony Iommi, Dimebag Darrel, and Phil Anselmo, I hung a Pantera flag behind my futon.

BEFORE SCHOOL STARTED, I drove around a lot, trying to understand the layouts of Denver and Aurora. In the business sections of Aurora, the blocks are huge. Trying to live here without a car would be a massive pain in the ass. Even though it's a suburb of Denver, Aurora covers more square miles. As a whole, Aurora and Denver span more than sixteen times as many square miles as Rock Springs.

One day, I left my apartment shortly after noon. Instead of looking up the address of a grocery store, I decided to just drive around and find one. I turned west onto Colfax, a main street, toward downtown Denver. Fast-food places, liquor stores, head shops, tattoo parlors, and used car dealerships lined both sides of the street. As I got closer to Denver, I noticed fewer windows with bars on them, and the buildings looked nicer, with newer paint and signs. I also noticed fewer crackheads on the sidewalks.

I turned north onto Colorado, passing apartment buildings, gas stations, big houses, and a large park. Soon, I reached I-70, and industrial yards surrounded me. I did a U-turn and headed south.

Several blocks after passing Colfax, I finally found a King Soopers, but I passed it—two more U-turns before I made it into the parking lot. I stocked up on frozen dinners, Chef Boyardee, and sugary fruit juice.

Trying to find my way home, I turned onto a street that dead-ended in a labyrinthine residential neighborhood, and it took me twenty minutes to start heading in the right direction again. It was past four by the time I got back to my apartment.

This became a routine. Instead of going to the same store again, I'd try to find a different one, often getting lost in a sea of traffic, buildings, and confusing streets. I hated getting lost, but I also knew that I wouldn't learn much about my new surroundings from looking at a map.

THE COLORADO FILM SCHOOL campus was only a few blocks from my apartment complex. Buildings of the defunct Lowry Air Force Base had been converted to house the film school and a branch of Community College of Aurora in 1994. Built in 1938, Lowry was originally used to train bomber crews.

On the first day of school, I parked in front of the yellow brick buildings of Lowry Base, now Colorado Film School. Dead grass surrounded the squat buildings, and a few liquor stores beckoned from across the street, their neon lights glowing. To the west you could see the buildings of downtown against the backdrop of the Rockies. I knew that cool shit was always happening in Denver, but it seemed out of my reach.

On the first day of film school, I made a few friends, Steven and Dave. Still, I realized that I didn't want to be there within a month. Most students wanted to make feature-length movies, whereas I only wanted to study digital editing. But I had to learn about lighting, script writing, and camera techniques, too. The only film-related work I actually finished in Aurora was converting my BMX video, which had previously been on VHS, to DVD.

When I should've been doing homework, I sat on my futon, thinking about Lindsay, listening to metal, and playing *Tony Hawk's American Wasteland* on PS2. I constantly imagined what it would be like if Lindsay moved to Aurora.

In my apartment, I could only fall asleep while watching TV. I didn't have cable, so I just watched *The Lord Of The Rings*, *Detroit Rock City*, and Pantera's *Home Videos* over and over. My life was a shitty, predictable song on a repeating loop.

ALTHOUGH I LIKED TO believe I was a nonconformist, I really just wanted a stereotypical college experience, minus the schoolwork. I wanted college to be like it was in comedies like *Animal House* and *Road Trip*—a constant party.

Half of my classes were at the Lowry Base, and the other half were at the main branch of CCA, in eastern Aurora. The main campus consisted of a few nondescript white buildings in a business park. The nearby glass-and-concrete buildings all looked new. Manicured grass, trees, and bushes surrounded each building. People zoomed in and out of parking lots, all seeming like they were going somewhere important. Driving through the business park, I usually felt like I was in someone's way, going too slowly or otherwise holding up traffic.

On my first day of classes at the main branch, I hoped and expected to see hot girls everywhere, girls that wanted to date a metalhead. Instead, most of the students were older than me, walking to class with their heads down. I saw a few cute girls, but none of them seemed to care that I existed. I had the same experience in my classes—a few attractive women who didn't seem at all interested in me.

Most students worked full-time jobs, and many of them were married or in serious relationships. I wanted a fantasy, but life at CCA was mundane. Having held out hope for so long that life outside Rock Springs would be amazing, I began to realize that, no matter where you go, life is mostly boring.

JARED WAS GOING TO school in Thornton, thirty minutes west of Aurora. For the first few weeks after we moved, Jared and I rode together a lot, hitting the amazing concrete skate parks in and near Denver. We had a few fun sessions, laughing and pushing each other to do new tricks. But Jared was going through an intensive two-year drafting program, and he was serious about school. He also got a job at FedEx and, soon, didn't have much time to ride. When we rode together, my choice to become a drunk hung in the air between us. Jared was worried and disappointed, but he knew that, if he said anything, it wouldn't have made a difference.

During that first month, I often rode alone at the Aurora skate park, although bikes weren't allowed. This park was amazing, with a peanut bowl, snake run, and seemingly limitless possibilities for lines—a maze of transitions, flat banks, and ledges. But I quickly found myself repetitively doing the same tricks on the same obstacles, and I'd get pissed at myself for not diversifying my riding more. I could've practiced the rudimentary tricks I needed to know to progress—tricks I should've learned years earlier—but I wanted to look like a badass, not a newbie. The last few times I went to the Aurora skate park, I spent as much time staring at the yellow grass surrounding the park as I did riding.

SHORTLY AFTER STARTING SCHOOL, someone told me about Wax Trax, an amazing record store on Denver's Capitol Hill. The first few times I went in, I browsed the rock, hip-hop, indie, and industrial sections, quickly getting overwhelmed. I always ended up in the metal section, looking through racks of familiar music. Soon, I started going directly to the metal CDs without looking at anything else.

A clerk with shaggy blond hair and intricate tribal tattoos crawling up his arms would tell me about doom bands that I hadn't listened to—Yob, Grief, Electric Wizard, and several others—and I began looking forward to talking to him as much as buying new music.

I DECIDED TO GET another tattoo at the end of September. A few years earlier, I'd bought a plastic figurine of a skull that Metallica used on merchandise for their Damage Inc. tour—the 1986 tour that followed the release of *Master Of Puppets*, easily my favorite Metallica album. I wished that Metallica had never departed from the punk-infused thrash that made them famous in the eighties, a style that captures what it truly means to destroy.

I drove west on Colfax after school one day, stopping at a tattoo parlor called Bound by Design. I didn't know if this was a good shop; it just looked cool. A large metal sign with red letters hung above wide windows that looked onto the dirty sidewalk.

Inside, I showed a tattoo artist the plastic skull so he could draw it onto wax paper. Two baseball bats, each with nails jutting from the top, penetrated the skull. Jagged teeth sprouted from the skull's upper jaw.

"Where do you want it?" the artist asked.

"On my right forearm." I thought the guy would be impressed, that he'd say something like, "Damn, you're hard-core." Instead, he smirked as he drew the skull, probably thinking, "This kid is a dumbass."

He pressed the stencil onto my skin. The skull covered the majority of my right forearm. Loading his tattoo gun with black ink, he said, "You sure about this?"

I felt a tinge of apprehension, which I'd also felt before getting my other tattoos. I smothered this feeling by telling myself that I'd never change. As the artist tattooed my skin, anxiety about my place in the world didn't seem as intense.

WITH MY FILM SCHOOL friends, Steven and Dave, as well as Jared and his girlfriend, Jessica, I went to Casa Bonita one night, a shitty Mexican restaurant in west Denver with cliff divers and magic shows. I had met up with Jared and Jessica in Thornton. One of Jared's roommates bought a fifth of Captain for me, and I downed most of it within fifteen minutes. My mantra for social situations at the time: What would Dimebag Darrel do?

Jessica was from Rock Springs, too, and she'd graduated with Jared and me. She'd moved to Fort Collins, an hour north of Denver, for school, and she and Jared had decided to stay together. When I hung out with them, I always wished that Lindsay would have give a long-distance relationship a chance.

Jared had to help me down the stairs from his apartment and into his car. Sitting in the backseat, I said, "Put on some fucking Slayer, Jared." Jessica and Jared laughed, but I could feel disappointment underneath Jared's laughter. I thought about his dad driving home drunk every night, constantly flirting with death. Looking at Jessica, who'd always been a straight-A student, I wondered about the point of putting so much work into life when we're all just destined to die.

At Casa Bonita, I followed Jared and Jessica inside, stood in line, and drunkenly ordered some food. Steven and Dave had gotten a table near a magician, who was putting on a show. Children and parents gathered around the middle-aged man, clapping as he performed card tricks and pulled a long piece of ribbon from behind a kid's ear.

"Fuck yeah," I said, clapping loudly. "I fucking *love* magic. Do another trick."

"J. J.," Jared said, speaking under his breath and trying not to laugh. "Shut up. You're going to get us kicked out."

I kept talking shit to the magician, who, red-faced, tried to ignore me. Moms and dads glared at me. Jared, Steven, Dave, and Jessica were all laughing.

Looking back, this memory almost doesn't seem real. I can smell the dirty water that the cliff-divers had jumped into, as well as the greasy food. But I also have a hard time convincing myself that I was the little asshole shouting at the magician. While I know this person is still part of me, he also seems like someone I've imagined.

When the waiter brought out our food, he told Jared that, if I didn't quiet down, he was going to call the cops.

I passed out, face down on my burrito and refried beans.

I woke up about fifteen minutes later, needing to throw up. I stumbled to the bathroom, Jared following. In a hallway, I waterfall-puked onto the clean black-and-white tile, giggling as I picked strands of hair from my mouth. Jared walked me to the bathroom, where I covered a toilet with puke.

He decided that we should leave, leading me outside after getting Jessica. Even though I knew he was irritated with me, I also felt a sense of stability as I held onto Jared's shoulders. Two cop cars pulled up as he walked me through the doors. Jared told me not to say anything. We walked past them and to his car.

At Jared's apartment, I woke up after an hour or so. He and Jessica were asleep, and I decided that I wanted to sleep in my own bed.

In my truck, I put Every Time I Die's *Hot Damn* in my CD player and skipped it to "I Been Gone A Long Time." I found I-25, then I-70, then I-225 as I listened to the band's chaotic hardcore and filthy Southern breakdowns.

I headbanged during my favorite parts, nearly swerving into metal guardrails lining the interstate.

I WANTED TO GET drunk every night, but I was only nineteen, and I didn't know anyone who'd buy booze for me regularly. I'm not sure why I didn't hang out in front of a liquor store, asking people to buy. Walking in the hall of my apartment building one day, I saw the small black guy who'd tried to sell me weed when I moved in. I asked him if he'd buy some beer for me.

"Yeah, I'll buy some shit for you. You'll need to buy me a Mad Dog, though." Later, when I told my friends about this, they started referring to the guy as Mad Dog, and I did too. We'd joke about how Mad Dog would be a perfect shitty rapper, not thinking about how racist our jokes were.

He got in my truck, and we drove to a nearby liquor store, Lamb of God's *Ashes Of The Wake* playing in my CD player. Randy Blythe screamed about governmental folly while the rest of the band played super-fast thrash and mind-numbingly technical breakdowns.

"I don't get why so many white people are pissed off all the time," the guy said.

He bought me a thirty-pack of Keystone and a blue Mad Dog for himself. I got drunk that night and a few nights afterward, but I didn't want to keep asking the guy to buy booze for me, afraid that I'd piss him off.

MYSPACE WAS JUST BECOMING a craze during this time. I signed up, hoping to get laid. In the music section, I listed off my favorite bands in descending order, making sure to get the list perfect. My movies section: *Evil Dead*, *Detroit Rock City*, *The Lord Of The Rings*, *Dogtown And Z-Boys*, and *Army Of Darkness*. I adjusted my hair to make it look shaggier before taking a picture of myself in front of my Pantera flag. After careful deliberation, I decided to wear my favorite Sabbath shirt in the picture.

I'd spend hours on Myspace, examining profiles of cute girls. One day, I found a girl from my math class on the site. She was emo, with dyed-black hair and star tattoos on her arms, and she always wore thick eyeliner. After she accepted my friend request, we exchanged a few messages. She used a Good Charlotte album cover as the background of her page, and I wondered how she did this, wanting to customize my background, too.

When I tried to talk to her in person, I felt awkward and sad in a way that I couldn't quite pin down. She was cute, but she also made me think about how lonely I truly was. I probably represented the same thing to her. After we talked in class, I noticed her emptily staring at the cover of her notebook, not listening to our precalculus teacher. We said hi or nodded to each other in the rest of our classes, but neither of us tried to strike up conversation again.

THE PARTIES AT GARRETT and Tyler's apartment got crazier after I moved. They'd call me most nights and tell me how much more fun they'd have if I was there. Although I hated Rock Springs, I ended up going back every few weeks. When I thought about the parties I was missing, I'd feel a giddy restlessness. I wanted a part in any crazy story that took place at the apartment.

I'd usually drive back on a Friday afternoon, getting to Rock Springs around ten or eleven. When I walked into Garrett and Tyler's apartment, a womb-like warmth would envelop me. Steve, Tyler, Garrett, and Nate would feed me rum. We'd hug and tell each other how badass we were.

More and more people in Rock Springs started to find out that Garrett and Tyler were always down to party. Walking into the apartment after driving six hours from Aurora, I'd see some people I knew and several others I'd never seen before.

Getting wasted with some of my high school classmates, we'd talk to each other as if we were old friends. Outside the apartment, we never would've hung out together. Hitting on girls from school whom I'd been afraid to talk to when I was sober, I often thought, *Remember me, how I used to be straight edge? Look how crazy I am now.*

Garrett and Tyler planned an epic party for Halloween. I thought about my costume for weeks in advance, eventually deciding to be Hulkamania-era Hulk Hogan, my favorite wrestler when I was four and five. At a costume store in Denver, I found a handlebar mustache that perfectly matched my blond hair. I had a pair of black-and-neon-green spandex pants that I'd bought a few years before, on a BMX road trip, and I bought a tight yellow T-shirt, ripped off the sleeves, and wrote "Hulkamania" on the front, in black marker.

Driving to the party on a Friday night, I stopped at a truck stop in Rawlins, a little town ninety miles east of Rock Springs. Wanting to show up at the apartment in costume, I put on my spandex and sleeveless shirt in a stall in the men's room. Looking in the mirror, I carefully glued on my mustache with spirit gum. A few truckers came in, each one staring at me. Outside, biting Wyoming wind flooded through my spandex as I walked to my truck.

I thought about my dad and Lindsay's dad when I passed Point of Rocks—the tiny community near the power plant where they'd both spent a huge part of their lives. From I-80, hills obscured the plant, but I could see the blue glow it cast into the night.

Giddiness fluttered in my stomach as I climbed the stairs leading to Garrett and Tyler's apartment. "Oh shit!" Garrett said when I walked through the door. "Motherfucking Hulk Hogan's up in this bitch."

Steve came up from behind and lifted me in a bear hug. He held up a handle of Jagermeister. When we'd seen Slayer in Salt Lake a few years earlier, the tour was sponsored by Jager, so drinking this sweet liquor always seemed like a very metal thing to do.

I kept going to the bathroom to look at myself and jokingly flex my scrawny arms. Halloween has always been one of my favorite holidays—a day to pretend that I can be whomever I want.

Within an hour, I passed out in Garrett's room.

DURING THE WEEKEND OF the Halloween party, I took my drums with me back to Aurora. I'd been exchanging emails with a guitarist from Clusterfux, a crossover thrash band that needed a drummer. Listening to their music, which sounded like Cro-Mags, D.R.I., and Slayer, I knew that I couldn't play it—it was blazingly fast, with a lot of double bass—but I still decided to try. At this point, one of the only things I knew for sure was that I wanted to play music.

Driving to Aurora after Halloween, I kept looking in my rearview mirror to make sure that my drums hadn't bounced out of my flatbed. Winter had begun to slither over Wyoming. Small, hardened snowdrifts bordered the interstate. I'd covered my drums in old towels and blankets to protect them, but the coverings quickly blew off.

A week or so later, I was driving around downtown Denver, trying to find the warehouse where the Clusterfux guy lived. I made several wrong turns but eventually found it. Stickers of punk and metal bands, along with old school skate stickers, covered the faded green door of the warehouse.

"What's up, man?" the guy said when he opened the door. "You can just load your drums right in." He'd converted the warehouse into a jam space and apartment. He had a short pink mohawk that wasn't spiked, and the tuft of hair hung limply to one side of his head. He wore a black T-shirt under a sleeveless jean jacket that was covered in band patches—mostly punk bands from the eighties and nineties. A few black tattoos decorated his arms, and I remember thinking, *This guy is the real deal* as I carried my drums inside.

There were two Marshall full-stacks on either side
of the carpet where I set up my drums—the five-piece
Ludwig Rocker kit I had since I was twelve. As I set up my
cymbals, the guy asked, "Is that one of those cymbal kits
from Musician's Friend?"

"Yeah," I said, feeling like a poser for having such
cheap and generic equipment.

The guy had sent me a Clusterfux album a week or two
earlier, wanting me to learn the songs. I tried to play one
with him after I set up, but I could only make it through
a few bars before he said something like, "You flipped the
beat," or, "I think we got off time." I'd been trying to play
thrash for years, but I didn't have the stamina to play fast
for much longer than thirty seconds.

I eventually made it to the bridge of the song a few
times. On the recording, the drummer launched into a
double bass roll during this section. Like I'd tried so many
times before in my parents' basement—attempting to ape
Lars Ulrich, Dave Lombardo, and Vinnie Paul—I tried to
play a double bass roll but only succeeded in creating a
nonsensical jumble. I knew how the beat worked, I just
didn't have the leg strength or control to play it. Before the
roll, the drummer on the recording also played a triplet-
based fill that I couldn't pull off.

"Here," the guitarist said, setting his guitar against
his cab. "You just do the John Bonham thing before the
double bass part." I handed him my sticks and got up from
my stool. He played the fill and beat perfectly, explaining
how they worked afterward. Trying to play the song again,

I felt like I'd been spanked, bare-assed, in front of a full classroom. At the same time, during the few moments when we coalesced, I felt tinges of raw energy.

As I got ready to leave, I knew that I wasn't going to jam with the guy again, but I felt too awkward to say this to him. He was nice about how much I sucked, and willing to give me another chance. My hair, tattoos, and Slayer T-shirt probably told him that I was genuinely enthusiastic about music. In addition to practice, I knew that enthusiasm was the foundation of becoming a good musician, and the Clusterfux guitarist knew this, too. But I still felt embarrassed. During our phone conversations, I'd told him how much I loved Dave Lombardo and Vinnie Paul, not mentioning that I couldn't play like them.

"Just practice that double bass beat," the guy said before I left, "and we'll try again next weekend."

For the next two weeks, I made up excuses about why I couldn't come to practice. I finally told the guitarist that I was moving back to Wyoming, and I needed to pick up my drums. I convinced Jared to go to the warehouse with me so I could load out faster. The guy was very nice again, although I think he knew I'd been lying. As I broke down my kit and loaded it into my truck, I felt like I'd gotten caught jacking off. Even so, I still wanted nothing more than to play in a metal band.

AROUND THIS TIME, MY friend Steven decided to make a short movie, *Axe-Kaliber*, about a guitar-wielding hessian who fights evil with his shredding skills. Of course he chose me to play the metalhead.

I still have a copy of the movie. It begins with a shot of me walking on a sidewalk behind the Lowry dorms, where Steven and Dave lived. I'm a nerd in this part, wearing a tucked-in, button-down shirt, and my hair is pulled back into a ponytail. Lisa Loeb's "Stay" plays while I kick leaves, walking with an exaggerated hunch, like one of the awkward guys in *Revenge of The Nerds*. I find a guitar in the leaves, and the Lisa Loeb song fades away.

Holding the guitar, I walk behind a tree and jump out from the other side as a metalhead. My hair is down, and I'm wearing a black Lamb of God shirt. Iron Maiden's "Hallowed Be Thy Name" plays as I walk, headbanging and pretending to play a ripping solo. I make my way to the dorm building, still headbanging. I'm wearing my favorite pair of Levis, which have two holes near the right pocket.

There are a few closeups of my face. Staring at myself, I see stability in my eyes, and I doubt that I'll ever feel so certain about my identity again. I also remember how comfortable I felt around my film school friends when we were shooting this video—a social comfort that I can rarely attain now, and only in fleeting moments. Looking back on these memories, I've often told myself that I didn't know who I was. It's true that I inhabited a metalhead caricature, but my choice to do so stemmed from the fact that metal is truly part of who I am.

When I listen to my favorite bands from this time, it's easy to be critical of them. The anger and machismo in metal often seems silly. But I can't deny that this music still connects to something deep within my psyche. To me, heavy metal has always been about finding meaning in ugliness. Slayer, Black Sabbath, Pantera, and old Metallica—these bands are all raucous, playing chord progressions and using song structures that make most trained musicians sneer. After a while of listening to Metallica, Slayer, and Pantera's manic thrash, or Sabbath's plodding doom, the harsh sounds become beautiful. Metal taught me that one way to find meaning is by reshaping surrounding negativity into art, which is a process of owning that negativity. This music also helped me realize that one of the purest places of existence is the ledge between life and death, a place where thought melts away and only action matters.

In the movie, I walk through a narrow hallway, where I see Steven's friend, Robbie, who's pretending to be an evil guitarist. He wears a jean jacket with no shirt underneath, and a black bandana is tied around his head.

Judas Priest's thrashing anthem, "Metal Meltdown," replaces the Iron Maiden song as Robbie and I begin our guitar battle. After each of my solos, a red flash shoots from my guitar, and a blue flash shoots from Robbie's after each of his. We act like these flashes hit us, recoiling as if getting punched. We bludgeon each other a few times before I play my most furious fake solo yet, headbanging and holding my guitar in the air like Dimebag. My metal madness makes Robbie explode, and I walk down the hall, still pretending to shred.

AFTER STEVEN FINISHED THIS video, I tried to play with another metal band, the guitarist of which I'd also met online. I'd been wanting to play in a Sabbath-worshipping doom band ever since discovering this style, but I couldn't find anyone who wanted to play sludge metal. When I saw Crowbar, Eyehategod, and Down in this guitarist's list of influences, I replied immediately, trying to ignore that he also listed death metal bands like Obituary, Deicide, and Cannibal Corpse—bands that played even faster than Slayer and Pantera, with more double bass.

I drove to Lakewood, a western suburb, to meet the guitarist. Like the Clusterfux dude, he was super nice. He covered his frayed, blond mullet with a camouflage hat, and he wore a faded Obituary shirt and slim-fit Wranglers. He looked like he could've been a redneck from Wyoming, but he talked with a Southern California drawl, punctuating most of his sentences with 'bro' and 'man.'

I followed him into a small brick building, which housed several rehearsal spaces. The opening of "War Pigs," one of my favorite Sabbath songs, blasted from one of the rooms. The guitar, bass, and drums sounded spot-on, and the vocalist mimicked Ozzy with eerie accuracy.

"A Sabbath cover band," the guy said, nodding at the room as he opened the door of his practice space. I wanted to be in that other room, jamming Sabbath. "I know it's pretty small," he said about the tiny, plywood-walled rehearsal room. "The old drummer we played with just set up in that corner."

He introduced me to the bassist and singer, who were both in their early thirties. They helped me unload, and I set up my drums between the guitar and bass amps, barely having enough room to move my arms. I hit my elbows against the back wall a few times as I warmed up, trying to impress these guys with my simple drumming.

They played one of their songs for me. I felt anxious during the fast sections, but there was a sludgy, mid-tempo breakdown in the middle of the song, and I immediately knew what to play during that part.

During the fast parts, I nervously stomped my double bass pedal, hoping that I'd suddenly be able to pull off fast rolls. As the band launched into the breakdown, I effortlessly found a groove. I beat the shit out of my drums, my arms propelled by the Crowbar-style riff. When the band transitioned into another death metal section, anxiety replaced the energy that I'd felt during the sludgy part.

"Fuck yeah, man," the guitarist said afterward. "You nailed that breakdown. And you'll get the other parts."

We tried the song a few more times. I became increasingly sloppy, and my arms started to feel like they were made of Jell-O.

We took a smoke break. Standing outside, I bummed a cigarette from the guitarist. I'd recently decided to start smoking, even though I only liked it when I was drunk. It was something to do, and I thought that I looked cool doing it. Some of the drags tasted good, but I also gagged after inhaling a few times, trying not to let these death metal dudes notice. They all told me that they were psyched to meet me, that they couldn't wait to play a show together.

Back in the jam space, I showed the guitarist my Black Sabbath tattoo after he asked about it. "Fuck yeah, bro.

That's sick." He picked up his guitar and started playing "Sweet Leaf," a classic Sabbath jam about the magical powers of weed. Although I'd never played it before, I knew all the changes, as if the song had been written into my DNA. I'd felt too tired to move fifteen minutes earlier. Now, I felt like I could play forever.

We jammed the song for a few more minutes before he tried to teach me another original. Again, anxiety rose in my chest as I tried to play the fast sections, and I knew this band wasn't right for me. After practice, I loaded my drums back into my truck, knowing I wouldn't jam with these guys again.

SLAYER PLAYED DENVER IN November, and I'd been giddily looking forward to the show since finding out about it three months earlier. Lindsay, who'd never been to a metal concert, decided to go with me. I was more excited to hang out with her than to see Slayer, although the thought of seeing the thrash legends again also made my veins buzz.

Since we'd moved out of Rock Springs, Lindsay and I had been talking and arguing on a regular basis. Most of our arguments stemmed from my being an immature asshole, but I also think both of us were frustrated by how badly we wanted to be together.

A week or so before she came to Denver for the concert, Lindsay had gotten me a kitten, which someone gave her outside a convenience store in Wyoming. I'm allergic to cats—once, when I was five or six, I had to get rushed to a hospital and put on a respirator after staying one night with my aunt, who had a cat—but I thought the kitten was a sign that Lindsay wanted to get back together. I hadn't been around cats much until I started hanging out with her, and I quickly fell in love with them—little fur balls of anarchy.

On a gray Colorado day in November, I met Lindsay at a gas station on Colfax. A tiny black kitten with blue eyes ran around the backseat of Lindsay's car. When I tried to pet her, she scratched the back of my hand.

Lindsay hadn't seen the Metallica tattoo on my forearm, so she asked me to show it to her. "Oh my God, J. J.," she said, tracing the slightly raised black lines of the skull with her fingers. "It's really big."

She followed me to Aurora. Inside my apartment with her, I felt more comfortable than I had in the past three months. The kitten, which Lindsay had named Crazy Mary, after a Pearl Jam song, tore around on the dingy pink carpet. Watching her, Lindsay laughed and said, "I hope you know what you're in for, J. J. Kittens are fucking crazy."

We drove to the Fillmore after getting some burgers at Good Times. The doors weren't scheduled to open for another four or five hours, but we wanted to get in line early so we could get spots next to the front rail.

Lindsay was one of the few girls in line. By the end of the night, there were still eight or nine times as many men as women at this show. Looking at Lindsay, I felt proud, knowing that the guys around us were jealous. It was warm for November, and the Colorado sun eventually pierced the gray veil that had been hanging over the city, shining down on the leaf-strewn gutters of Colfax.

Lindsay and I told each other stories about things we'd seen or done since starting college. Underneath her laughter and banter, I sensed uneasiness. She knew that I cared more about drinking than school, and also that I'd only been attending class sporadically, not bothering with homework after the first few weeks.

When a security guard finally opened the doors, Lindsay and I walked directly to the rail next to the stage. Mastodon was scheduled to play first, a band I'd been listening to a lot. They interweave several layers of rhythm while also knowing exactly when to simplify, and just be heavy as fuck. The intricate guitar harmonies, odd time signatures, and subtle, jazz-style drumming on *Leviathan* and *Remission* confused me, but in a way that kept me coming back to the albums. They're definitely a metal band, but I'd never heard metal like this.

I studied each member of Mastodon while they set up. Brent Hinds, the lead guitarist, had tattoos of geometric patterns covering his arms and hands, patterns I'd later associate with LSD. The drummer, Brann Dailor, had short blond hair and tattoos covering his arms and neck. Each member of the band wore tightly fitting clothes, and I remember thinking about how good-looking they all were in comparison to most metal musicians.

Speaking into my ear so that I could hear her over the house music, Lindsay said, "That drummer is hot." She was wearing the red camisole that she'd worn on the night of our first kiss. As Mastodon played a set of polyrhythmic prog-metal, I headbanged, holding my head in front of the rail. I also kept glancing over at Lindsay, thinking about how much I wanted to lose my virginity to her.

Mastodon had recently released *Leviathan*, but they weren't metal stars quite yet. I was one of a handful of people in the front row rocking out. Most of the Slayer fans were still trickling into the Fillmore. When Mastodon finished their set, which I loved, although a lot of it sounded like chaos to my ears, I called out to Brann Dailor, holding my hand in the air and hoping he'd throw me a drumstick. I'd only read his name in magazines, and I pronounced it 'Bran,' like oat bran, instead of how it's supposed to be pronounced, 'Brawn,' which I'd learn later. He threw a stick directly to me. Reaching up to catch it, I felt like Jam in *Detroit Rock City* when he catches Peter Criss's drumstick. I slid the stick into the front of my jeans so I wouldn't lose it.

Killswitch Engage, a popular metalcore band, followed Mastodon. As roadies set up their equipment, people swarmed to the front. Lindsay and I were smashed against the rail before Killswitch even started. For us, live music was as much about pain as pleasure. We'd often brag about the bruises we got from shows—bruises earned by getting crushed on the rail. Waiting in line was also part of this pain. Pain, expectation, and waiting made concerts more meaningful for us, like we'd earned the pleasure we got from the music.

When Killswitch launched into a chugging ballad, a wave of dudes surged forward. My ribs pressed into the rail. Soon, I couldn't tell if my feet were touching the ground. Red-faced, Lindsay fanned air onto herself, having a hard time breathing. I worried that she was going to get one of her ribs broken. She lifted her arms up for a security guard to lift her out, and, after a minute or two, I did the same.

Throughout the rest of Killswitch's set, I walked through the crowd, searching for Lindsay. I walked around the edge of the mosh pit, getting shoved a few times by guys who were way bigger than me. I liked Killswitch Engage, but I also remember thinking, *Fuck this scene and its macho bullshit.*

Although similar thoughts had come up at other metal shows, I was usually able to move past them and just get into the music. I think having Lindsay here made me see this world in a different light. She'd often told me that she liked metal, but it was too angry to listen to all the time. She also told me that, before we started talking to each other in high school, she was scared of me because I always looked pissed. Looking for Lindsay during Killswitch Engage's set, I think I was beginning to admit that she was right to be scared of the anger that was such a huge part of my identity.

I finally found Lindsay near the back, a few minutes before Slayer started. She hugged me. "There you are, J. J.," she said, her voice tinged with a playful warmth that I hadn't heard in quite a while. "I was looking for you, but this guy ended up buying me some shots of Jager." The insecure metalhead in me was jealous, but I also thought about how badass Lindsay was, going to a Slayer show, getting in the front row, and taking shots of Jager from some dude who she'd never see again. At this point, she'd gotten drunk a few times but didn't want to drink with me, probably because she didn't want to encourage my choice to become an alcoholic.

After Killswitch finished their set, I excitedly watched roadies set up for Slayer. A half-hour later, the intro to *God Hates Us All* started to play through the house speakers, muddied by the din of fans' voices. A sea of black T-shirts filled the two-tiered, old-style ballroom, and I felt the sense of community that I'd always loved about metal. We were all here to worship Slayer.

The venue lights shut off for a few minutes, coming back on as Slayer started attacking the crowd with old school thrash. The original drummer, Dave Lombardo, had recently joined the band again. To celebrate, they were playing *Reign In Blood*, my favorite Slayer album, in its entirety.

The changes, lyrics, and riffs on this album were written into my bone marrow. I headbanged wildly, knowing that Lindsay loved to watch me rock out. We stood off to the side of the mosh pit, not wanting to get bludgeoned. Sweaty men collided with each other, running around in a huge circle. Looking into their faces, I saw a violent and moronic crowd consciousness. But watching them also motivated me to keep swirling my hair, pushing past the warm pain that latched onto the back of my neck.

As Slayer played the title track of *Reign In Blood*, easily my favorite song of theirs, fake blood sprayed from sprinklers above the band, soaking the members and their instruments in crimson. I stood behind Lindsay, wishing that she'd turn around and kiss me.

On the drive back to my apartment, I hoped that we were finally going to have sex. When we got there, Lindsay quickly fell asleep on the futon.

She left early the next morning. Outside, just before getting into her car, she said, "Take good care of Crazy Mary, J. J."

That day, I decided to rename my cat. I chose Ozena, the title of a Superjoint Ritual song about necrophilia. The band was Phil Anselmo's brainchild and, in my mind, another example of his genius. In the midst of dirty, discordant punk in "Ozena," he screams, "Sex was meant to kill you."

SHORTLY AFTER THE SLAYER concert, I got another tattoo: Black Sabbath's fallen angel on my right shoulder. His bat-like wings spread from my shoulder blade to the top of my pectoral muscle, and he's leaping like a ballet dancer. I loved how the effeminate angel signified a band as badass and manly as Sabbath.

ONE WEEKEND, MY BUDDIES from Rock Springs, Mike and Matt, came to Denver. Matt was Jessica's younger brother, so they stayed with her and Jared in Thornton. On Friday night, while we were watching TV at Jared's place, Mike said, "I brought some weed if you guys want to smoke." I felt an anxiety born of fighting for years with my dad about his pot smoking. But I also felt curious, not quite able to remember what it felt like to get high. Matt made a pipe out of a pop can.

After he and Mike had each taken a few hits, I said, "Let me try that shit." Eating canned fruit at his kitchen table, Jared looked at me. Mike showed me how to take a hit. I inhaled and coughed immediately, the sour smoke scratching my throat.

Within minutes, I was laughing hysterically. My friends' faces took on a cartoonish sheen, as if they'd been transformed into Pixar characters. I was amazed by how much easier it was to get high than drunk. Jared was the only person in the room who really understood what it meant for me to get stoned, to envelop myself in the smoke that consumed my dad's brain. But I felt blissfully disconnected from his concern.

I got high a few more times over the weekend. Immediately after Matt and Mike left, I drove to a head shop on Broadway and bought a black-and-red pipe with a humongous bowl—a pipe that my buddy would later name Carnage, after the Spiderman character.

Driving back to Aurora, I wondered how I could get weed. And then I thought about the dude who'd bought me beer a month or so earlier. I didn't know how weed culture worked, and part of me worried that I'd irritate him if I asked for pot.

Even so, when I got home, I went straight to the guy's door and knocked. A slow, bass-heavy backbeat thumped against his walls. I knocked again, harder this time. He cracked his door, blurry eyes not quite focusing on me. "What's up, man?"

"I was just wondering if you have any green," I said. On my way to Aurora from downtown, I'd been wondering what word I should use to refer to weed, finally deciding that green sounded cool.

"Shit," he said, motioning for me to come inside and shutting the door behind me. "How much you want?"

I stood in the corridor, not sure if I should cross my arms or keep my hands in my pockets. His apartment was the same as mine, but inverted. Instead of the kitchen to the right and bedroom to the left, his kitchen was to the left, bedroom to the right. A large velvet print of Tupac hung above his couch. I remembered hearing people in high school talk about eighths and quarters, not knowing what these measurements meant. "Like a quarter or an eighth?"

"That's what, like five blunts?"

"Uh… Yeah."

He opened a kitchen drawer, revealing a saran-wrapped brick of swag. He broke off several large chunks and placed them in a different piece of saran wrap. "That's going to be twenty." After I gave him the cash, he said, "You know where to come when you need more."

Walking to my apartment, I felt like a little kid about to tear into a mound of Christmas presents. Inside, I stuffed a few chunks of pot into my pipe, not sure if I was loading it the right way. Before I took a hit, I blasted "Sweet Leaf" on my computer.

A whirlpool of pot smoke and riffs I could feel in my gums.

I didn't know that you had to take out the seeds. Holding my lighter to the bowl, I watched brown seeds crackle and expand under the flame, thinking that they got me more stoned. Over the bedrock of Bill Ward's heavy-ass grooves, Ozzy sang, "You introduced me to my mind / and left me wanting you and your kind."

Sitting on my futon, I stared at the TV, which I'd left on. Letters on the pause screen of *Tony Hawk's American Wasteland* spun in a kaleidoscopic dance, and I remember thinking, *This is who I was meant to be.*

MY FILM SCHOOL FRIEND, Dave, started coming over to get high and listen to metal. We'd watch Pantera's *Home Videos*—several hours of live shows and footage of Pantera fucking around—laughing hysterically at the ridiculous shit Dime, Phil, Vinnie, and Rex did when they were wasted.

There's a weed-smoking montage at one point in the videos, during which the Pantera dudes all take hits from bongs, joints, pipes, and blunts. Dave and I loved to smoke with the band during this section. A scene from a nineties Pantera concert ends the montage. Phil wheels out a rack with a Pantera flag hanging from it. The rack has four arms, each one holding a lit joint. The crowd cheers as each band member takes huge hits, blowing smoke into the already smoke-dense air. On the flag, there's a huge pot leaf beneath the Pantera logo. This scene always made me wish that I was at this concert.

When Dave and I weren't watching the *Home Videos*, we'd listen to stoner metal. One of our favorite heavy bands was Sleep, who I'd found out about a few years earlier from a BMX video. Weed turned Matt Pike's cough syrup riffs into a padded room.

Stoned, I'd study the cover of Sleep's *Holy Mountain*, which is a collage of pot leaves, mushrooms, planets, and random religious imagery. Looking at this cover one night, I noticed a keyhole with an eye behind it, and I thought about how I'd finally found the missing key to my personality. I'd been fighting who I truly was for a long time. My dad was a stoner, and hardly anything excited me as much as weed-laden doom metal. Nearly all of my favorite musicians smoked pot.

I was destined to be a stoner.

I started going to my neighbor's apartment multiple times a week. As I walked back to my apartment each time, I wanted to skip down the hall with my saran-wrapped goodies. I completely stopped going to class. My typical day for the next month: I'd wake up, think about how much pot I had left, get high, jack off, and play video games, trying to stay stoned all day. Looking at my bloodshot eyes in the bathroom mirror, I believed that I was a completely different person from the person I had been just a year earlier.

Getting high alone, I'd also watch *Dogtown and Z-Boys*, a documentary about the birth of modern skateboarding, often crying during the section about Jay Adams. Neil Young's "Old Man" plays as Adams destroys pools and other obstacles on his skateboard. The other Z-Boys talk about how Jay was the most talented Dogtown skater but always cared more about partying than trying to make a living with his skating.

My dad used to bomb hills on his skateboard during the seventies, and I always thought of him during this section. I felt like I was finally beginning to understand him.

AT ABOUT NINE ONE night, I decided to drive to Wyoming for a party at Garrett and Tyler's. When I walked outside my building, I saw five or six raccoons rummaging near a dumpster. As I stared at their hands and hides, disgust crawled over my skin like a blanket of maggots. I ran back inside, locking my door behind me.

SHORTLY AFTER DECIDING TO become a pothead, I went to a party with Steven and Dave. Steven needed a party scene for a movie he was making, and he wanted to use me as an extra. Someone at the party bought a Camo forty for me, and I downed most of it within ten minutes.

Amber, a cute punk girl, lived at the apartment with a few roommates. Star tattoos decorated her wrists, and she had short brown hair. While Steven tried to get the shots he needed, I shamelessly hit on Amber, talking too loud and ruining the scene several times.

I quickly found myself in her room, getting stoned. I'd only gotten twisted a few times, but I immediately fell in love with the way the world seemed to ooze and shift when I was high and drunk.

My pick up line: "Where's the party at?"

Before I had time to say to myself, *Holy shit, you're about to have sex!* we were naked. Just as I found a groove, an older guy opened the bedroom door.

"What the fuck, Amber? You in here fucking?" It was her dad's old friend who'd randomly decided to visit. She pushed me off and told me that we wouldn't be able to finish. A few minutes later, Steven burst into the room, wielding his camera. To cover up, Amber put on my T-shirt, and I put on her silk nighty.

The next day, watching footage of myself sitting on Amber's bed in her pink nighty, I laughed with Steven and Dave. I also wondered if it counted—if I'd actually lost my virginity—finally deciding that it did. I felt like a badass. Metalheads were supposed to fuck as many women as possible. But hints of guilt tainted this pride, and I thought about how I should've lost my virginity to Lindsay. Although I tried to drown this thought by telling myself that I should be proud, it kept surfacing.

I WENT TO A Gwar show a week or so afterward. The band is known for dressing up in ridiculous costumes and hosing the crowd with fake blood. I didn't like that they were a joke band, though. Gwar plays with the idea of performance in metal culture, and maybe I didn't like them because I didn't want to admit that part of my identity was a performance. But I figured that I had to see them at least once. Most of my metal heroes loved Gwar, including Dimebag Darrel, who often wore Gwar shirts in pictures and videos.

A few weeks earlier, I'd seen Damageplan—a radio-friendly nu-metal band that Dime and Vinnie had started after Pantera broke up—with Dave. In my mind, Damageplan didn't even come close to comparing to

Pantera, but I knew this show would probably be my only chance to see the Abbott brothers play live. Phil didn't get along with Dimebag or Vinnie, and vice versa. Although I held out hope for a Pantera reunion, I knew that it was unlikely. But I still worshipped Dime and Vinnie, often playing air guitar and drums in my apartment along with my favorite Pantera riffs during the days leading up to the show.

Dave and I stood in line for an hour or so at the Ogden, waiting to see Damageplan. I'd met a few Denver metalheads at other shows, and Dave and I talked to these dudes, trying to ignore the homeless crackheads and drunks roaming Colfax. Like me, most of the people in line were wearing Pantera shirts. I showed my CFH tattoo to some of my fellow fanatics, getting responses like, "Fuckin' A, brother," and, "Hell yeah. That's awesome." A few fans also showed me their CFH tattoos. I felt comforted and welcomed by these people, a rare feeling in a city that mostly seemed indifferent to me.

As Damageplan played their first few songs, giddy pulses tickled my stomach. But the novelty of seeing Dime and Vinnie in person soon wore off, and I started to feel pity for them. Dimebag had gained a lot of weight since the last pictures and videos I'd seen of him. He had the same long, curly hair and dyed-red goatee that he had for the past fifteen years. He acted out the same onstage antics—throwing cups of whiskey into the crowd and headbanging wildly—as he does in the *Home Videos*.

Hearing Damageplan's music before this show, I thought that they were just trying to pick up where Pantera had left off, but in a watered-down way. Watching them, I realized that Dime and Vinnie couldn't move beyond the past. The singer, with a shaved head, tattoos, and tough-guy persona, aped Phil's moves, which became more obvious when the band played a few Pantera songs—"Becoming," and one or two others. As I thought about how Dimebag and Vinnie were smothering themselves with their own shadows, I felt disloyal, like I was betraying my family.

Later in the set, Dime, Vinnie, and the bassist came onstage without the singer. Dime started playing the opening riff from Ted Nugent's classic, "Stranglehold." Vinnie and the bassist held a solid groove while Dimebag launched into a series of shredding solos. The pity I'd been feeling dissipated as I watched two brothers who just fucking loved to jam. Sibling musicians can attain a tightness that borders on psychic interconnection. During the next few months, I'd try to think about these moments and forget what I'd seen and thought about throughout the rest of the set.

At the Gwar show in December, a few weeks after the Damageplan concert, I watched the band dismember papier-mâché celebrity caricatures and spray the crowd with fake blood. After an hour or so, Gwar left the stage and came back without their costumes on. In costume, they looked like characters from *Army Of Darkness*, but now they all looked pitifully normal.

"We just got some really fucked-up news," the singer said. "Dimebag Darrel just got shot." People in the crowd laughed and shouted, thinking it was a joke, like the rest of the set. "No, I'm not fucking with you. Dimebag Darrel from Pantera just got shot and killed at a show in Ohio." The crowd, which had been irritating and raucous the rest of the night, hushed.

"We're going to play a few more songs tonight, dedicated to Dimebag." The singer looked up to the rafters and pointed. "This is for you Dime, my brother."

I left the Ogden and drove home, trying to convince myself that this was just another bad Gwar joke. In my apartment, I watched a few online news clips, piecing together the story of Nathan Gale shooting Dime at a Damageplan show, during the same tour that I'd seen him on a few weeks earlier.

I bawled as if I'd lost a family member, also chiding myself for feeling so pained by the death of someone I'd never met. I got high and listened to Pantera, trying to replay those ecstatic moments when the power of Dime and Vinnie's jamming had enveloped me. But I also thought about the moments when I saw Dimebag as a husk of himself, trapped in the shell of a character he'd created.

TYLER CALLED ME A week or so later. He'd been planning to move to Austin in January with Garrett and Nate, and they'd been talking about it since I started drinking with them. Tyler thought his band, The Scissorhands, was destined to make it in Austin.

"Our dad's not going let Nate move with us anymore," Tyler said, a jumble of music and voices in the background.

"Damn, dude. That sucks."

"You're the first person I thought of, J. J." I almost laughed at the earnestness in his voice, but I also felt flattered. "I know we'd be fine with a badass like you playing drums for us. There's no way we *wouldn't* make it." I'd jammed with him and Garrett a few times, just messing around. Compared to the stressed-out struggle of trying to play thrash, their generic, mid-paced grunge songs were easy.

Without hesitating, I told Tyler that I'd move with him, already thinking about how I'd have tell my parents that I was dropping out of school and moving to Austin. Even though I didn't like The Scissorhands' music very much, I also heard potential in their songs.

During the next few days, I canceled my lease and called my mom, finally telling her that I hadn't been attending class for the past six weeks. She and my dad were pissed, but I don't think they were surprised. When I told them that I was moving to Austin to play drums, they knew me well enough not to try to change my mind, even though it was a stupid idea. I moved back to Wyoming to save money and practice with The Scissorhands.

A movie of me onstage in front of thousands of people, rocking out like Dave Grohl, repeated in my head. Now, it's easy to mock myself for believing that I'd become a rock star, especially considering how much I sucked at the drums. But, in a way that I didn't know much else at the time, I knew that I wanted to be a drummer, and that I needed to find out what I was made of.

ON DESTRUCTION

I FIRST EXPERIENCED THE RUSH of vandalism during the summer of '97, right after I finished elementary school. At the end of sixth grade, teachers told us that, in junior high, we'd have lockers and class periods—each class in a different room. Classmates told me that their older brothers and cousins regularly got stoned and drunk in junior high, and also that junior high girls would let you go further than kissing. Although curious, I was mostly scared.

Before the end of grade school, a few kids had bragged about sneaking out of their parents' houses during sleepovers. One night, shortly after summer break started, I stayed at my friend Glen's house. Glen and his other friend had snuck out a few weeks earlier. In nearby neighborhoods, they rang people's doorbells and ran away.

"Let's sneak out tonight," I said.

At one o'clock, a few hours after Glen's mom went to bed, we skulked through his house and out the back door. We stealthily climbed over his backyard fence. Streets and sidewalks opened into the night. The patter of our shoes was amplified, sounding like little pieces of plywood slapping concrete.

Glen rang someone's doorbell. When lights in the house came on, we bolted down an adjacent street, laughing hysterically. We each rang a few more doorbells before going back to Glen's house. Following him, I held my breath as I crept through the barely-opened back door. Plastic blinds ticked against the door's window.

Glen's mom made us pancakes the next morning. Sitting at the kitchen table, Glen and I burst into laughter when we looked at each other.

We switched between sneaking out of my parents' house and Glen's mom's house. Soon, ringing doorbells didn't give either of us much of a rush. One night, I kicked over someone's trashcan, and Glen kicked over a trashcan at the next house. He then ripped open the garbage bag and scattered trash all over the groomed front yard. The next time we snuck out, we started letting air out of people's car and truck tires. For the next few weeks, we rang doorbells, let the air out of tires, and knocked over trashcans.

Destroying a wooden yard display one night was our turning point into real vandalism. A fake water well made out of latticed particleboard sat in a yard near the only Mormon church in town. Painted baby blue, the thin wood encircled a miniature hay bale. Carefully painted Precious

Moments children played hopscotch on a crosspiece that hung over the hay.

I ran up to the fake well and started pushing. Glen helped. We tipped the well onto its side, and Glen rolled it across the lawn. Wood cracked with each rotation. We stumbled away, unable to run because we were laughing so hard.

A FEW DAYS LATER, Glen and I jumped on his trampoline.

"You know what we should do the next time we sneak out?" I said. "We should fuck up someone's mailbox." I'd wanted to destroy a mailbox ever since I watched *Stand By Me* when I was seven. To a soundtrack of Jerry Lee Lewis's "Great Balls Of Fire," Kiefer Sutherland and his posse, The Cobras, drive down a rural road, playing mailbox baseball. Leaning out of a speeding convertible, Sutherland hits mailboxes with a wooden bat. The metal boxes fly off their posts. To me, he looked incredibly badass, like he wasn't afraid of anything.

Glen loved the idea.

I had a few baseball bats at my house, so we decided to stay there on the upcoming Friday. During the early evening, we set two metal bats near my backyard fence because we didn't want to rummage for them in the cluttered garage while my parents were asleep.

We only waited about a half-hour after my parents went to bed before we snuck out. With our bats, we crept through my back gate and into the waiting neighborhood. Like the first night I snuck out with Glen, streets I saw every day seemed like they might lead to places I'd never been.

We cut down a side street half a block away, stopping in front of a silver mailbox. A streetlight stood directly over it. Holding the bat over my head, about to swing, my mind pushed past a barrier. In the space of that moment, I knew exactly where I was and what I was capable of doing.

I swung down as hard as I could.

Stinging vibrations shot through my hands. Unlike the mailboxes in *Stand By Me*, this one didn't budge. But I badly dented the top. Glen swung from the side, smashing the mailbox door. The clank of metal against metal echoed down the street. I pictured sonar waves emanating from the mailbox.

We sprinted for two blocks. Glen noticed a large gold mailbox and hit it, letting out a grunt as his bat connected. I hit this mailbox from the side, like I was swinging at a baseball, almost dropping my bat because of the sting.

Three or four blocks away, lawn lights decorated a walkway leading to someone's front door. "Let's golf those lights," Glen said.

Swinging our bats like golf clubs, we each hit a few lights, sending them into the brick wall of the house. Shards of plastic and glass shot from our bats.

"Hey!" Next door, a short, muscular guy had been watering his lawn. Glen and I bolted. The guy was about fifteen feet away, but he was fast, and he'd gotten the jump on us. He lunged at Glen, tackling him onto the sidewalk and pinning his shoulders against the ground. Not sure what to do, I just stood there, a few feet away from them.

"Hit this motherfucker!" Glen screamed.

"Put down your bat. I'm putting both of you under citizen's arrest."

I tightened my grip before dropping the bat onto the street. I thought about running away, but I didn't want to leave Glen. A fat middle-aged guy, wearing a white T-shirt and boxers, came out of the house with the lawn lights. He grabbed me after his neighbor told him what Glen and I had done.

Waiting for the cops, the men held our arms behind our backs.

*

NATE AND I WOKE up early. Beer bottles littered the coffee table, TV, and carpet of Garrett and Tyler's apartment. We held beer bottles up to the light, finishing off the wounded soldiers without cigarette butts or ash in them.

I'd been living back in Rock Springs for the past three weeks. Tyler, Garrett, and I were moving to Austin in two more weeks.

Nate and I only caught a slight buzz from the wounded soldiers. I didn't have any weed left, and neither of us could buy booze. A few nights earlier, we'd both huffed computer duster for the first time. With a few other friends, we passed the canister around a circle. After sucking duster into my lungs, my voice sounded tar-soaked, as if I was in a slow motion video sequence—the reverse effect of inhaling helium. I quoted some of Cheryl's lines from *Evil*

Dead, sending everyone into hysterics. My voice echoed off the walls of Garrett and Tyler's apartment.

On this morning, a few days after trying the inhalant, I said, "We could go to Kmart and buy some duster."

In Nate's Grand Cherokee, I put Guns N' Roses' *Use Your Illusion* in the CD player, skipping forward to "Live And Let Die," a song that Nate and I'd been listening to on repeat. Nate put on his aviator sunglasses. Driving through Rock Springs on this late December morning, we sang along to the lines, "You used to say live and let live / But if this ever-changing world in which we live in / makes you give in and cry / say live and let die." I liked Paul McCartney's original version of the song, but the Guns N' Roses cover seemed more powerful. As Axl carries "die" into the chorus, Matt Sorum leads Slash and Duff into plodding rock-and-roll, pulverizing his drums.

I found a three-quarters-full bottle of mouthwash in Nate's center console. In junior high, kids had said that they got drunk on mouthwash. I took a pull and handed the small bottle to Nate. We finished it on our way to Kmart.

We found duster in the electronics section. A clerk at the checkout stand asked to see my ID—you had to be eighteen to buy duster. Nate and I didn't try to hide our laughter. The clerk handed back my driver's license after checking it, not making eye contact with me.

Sitting in Nate's Jeep, we listened to "Live And Let Die" again. Just before I took a massive hit of duster, I saw Nate and myself sitting in the near-empty parking lot from a zoomed-out perspective. Pressing the button on top of the canister, I sucked duster through the nozzle. The world spun around me, but I felt cemented in place.

WHEN I MOVED BACK to Rock Springs from Aurora, my second cousin, Paul Jr., gave me a job with his vending company. Paul Sr., Grandpa Don's younger brother, was easily the most successful Anselmi in Rock Springs. During his life, he built and ran an American National Bank, Holiday Inn, Comfort Inn, laundromat, and an apartment complex.

I didn't know Paul Jr. very well when I started working for him, but I knew his backstory. Paul's arcade had gone out of business three years earlier, at which point he started Golden Opportunity Vending. He had arcade games and vending machines in businesses throughout Rock Springs. It was my job to collect quarters from Paul's games and vending machines, and also to restock his soda and snack machines. Golden Opportunity was a business of cheapness and marginal profit, constantly reminding me of the contrast between Paul's life and his dad's.

When I was in junior high, I'd overheard Grandpa Don and Uncle Nick talking and laughing about Paul's life as if it was a sitcom. Paul began partying hard in high school and never really stopped. From the beginning of his life, people in my family, as well as in Rock Springs, doubted that he could ever live up to his father's success. After he dropped out of college, the expectation solidified that Paul was doomed to be a fuck up.

I worked about twenty-five hours per week for Paul. I also spent a lot of time hanging out with him at his apartment after work, drinking vodka and 7-Ups and popping Percocets and OxyContins that he gave me. I'd never gotten high on pain pills before I started working for Paul.

Seeing perfect double—not two blurred versions of things, but two clear versions—I'd look at the pictures hanging on Paul's walls. In one, he and his dad stood with an arm around each other, both holding a drink. Paul had a large gut and stood over six feet tall. Even so, he looked small next to his dad. In another picture, Paul and my dad, both in their early twenties, held up some fish they'd caught. Their eyes were ridiculously bloodshot, and the right side of their upper lips curled up into the smart-ass Anselmi smirk that I saw in the mirror when I was stoned.

I always felt eerily comfortable hanging out with Paul, and I'd often think, *Maybe I really am doomed to become another fucked-up Anselmi.*

ONE NIGHT, SOME STONER girls invited Nate and me to a party at the Outlaw. We hung out in the motel room for a while, drinking beer and getting high. Everyone at the party knew that Grandpa Don had built the Outlaw, and that Uncle Nick now ran it. One girl said, "It's hilarious that you're getting all wasted in your family's motel."

I thought about working for Uncle Nick three years earlier. About two months after I started the maintenance job, two of my coworkers and I mopped a stretch of tile. Uncle Nick came up to me and grabbed the mop from my hands.

"Don't you know how to mop a floor? You do it up-and-down, not side-to-side like an idiot." He demonstrated the proper way to mop while my coworkers laughed under their breath. "See?" he said, dragging out the last part like Grandpa Don used to. "You don't pick up any dirt doing it the other way."

Getting fucked-up in the motel room, I also thought about Uncle Nick's wife, my aunt Nina, and Grandma Vera. I'd last seen both of them six months earlier, at my high school graduation party.

"What school are you going to again?" Aunt Nina asked me.

"Colorado Film School. It's a branch of Aurora Community College."

"Oh, great. You'll save a lot of money going the community college route. Luckily, John has a scholarship at Yale, and Michael has a scholarship at Notre Dame. Otherwise, I'm not sure how we'd afford it," she said, laughing. She referred to her sons, my cousins.

"Just don't end up like your dad," Grandma Vera had said.

Nate and I each shotgunned a few beers then went outside to smoke. Before going back into the room, I said, "Let's go over to the pool." As we walked to the other side of the motel, Nate asked me what I was going to do, but I didn't answer.

A large potted tree, which was about eight feet tall, sat near the indoor pool. Its branches hung over a beige patio table and chairs. I picked up the plastic pot that held the tree. Laughing, I almost dropped it as I tottered to the pool.

I threw the tree into the deep end. For a moment, it seemed to hover above the calm pool. Then the pot hit the water, making a loud *plunk*. Waves rippled to the shallow end. Still upright, the tree sunk to the bottom, its branches wavering. Dirt tendrils reached out from the pot.

Nate and I hurriedly left the Outlaw.

Okay, I was an asshole. Throwing the tree into the Outlaw pool was a petulant attempt to get revenge on Grandpa Don, Grandma Vera, Uncle Nick, and Aunt Nina. I didn't have much respect for other people's property, and I think this was partly a reaction to the Anselmis' materialism. Although it's also true that I used my clothes, CDs, drums, and bike to define myself.

As I looked at the submerged tree, I didn't think about who'd have to clean up after me, even though it wouldn't have been Uncle Nick, and I knew this. But this act of destruction made me feel like I was capable of controlling my own life, at least in a small way, and I'd be lying if I said that I no longer get the urge to destroy things.

GARRETT, TYLER, AND I practiced in the back of Tyler's dad's carpet store. I didn't have much trouble learning The Scissorhands' songs. Locking in with Garrett's thumping bass and Tyler's distorted guitar, I felt solid, like I couldn't fuck up. Soon, I knew exactly what was going to happen in each song. Tyler basically wrote dumbed-down versions of Nirvana and Velvet Underground tunes. Garrett played exactly what Tyler told him to play, and I put in obvious fills wherever I could. But I felt a natural energy in the music when we were tight.

Before moving to Austin, we played a show in the carpet store for our families, and my dad filmed it. Watching the video now, our overall sloppiness makes me cringe, and it's hard to believe that I actually thought we'd make it. Our families gather around us. Garrett and Tyler's dads stare at their sons, both of them looking irritated. As he sings, Tyler looks embarrassed, keeping his face covered with his hair. Garrett's feet are glued to the ground, and he seems relieved when each song ends.

Dad zooms in on me as I flaunt my rudimentary drumming. I smile idiotically, hair partly covering my face. Today, for better or worse, I'd be feeling awkward along with Garrett and Tyler. At the time, I just let myself have fun. Of course I was a dumbass for believing that we'd get anywhere with such generic and predictable songs, especially in a place like Austin, where the standard for musicians is super high. But I could also inhabit individual moments in a way that I'm not sure I can anymore.

After each song, Dad says things like "Right on, Jay" and "Far out," while Garrett and Tyler's families awkwardly clap.

LINDSAY WAS BACK IN Rock Springs for winter break, and I hung out with her whenever I could. Watching TV at my parents' house one night, Mom asked Lindsay what she thought about me moving to Austin.

"J. J.'s going to do whatever J. J.'s going to do," Lindsay said.

For a few nights, Lindsay convinced her mom, Linda, to let us drink at her house. These were the first times Lindsay and I drank together.

Sitting next to her when I was sober, I'd let fear push me away from the threshold of action, always wanting to kiss her but only making a move a few times. Drunk, Lindsay and I made out like we'd always wanted to, and I don't remember thinking twice about trying to kiss her on those nights.

If she'd asked me to stay in Wyoming, I might've considered it.

SHIT-FACED, I CONVINCED GARRETT, Tyler, and Nate to go on a drive with me one night. In my truck, I blasted Every Time I Die's *Hot Damn*, headbanging along with their Southern-fried breakdowns. One time, I lost myself in the music and nearly hit a guardrail.

"Shit!" Tyler said. Sitting in the passenger seat, he grabbed the wheel and steered us back into the right lane.

A few minutes later, I pulled onto the main drag, still feeling energized by Every Time I Die. Kmart's illuminated red sign stood out against the backdrop of the Wyoming night sky. I drove into the empty parking lot, glancing at Paul Sr.'s bank, which sat across the street.

Several cement splash blocks were stacked against the side of the Kmart building. I drove over to them, not answering my buddies' questions about what I was doing. I got out of my truck, leaving the door open. As Every Time I Die's nasty hardcore disrupted the quiet night, I picked up one of the cement slabs, held it over my head, and hurled it onto the ground. I could feel the sound of cement smashing against asphalt. The rectangular slab shattered into chunks, becoming something new, something it wasn't before.

I drove away, electrified.

THREE OR FOUR NIGHTS later, Garrett and Tyler threw a going away party at their apartment. John, a high school enemy of Tyler and Nate's, had recently moved into the same building. He was muscular, often wearing wifebeaters to show off his large arms. John showed up at the party, and, without saying anything, punched Nate in the jaw. Nate tried to fight him, but some bigger guys broke them up. John's shirt got pulled up, revealing a handgun that he had strapped to his back.

The next time I saw Nate, two nights later, he had a swollen black eye and deep bruises on his back and chest. "My dad beat the shit out of me because I've been coming home wasted," he told me.

It was one of the last times Nate and I would hang out. Drinking Captain Morgan at a friend's house, we listened to Electric Light Orchestra. Nate danced furiously. Trying to pull off a spin move, he sent himself into the arm of a nearby couch, hitting his head.

After an hour or so, I told Nate that I felt like fucking something up.

"Like what?" he asked, laughing.

"I don't know. What about John's truck?"

Driving to John's apartment complex, we listened to "Live And Let Die" on full-blast. With a cigarette in my mouth, I played air drums during the chorus.

Nate parked a block away from the complex. We finished our cigarettes after getting out of the Jeep. Puffs of smoke became plumes in the frigid Wyoming air. Knowing where he usually parked, we walked straight to John's Silverado. Frost on its silver hood dimly glimmered under a streetlight. The truck's black rims were spotless, and two chrome exhaust pipes extended from beneath the tailgate.

I noticed two rows of large rocks that lined a walkway leading to the apartment buildings. We looked around the complex to make sure no one was watching. Knees bent, we each carried a rock to John's truck.

I held the rock over my head before hurling it into the windshield. As it left my fingers, ripples of air seemed to reach from the rock, as if it had broken an atmospheric surface tension. Aside from other moments of destruction, I'm not sure if I've ever had a clearer, more immediate sense of my capability to imagine change and make it real.

Hundreds of cracks stemmed from a gaping hole in the windshield.

Nate shattered the driver-side window. To my ears, the cymbal crash of breaking glass was musical. His rock bounced on the seat and clunked against the passenger door.

JUST BEFORE NOON THE next day, Nate called me.

"John's at my dad's carpet store with a few cops," he said. "He knows it was me. I'm going down there to turn myself in, but you don't have to come if you don't want to."

"There's no way they can prove it was us, though. They're not going to fingerprint those rocks, and no one saw us. They can't prove shit."

"I'm still going down there to tell them the truth. My dad can tell when I'm lying."

I met Nate at the carpet store. We smoked in the parking lot before going inside. Holding his cigarette to his lips, Nate's hand trembled.

Along with John and two cops, Nate's dad glared at us when we walked into his office. John said that he wouldn't press vandalism charges if we gave him the money to fix his windows. Even while writing John a check for 500 dollars—about half of what I'd saved for Austin—I didn't regret destroying his windshield.

THE BIG TEXAN I

DRIVING TO AUSTIN IN January, Garrett, Tyler, and I stopped at the Big Texan, a mishmash of Texas clichés in the form of a restaurant, motel, gift shop and shooting gallery. Ever since we crossed the New Mexico/Texas border, we'd been seeing signs for the Big Texan steak challenge on the side of the highway—"Free 72 oz. Steak" in large yellow letters and "If eaten under an hour" underneath, in fine print.

The Big Texan hunkers on the edge of Amarillo, a small city amidst the barren plains of north Texas. A large metal cowboy stood in front of the Big Texan, beckoning us from the interstate. Towing a U-Haul behind my truck, I followed Tyler and Garrett, who were in Tyler's 1978 Chevy van, to the Big Texan.

The restaurant building was painted bright yellow. A large sign hanging above the entrance proclaimed "The Big Texan" in bright blue letters. Cow skulls adorned the top of a white railing that bordered the restaurant porch. A brown plastic steer, probably over six feet tall, grazed a parking space in front of the restaurant.

Plywood rodeo scenes with holes where the cowboys' and cowgirls' faces should've been stood next to the steer. Garrett, Tyler, and I took turns standing behind these cut-outs, taking pictures of each other with a disposable camera. I thought about how funny it would be, after we became famous, to look back at these pictures.

"One of us has to try the challenge," I said.

"Fuck that, dude," Tyler said, stubbing out his cigarette.

"Yeah, that shit would be disgusting," Garrett said.

I decided to take on the steak challenge: if you eat a seventy-two-ounce cut of prime rib and two side dishes under an hour, you get the fifty-dollar meal for free, a T-shirt, and your name added to the list of successful challengers, written on a wall inside the restaurant. On some level, I felt like I had to try it, if only for the story I'd be able to tell afterward. I was also in the habit of biting off more than I could chew and not giving a shit about the consequences—a habit I'd continue in Austin.

After I told the hostess that I wanted to try it, she talked about some notable moments in the steak challenge history. An eighty-year-old woman held the record for eating the steak the fastest. She wolfed down the slab of meat in less than ten minutes. Andre the Giant had once taken on the challenge, eating two steaks in under an hour. He ate them with his bare hands, dunking the massive steaks in goblets of red wine to soften the meat.

Garrett, Tyler, and I laughed as we listened to the middle-aged hostess tell us these stories. She led us into the dining room.

A stuffed grizzly, its mouth contorted into a savage roar, stood on its hind legs, welcoming patrons into the dining room. The room was furnished in faux-rustic wood. Deer, elk, moose, bison, and other animal heads hung on a railing that lined the second floor, each one blankly staring. I only expected to see stereotypical tourists in the restaurant, but there were equal amounts of burned-out parents with excited children as well as plains-hardened Amarillo locals—men and women wearing genuinely shabby ranch attire, and several other people with the haggard circles of blue-collar labor beneath their eyes.

The hostess led Garrett and Tyler to their table, taking me to a different one in the middle of the room. Two big digital clocks stood atop poles on either side of this table, which sat on a cowhide-carpeted pedestal. A large plastic trashcan sat next to each of the two chairs behind the table.

The burly cook looked at me after the hostess told him that I wanted to try the challenge. The grills were right behind my table. Shaking his head and chuckling, the cook slapped a doormat-sized steak onto the grill. I thought about the scene in *The Great Outdoors* when John Candy takes on a similar challenge, barely finishing his meal before vomiting outside the restaurant.

When my steak was cooked, a waitress plunked an overloaded plate onto my placemat. Ringing a small dinner bell and standing in front of the cowhide pedestal, she said, "Can I get your attention, ladies and gentlemen? This young man is going to take on the Big Texan challenge. Let's hear it for him before I start the clock." A few awkward claps hung in the air.

As the digital clocks counted down from an hour, I stuffed large slices of meat into my mouth. The first sixth of the behemoth steak wasn't too bad—bland, but still resembling the taste and texture of good prime rib. Soon, each piece began to feel increasingly tough and rubbery, though. The muscles in my jaw stiffened and popped. Although I drowned each piece in au jus, I felt like I was eating a steak that had been used for years as a welcome mat.

I got through a third of it before switching to a side dish: the shrimp cocktail. The shrimp were small and slimy, looking like big maggots. As soon as a shrimp touched my tongue, I retched. Garrett, Tyler, and the rest of the patrons watched as I regurgitated steak into one of the blue trashcans.

THE CO-OP

BEFORE WE LEFT WYOMING, I got a haircut. But I still kept my hair shaggy. I wanted to look like a seventies rocker. I started wearing tight jeans almost exclusively, and I listened to Bad Company's "Shooting Star" on repeat, convincing myself that the narrative of rock stardom and excess in the song was my destiny. After we left Rock Springs, I cried a little when I heard the lines, "Mama came to the door / with a teardrop in her eye / Johnny said, 'Don't cry, Mama / just smile and wave goodbye.'"

When we got to Austin, I thought the city would immediately embrace us, even though Denver hadn't opened up for me like I thought it would. I followed Tyler's van into dense traffic on I-35. I tried to change lanes, but no one would let me in. People honked when I cut across two lanes. We rented a hotel room near the interstate.

"We'll start looking for apartments tomorrow," Tyler said.

That night, we drove around Austin in the van. Both Tyler and Garrett were a few months away from turning twenty-one, but Garrett was the only one of us with facial hair—the only one who could grow real facial hair—so I nagged him to try to buy booze. After twenty minutes of listening to me say, "Come on, dude. Just try it," Garrett walked into a gas station and came out empty handed.

We ate at a hip restaurant near Sixth Street. The waiter, as well as a few customers, smirked at us. I didn't want to admit that, even if people in the restaurant knew we'd just moved from Wyoming to Austin to make it, they wouldn't have been impressed.

Sober, I usually felt awkward around Tyler and Garrett. I'd run out of weed before we passed the Colorado border. By the time we got to Texas, I'd smoked every bit of resin in my pipe that I could reach with a paperclip. Still, that night in the hotel room, I repeatedly sucked a butane flame into my pipe, hoping for at least one resin hit.

THE NEXT DAY, EATING at Long John Silver's, we browsed apartment ads, most of them for apartments in generic complexes. I pictured us in a one-bedroom with beige carpet and walls. Chain-link fencing surrounded my imaginary complex, and I thought about how isolated I'd felt while living in Aurora.

We drove around Austin, trying to find "For Rent" signs. I noticed a head shop and convinced Tyler to stop. Cream's "Sunshine of Your Love" drifted through speakers

8xz12(3)9qpw

in the upper corners of the store. I'd only been a pothead for about two months, so marijuana culture was still a novelty to me. Plastic bongs lined a shelf in front of a Bob Marley flag. The bong company used a skull as their emblem, which I thought was rad. I bought a red bong for ten bucks. Before leaving, I asked one of the clerks for a job application.

As we looked for apartments, I wondered what I should name my new bong. A stoner friend in Wyoming had told me that it's bad luck to have a bong without a name.

In the afternoon, at a public library, Tyler found an ad for the Austin Musician's Co-op. He told us about it after talking to someone who lived there. "I guess they have practice spaces, and they put on these shows every week. The guy said we could go take a look today."

Excited, I imagined a dirty warehouse inhabited by crust punks and metalheads. A few weeks later, after we'd been voted into the co-op, I didn't think about how unbelievably lucky it was that Tyler had found the ad. We were supposed to find the co-op, I thought. It was part of our destiny.

After several wrong turns, we reached the one-level building at 54th and Guadalupe, which had originally been an old folks' home. A large eighth note was messily painted on the east wall.

"Hey, what's up? Are you the guys who just called?" asked a lanky guy with shaggy brown hair. Sitting behind a counter near the front door, he wore faded Wranglers with holes in the knees and a tight T-shirt. "My name's Rich." I correctly predicted what style of music Rich played— hopeful, yet broken-down alt-country, similar to Lucero.

Rich gave us a tour of the co-op. The tile-floored building consisted of three different branches, and there were about twenty-five rooms for tenants, as well as a kitchen, computer room, hostel, stage area/lounge, front and back patios, and a few rehearsal spaces. After showing us one of the empty bedrooms, Rich led us through the restaurant-sized kitchen. Next to the kitchen was a small stage area with tables and chairs in front of the stage. Tie-dyed sheets decorated the walls, and there was a four-piece drum kit onstage. I saw myself whaling on the kit, hundreds of people cheering. Most tenants were at work, so the co-op was quiet and almost empty.

"It takes two weeks before you can get voted in," Rich said. "Until the vote, you guys can live in the hostel." He explained how the co-op worked: a thousand dollars per room in rent also paid for food. Each tenant had to complete a chore—ranging from things like cooking to sweeping and mopping floors—and you'd get assigned a different chore every month. Practice spaces were available throughout the week, and there was a weekly open mic night. If asked, I would've said that I didn't give a shit about politics. I didn't understand that collective living in America is subversive. The co-op just seemed really cool, and I immediately felt like I could be myself here.

A cute girl, Landry, was painting flowers on a wall in one room, and Rich introduced us to her. She wore a puka shell necklace, khaki shorts, and had beautiful, tanned legs. Like me, she was nineteen. To my disappointment, I'd soon find out that Landry and Rich were dating. "So, you guys are from Wyoming?" Landry asked. "That's way cool."

Most tenants said something similar when we met, not questioning why we'd moved to Austin. Landry told us that she played guitar and sang after asking about the type of music we played. I could hear her playing angst-ridden love songs. Most of her songs, I'd learn, were about her first love.

Using money we'd saved from our jobs in Rock Springs, Tyler and I paid for three beds in the hostel. Before we moved, Garrett had spent most of his earnings from his maintenance job at JCPenney on his shitty Olds Mobile, which he just ended up abandoning.

We drove to the hotel to pick up my truck and the U-Haul. Back at the co-op, Tyler asked Rich when we'd be able to practice.

"You guys can jam right now if you want."

We unloaded our stuff into an empty room after Rich unlocked it for us. We'd packed all of our gear into Tyler's van. During the trip, our equipment had become jumbled, unlike the tightly packed vans of professional musicians that I'd seen. Crumbs, fast-food wrappers, and cigarette ash littered our equipment. Microphone stands, amps, speakers, and guitars covered my drums and cymbal stands, and I hoped that my cheap gear hadn't gotten fucked-up.

We played the eight or nine Scissorhands songs I knew. Drumming along to predictable changes and chord progressions, I felt ecstatic, like great things were about to happen. I headbanged while Tyler climbed on my bass drum and jumped off.

"That was great, you guys," Landry said when we finished. The practice room was next to the room she was painting. "This place has enough singer-songwriters. I'm glad a real rock-n-roll band is finally here."

BY THE NIGHT OF the first open mic, two or three days after we found the co-op, we'd gotten drunk or stoned with several tenants, but I still hadn't heard most of them play. Aside from co-op tenants, another twenty people or so showed up.

Originally from Brooklyn, Rich exhibited the mix of irony and sincerity that I've seen in most people who play alt-country. But I liked this predictability. He stomped a two-step rhythm after shouting "Woo!" in an exaggerated Southern drawl. Hanging out with him one night, we passed a jug of Carlo Rossi wine around a fire pit. I chugged it, trying to drink more than anyone else. Rich said, "That's what I'm talking about right there—a Wyoming chug."

Sarah, who had a large Cheshire cat tattooed on her right bicep, played fiddle with Rich, upstaging him with ripping solos during a few songs. When she first met Garrett, Tyler, and me, she'd said, "Look at your guys' hair and tattoos. You look like Detroit rockers." I thought about *Detroit Rock City*. Sarah asked me if she could look at the tattoo on my right forearm. I held my arm out, and she traced the skull with her index finger. "Very cool," she said.

Jarrell, one of the two black people in the co-op, played a mix of roots, jazz, and rock on piano and guitar. Playing piano, he tipped back in his seat, moving with the music. Most of his hair was clumped into one massive dreadlock, and he sold swag weed—fifteen bucks for a quarter-ounce. A month or so after we moved in, Jarrell made a few derisive comments about my lack of musical skill, which happened after a few other tenants had also been critical of my drumming. But I just saw Jarrell as a happy-go-lucky pothead during the open mic.

Pod was a white dude with blond dreadlocks, often wearing the blue-and-white poncho that he wore on this night. As with Jarrell, I mistakenly thought of Pod as a stereotypical stoner. Instead, he'd be another of the tenants that poked through my self-delusion, making me realize how far I had to go before I could call myself a real musician. He played kooky folk ballads on this night, singing in a gruff mountain man voice.

Belting Jewel-esque melodies, Landry fingerpicked her acoustic guitar. She looked me in the eyes throughout the set. Even though she was dating Rich, I constantly flirted with Landry.

Wearing a tie-dyed shirt, James played a Grateful Dead cover and a few blues standards. He was short, with curly black hair that covered his ears and a wisp of a mustache. As with Jarrell and Pod, I liked James because he seemed like a walking stoner caricature. Although we were the same age, he'd soon become my weed and music coach. He taught me how to roll joints, and he introduced me to LSD. Listening to music in his room, he'd point out aspects of Sabbath and Zeppelin that I hadn't noticed. But he also mocked me and my enthusiasm for heavy music, and I took his words way too seriously.

Over awkwardly generic rock, Paige flaunted her singing. She was tall, thin, and blond. Someone would later describe her to me as the diva of the co-op. Paige's room was directly across the hall from mine. When she learned about auditions for a reality TV show in which a new singer for INXS would be chosen, she practiced "New Sensation" relentlessly. I can still hear Paige singing the song whenever it plays on the radio.

Luke, a large guy in his mid-thirties with stringy, shoulder-length hair, played bass in Paige's backing band. I saw Luke as the wise older stoner. He blew glass for a living, and food stains always speckled his baggy shirts and cargo pants. In his drawling monotone, he'd tell me commonplace truths about weed, heroin, LSD, and music, speaking without a hint of irony.

Garrett, Tyler, and I set up after Paige's band finished. I felt like we were about to blow everyone's mind. Tyler played the opening riff of "Taking Your Name"—a song that consisted of blues-based hammer-ons and power chords. I jumped in with a dumbed-down Bonham fill, and a few people cheered. In my head, I saw a sea of flashing camera bulbs.

I boisterously played generic fills after every two bars. We were way louder than everyone else. Tyler and I swung our hair from side to side while Garrett nodded to the beat. When we finished our set, my brain amplified clapping and cheers from about thirty people into a roar. As we took our equipment offstage, Luke said, "That was awesome. The whole time, I was seeing flashes of Nirvana."

Listening to compliments from a few other tenants, I felt like I was discovering who I was meant to be.

A FEW DAYS LATER, Rich asked Tyler, Garrett, and me to post and hand out co-op flyers around Austin, and Jarrell came with us. Driving toward downtown, I put Eyehategod's *Southern Discomfort* in my truck's CD player.

"What are we listening to?" Jarrell asked while rolling a cigarette. A thick, earthy odor emanated from him.

"Eyehategod."

"Okay," he said, a mixture of surprise and distaste in his voice.

We left stacks of flyers at coffee shops and record stores. Walking around busy neighborhoods, stapling flyers to telephone poles, I stared at hot girls, who seemed ubiquitous in Austin. Jarrell and I shared a joint in an alley. After about two hours, with a fat stack of professionally-printed flyers left to hand out, all of us wanted to go back to the co-op, but Garrett, Tyler, and I didn't think we should say anything.

"What do you guys think about throwing the rest of the flyers away and just saying we handed them out?" Jarrell asked.

"Sounds good to us," Tyler said.

SHORTLY AFTER WE WERE voted in, I got a job bussing tables at Jovita's, a Tex-Mex restaurant. After a shift one night, I smoked a bowl in the restaurant parking lot so I wouldn't have to share my weed with any of my fellow tenants.

In the co-op kitchen, a vegan Indian dish rested on the stainless steel counter, and the food was still warm. I fixed a plate, thinking about how nice it was to have someone cook for me every night.

Garrett and I shared a small room, about the size of a dorm room. We didn't have a bed, so we switched off between sleeping on a couch, which had just been sitting in one of the halls, and the floor. I stepped over wadded clothes, record sleeves and CD cases. Bowls and plates were stacked on each side of the couch. Ash-speckled gobs of food were cemented onto the dinnerware. Garrett sat on dirty clothes, playing *Metal Slug 2* on his Sega Genesis, his glasses sitting just below the bridge of his nose.

"Sarah came by when you were at work," Garrett said, lighting a cigarette, although we weren't supposed to smoke inside. "She was all, 'Garrett, there's been a puddle of water in our hall for the past week. Aren't you supposed to be mopping the floors?'" Garrett spoke in a nasally voice, mocking Sarah.

"I haven't done my chore in like two weeks," I said, laughing. During the first two weeks, I'd been diligent about cleaning the floor and tables in the stage area. But I quickly stopped worrying about getting voted out. The co-op seemed like a place where consequence didn't apply.

When I finished eating, I set my plate in front of the couch. In the previous weekly meeting, someone had mentioned that a lot of plates and bowls had gone missing from the kitchen. I lit a cigarette. Exhaling, I watched smoke unfurl onto dirty dishes and clothes.

BY THE END OF the first month, I was jamming with other people more than with Garrett and Tyler. I practiced with The Scissorhands two or three times a week, but I wanted to jam every day. One afternoon, I jammed with Pod, James, and Jarrell. James began playing a funky, backbeat-driven bass line. His main instrument was guitar, but he was also an awesome bassist. I joined in, faltering before I found a groove. Pod played guitar and Jarrell played keys, both of them trading solos. A few times, someone looked at me and nodded, wanting me to switch the beat. But the jam stagnated. Eventually, each of us awkwardly trailed off.

James began playing a different bass line, and I played what I thought was a fitting beat. He stopped and said, "It's not a backbeat."

"You need to start jamming in some different time signatures," Pod told me. He unplugged his guitar and wrapped up the cable.

Later that night, sitting in the co-op parking lot and listening to Led Zeppelin's *BBC Sessions*, I hot-boxed my truck. I'd recently learned, from James, that John Bonham didn't play double bass. When I used to listen to Zeppelin, I always thought about how, compared to my favorite thrash drummers, Bonham's double bass was weak. Now, his single foot triplets, as well as his triplet patterns linking toms and the bass drum, mesmerized me. During complex fills, I also felt a tinge of anxiety as I thought about how I'd never be as good as him. I didn't compare myself to my favorite musicians nearly as much before living in the co-op.

Smoke poured out of my truck when I opened the door, reminding me of a scene from *Detroit Rock City*. Four friends, on their way to see Kiss, cruise down a highway in one of their mom's cars, pot smoke drifting from the windows.

James sat on the porch, smoking a cigarette.

"I've figured it all out," I said, sitting next to him. "I'm meant to be a drummer."

"Think so?"

Soon, thinking about several failed jams, criticism about my drumming from James, Pod, Jarrell, and a few other tenants, I'd anxiously wonder if I truly *was* meant to be a drummer. At the same time, even though I started to doubt my skill, I knew that music was in my bone marrow.

RATTY

J AMES WALKED PAST ME as I sat next to the co-op
stage, eating veggie enchiladas that one of the
other tenants had cooked. When I asked him if he
wanted to eat dinner with me, he said, "I'm going
to eat acid for dinner."

In junior high, I'd heard kids talk about acid—about
seeing talking zebras and fish jumping out of walls—
but I didn't think tripping was real, knowing that these
kids' stories were mostly, if not entirely, made up. After
watching several episodes of Vh1's *Behind The Music*
and TV specials about the sixties throughout the years,
I'd started to believe that people got fucked-up on LSD,
though I still got the feeling that most of the stories they
told about acid were exaggerated. I decided to find out
for myself.

I wolfed down my food and followed James into
his room. Standing in front of a Jim Morrison poster,

he held up a Clear Eyes container that was filled with a greenish-blue liquid. "I'll sell you hits for two bucks each," James said.

I walked across the hall and into our room, where Garrett was sitting on the floor and playing video games. I wanted someone to do acid with me, so I asked Garrett if he wanted to try it.

"Yeah," he said. "I'll do a hit."

Back in James's room, I handed him six dollars. "You've done this before, right?" he asked.

"Yeah. Just tabs though." I'd heard stoner kids in school talk about tabs of acid, not knowing what they meant.

James told me to open my mouth and stick out my tongue. His hand shook as he squeezed two drops from the vial. I watched him put one drop onto Garrett's tongue.

"So how long is it going to take to kick in?" I asked, smoking a cigarette outside with Garrett and James.

"I thought you said you've done it before," James replied, quickly. He dragged from his cigarette.

"No, I have. It was just a different kind," I said, looking away from him and at the cigarette butt-littered cement.

"It'll take about thirty to forty-five minutes."

A WEEK OR TWO earlier, I'd gone to a house party with Garrett, Tyler, and a few people from the co-op. Before we left, I drank an Olde English forty and took several bong rips of weed—the kind that sticks to your fingers. Walking to the party, I puked on the sidewalk after asking my friends if they ever felt like they were in a different universe.

A group of dudes stood in the driveway leading to the house, and I immediately recognized a few of them. Chase Hawk, Dave King, Brian Wizmerski, Bob Scerbo, and Magilla—some of my favorite BMX riders. I'd been watching videos of these guys and studying pictures of them in magazines since I was thirteen. Their faces looked unreal, almost cartoonish, like my favorite musicians when I'd seen them in person. They all wore hip clothes that tightly clung to their bodies.

"Holy shit," I said, walking directly into their group. "It's Dave King and Chase Hawk. And fucking Wizmerski!" I patted Dave's shoulder as if we were old friends. Austin has a world-famous BMX scene, and, during the past few weeks, I'd been seeing pro riders in grocery stores and other places but hadn't talked to any of them.

They laughed, and someone said, "Who the fuck is this kid?" I was wearing a Pantera T-shirt, a Pantera beanie, and baggy Levis, looking like the tool that I was.

Garrett, Tyler, and my co-op friends went into the house, where most people were hanging out. I stayed outside, smoking cigarettes and pot with the riders. Like Chris Farley's pathetic fanboy character on *Saturday Night Live*, I said things like, "Chase, remember, in the Manmade video, where you did that rail? That was badass."

I knew these guys were laughing at me, but I didn't care. I hadn't brought my bike to Austin because I decided to concentrate on music, and there wasn't enough room for it in the van or U-Haul. But BMX had shaped me, and I still respected what these guys could do on their bikes. Chase

Hawk and Dave King both focused on style, perfecting and personalizing classic tricks like tabletops and turndowns. I remember watching both of their sections in Manmade's *Chapter 2* over and over. In the air, they attain beauty. Like my metal heroes, they became my role models, and I filled in the gaps of their media-projected personalities with who I wanted and needed them to be. When I met them, I saw the characters I'd created.

As Dave passed me a pipe, Chase walked up to me and quickly reared back, as if he was about to punch me. I flinched, turning away when I saw his fist. Chase doubled-over laughing, and the other guys laughed hysterically, too. He acted like he was going to hit me a few more times, getting the same reaction from me and the other riders each time.

I'd showed up to the party twisted off my ass, almost asking for someone to fuck with me. Like most other BMX kids, I loved *Jackass*-style humor. Although I knew how quickly and easily this humor could go too far, I still thought it was hilarious to fuck with people. I didn't think about why I was attracted to this humor, or why it's so pervasive in BMX culture.

I started to feel uneasy, not sure if Chase was still joking after the third or fourth time. The riders surrounded me, and I tried to laugh with them. I kept talking about my favorite video clips of Dave, Chase, and the other guys that I'd seen throughout the years. Dave asked to see my tattoos, and none of the riders hid their laughter as I drunkenly explained what each one meant.

"Welcome To The Jungle" began pouring from a room in the house, drowning the din of the party. "Let's go rock out, Double Jay," Dave said. When I'd told him my name, he immediately started calling me Double Jay, a nickname that stuck in Austin. He was a big guy—taller than me and stout, with a beer gut, thick, hairy arms, shaggy blond hair and a five-o'clock shadow. He pulled my arm, hard, and I followed him inside the house.

On the dance floor, he grabbed my hair and jerked my head up and down, forcing me to headbang. During one of the downward thrusts, he punched me in the forehead. I stumbled outside, and he followed, saying, "Come back in, Double Jay. I thought we were rocking out."

I woke up the next day with Chase and Dave's numbers in my phone, and I somehow convinced myself that they actually wanted to be my friends. Or maybe I knew exactly what I was getting myself into.

AFTER I DOSED LSD for the first time, I decided to go to a party at the Ratty House, where Chase and some of the other riders I'd met lived. Driving down busy streets about twenty minutes after taking acid, electric waves crawled up my spine, and my legs felt weightless. I remember thinking that some serious shit was about to go down.

At the Ratty House, Dave King led me through the living room, where a DVD starring G.G. Allin—an old school punk rocker who used to take shits onstage—played on a dusty TV. Iron Maiden and Slayer posters hung on the walls, and immaculate BMX bikes lay on the ground. Dave took me to the back porch, where ten or so riders were drinking Busch and smoking cigarettes.

I told everyone I talked to that I was tripping. A few guys mocked my speech, which has always moved with the slow cadence of rural Wyoming. Dave rode a Razor scooter around in circles. He was over thirty, and seeing this burly man ride a children's scooter made me laugh my ass off. Chase, Dave, and the other guys looked fake, like CGI characters, which also seemed hilarious.

A tall, lanky guy named Josh, who was wearing a green sailor beanie and tight black Wranglers, told me that he and his buddy Mike had been looking for acid. "If you hook us up," Josh said, "you can smoke as much of this shit as you want." He took a fat bag of dank weed from his front pocket and placed it on the picnic table where we sat. I called James and then got into Josh's forest-green Subaru with him and Mike.

James met us outside the co-op. His pupils looked like two black orbs trying to consume his eyes. He'd taken around twelve hits, he said. In James's room, we smoked a bowl from his two-foot bong. Wanting to impress Josh and Mike, I inhaled a thick shaft of yellowish smoke in one breath, holding it in my lungs for a few seconds. One of them said, "Damn, dude. That was a big rip."

They each bought two hits of acid from James, whose look of concentration as he dropped the liquid onto their tongues made me giggle. I felt really stoned with hints of something new, but I wanted talking zebras. Watching Josh and Mike take two hits, I also felt like I needed to outdo them. I paid James to put two more hits on my tongue.

On the drive back to the Ratty House, Josh put in a CD and turned up the volume. Violently discordant guitar riffs, screams, and an onslaught of double bass. These sounds made anxiety course through my veins, but I also had to know the name of this band.

"It's called 'Curl Up and Die You Fucking Faggot Fucker,'" Josh said, bursting into high-pitched laughter. Knowing that he was fucking with me, I asked again, getting the same answer. The unease that I'd felt when I first met Chase and the other riders came back—a cold ooze that latched onto the back of my neck. I'd later figure out that we were listening to Converge, a chaotic metalcore band from Boston who'd eventually become one of my favorites, but also inseparable from those feelings of dread that I felt in Josh's car.

It had rained earlier in the day. When we got back to the Ratty House, I stared into a puddle in front of the porch. A burgundy coral reef of interwoven hexagonal patterns extended deep below the water's surface. Chameleons, salamanders, and other lizards inhabited the nooks and crevices of the reef, and the whole scene rotated in a slow, geometric dance.

"Hey," Josh said, holding open the front door and laughing. "What the fuck are you doing? Get in here."

I walked inside, mumbling about the lizards in the puddle. There were more people at the party now—a few other pro riders I recognized, some girls, and more dudes.

Taking bong rips with Chase in the kitchen, I quickly turned to my right when I saw cabinet doors opening, seemingly of their own accord.

"Whoa! How the fuck are those doors opening?" The guys around me laughed like hyenas. I'm still not sure, but I think they were just opening the doors when I wasn't looking.

Two of my favorite trail riders, Derrick "Maniac" Girard and Brian Yeagle, had come to the party. Fit and good-looking, they both wore tight jeans and had shaved heads. Someone dared Maniac to drink a few gulps of bong water. As he chugged the black liquid, I saw emptiness in his eyes, and I remember thinking that there was something dead in him. On any other night, I would've thought this was hilarious, along with the other riders.

There was a window next to the kitchen with a couch just beneath it. Getting a running start from the backyard, Yeagle jumped headfirst through the open window, landing on the couch. I don't remember either of them saying anything to me, but Maniac and Yeagle made me really nervous. They were known for having some of the biggest dirt jumps in the country—six- and seven-foot lips with thirty-foot gaps, snaking through dense Connecticut woods. Looking at pictures and watching videos of them throughout high school and junior high, I was amazed by their riding as well as their ability to sculpt dirt. They floated over each jump, nicking tree branches with their tires and zipping over the ground between sets. I loved to watch them whip their bikes sideways in the air and straighten out just before landing.

None of the Ratty House guys won contests like the X Games, but I considered them to be some of the best riders in the world. Chase, Dave, Yeagle, or Maniac could've learned contest-winning tricks like double backflips if they really wanted to, making it easier to earn money. But they didn't give a shit about the future. Watching videos of these guys now, I try to imagine how they feel in the air, and I'm still jealous of the union they attain with their bikes. They destroy themselves for those moments, knowing that beauty is inseparable from destruction.

Outside, I smoked a few bowls with Josh and Mike. Josh's tongue darted from his mouth like a snake's, and, when he laughed, I saw rows of sharp, reptilian teeth. A few of the other riders started mocking me again. I was still announcing that I was tripping to everyone I talked to, as if paying someone to put LSD on my tongue deserved respect.

Going to a party on acid is like wearing a sign around your neck that says "Please fuck with me," and I'm partly confused by my decision to ever go to the Ratty House, especially while tripping. But I sensed a yawning, destructive force inside Chase, Dave, and the other riders; and something in me gravitated toward this force.

Dave suddenly came up from behind and put me in a tight headlock. I got up from the table, and he started chasing me around the backyard, laughing and saying, "Come here, Double Jay. I'm not going to hurt you."

Back inside, I listened to music with a few riders. We talked about Eyehategod, Electric Wizard, Sleep, and other filthy doom bands. In a Superjoint Ritual DVD I loved, one I'd frequently watched while living in Aurora, Phil Anselmo says, "That's where true heavy metal lies—in the underground," with the authority and certainty that made me love him. Ever since hearing this, I'd imagined the underground metal scene in America as an actual place: a dingy basement where people talked about and listened to the heaviest bands. I'd become obsessed with finding this place, and, on this night, I remember thinking, *I've finally found the underground.*

The title track from Cavity's *On The Lam* slithered through speakers near the couch. I could feel the slow, churning riffs move across my brain tissue as if they were velvet ribbons. The guitars sounded like they were traveling through a wall of tar. Toward the end of the song, the band breaks down their already trudging tempo, creating a symphonic mass of distortion and Southern nastiness. In my mind's eye, I saw a group of good ole boys drinking whiskey in the woods and playing Cavity riffs on their fiddles. I knew that this was the type of music I was destined to play.

Dave introduced me to Katie, an incredibly hot girl. She was petite, wearing a white camisole and tight black pants. I told her that I was a drummer and asked if she'd ever done acid. I really wanted to invite her back to the co-op, but I felt awkward with Dave and the other riders watching me. Soon, Katie left, along with the other people who weren't staying the night at the Ratty House.

Sitting on the couch next to the kitchen, a rider with shaggy brown hair asked me if I knew about Floor, the band from Dave King's section in *Chapter 2*. As Floor's lyrics, "Crazy for the boy," played in my head, the guy asked me if I wanted to go into one of the bedrooms with him. "Are you into it?" he kept asking. Fear lodged in my throat while a magnetic urge pulsed in my stomach.

Josh told me that they were all bisexual or gay, which scared me in a way that almost seems comical now. I think I'd been curious about fucking around with another dude for a long time, but I didn't let these thoughts surface. Males dominate BMX and metal, and most guys in these scenes constantly try to impress each other. Underneath the tough-guy bullshit, it makes sense that a lot of guys in these worlds are attracted to each other on some level, but, like me when I was a teenager, won't let themselves admit it.

Sitting on the couch next to me, Josh pointed to my Pantera tattoo. "You know about the singer?" he asked. "We all know him." At the time, I was sure that he was telling me that Phil Anselmo is gay. I felt like a secret I'd sensed for a long time was finally being uncovered. A few more guys asked if I was "into it," but I couldn't go into one of those rooms.

The next thing I remember is sitting alone on the concrete floor next to the kitchen, deciding that I needed to leave. I walked outside, hoping my truck would start.

The starter had begun to shit the bed shortly after we'd moved to Austin. At least once a day, I had to push my truck and pop the clutch, usually with Garrett or Tyler's help. I also learned how to push-start it myself, parking downhill whenever I could. On this night, it started right away.

I put Mastodon's *Leviathan* in my CD player. Each song seamlessly drifted into the next, and I heard, felt, and saw completely new layers of their music. I passed an on-ramp to I-35, turned around, passed it, turned around, passed it, and continued this for about ten minutes before I finally decided to just go through town. At each stop light, I'd stare at the velvety mass of dancing geometric patterns in the concrete, asking myself, over and over, *Is this light really red, or do I just think it is?*

The sky was a pillowy gray blanket, and trees on the sides of the road writhed, branches wiggling like tadpoles. As the intricately layered prog-rock intro for "Megalodon" seeped through my speakers and changed into an onslaught of oddly timed metal, the road waved and dipped, perfectly on beat with the music. I'd driven on this road before, but I felt like I was seeing it for the first time.

I made it back to the co-op after an hour of making wrong turns. I sat in the parking lot, staring at a large white tree in the neighboring yard and still listening to Mastodon. The tree's branches and trunk glowed, illuminated from within. Brent Hinds's polyrhythmic guitar work in "Hearts Alive" expanded into a gelatin chandelier inside my brain.

He simultaneously fingerpicks and plays with a regular pick, creating several layers of sound. Listening to Brann Dailor's nimble, Buddy Rich-style fills and ghost notes, I saw a clear image of him playing. Wraith-like tentacles branched out from his body instead of arms and legs.

I'd always felt like "Hearts Alive" was just beyond my grasp. Tonight, the song opened into a kaleidoscopic room, and I thought about how beautiful it would be to live here. The song is epic, with transitions from mellow, jazzy sections into balls out rock-n-roll, and one of my favorite guitar solos. I was beginning to understand that heaviness is largely about context, that smartly crafted rock is often heavier than relentless thrash metal.

LSD has fucked me up in permanent ways, but it also changed the way I listen to music for the better. Tripping made me more paranoid and neurotic than ever before. At the same time, acid helped me understand how subtlety can challenge listeners in productive ways. When you have to listen closely, the overall experience is often more meaningful.

I went into our room and found Garrett drawing a large picture of a girl on our wall with magic marker. He told me that Tyler had gone to a party with some other co-op people. I wanted to be alone, so I went into Tyler's room, which was connected to ours by the bathroom, and lay down on a pile of dirty clothes. The stereo was on, and Jimi Hendrix's purple guitar notes danced on the walls.

Images of Josh and the other Ratty House riders flashed in my brain. I saw Josh unzipping his pants and playing with his thick cock. Blood rushed through my body, and I jacked off, coming hard and quick. On this night, I started to see sex as a bestial and chaotic whirlpool. The idea of being attracted to only women or men seemed absurd during these moments, and I kept saying to myself, *It's all the same. Guy or girl, it doesn't matter. It's all the same.*

Soon afterward, though, I'd collide against ideas of what I thought a man should be, ideas I'd been force-fed in Wyoming, ideas that were also reinforced by the worlds of BMX and heavy metal. I didn't think that straight guys should ever wonder about the pleasure you could experience with another man, and it would still take me quite a while before I could stomach the idea that sexuality can't be confined to rigid, black-and-white categories. Over the next few months, I'd fantasize about fooling around with a guy—often one of the Ratty riders—and feel oddly detached afterward. Not guilty necessarily, but empty.

The lines, "Would you look at me now? / Can you tell I'm a man?" from Pantera's "Suicide Note Pt. I" constantly repeated in my head. After Josh mentioned that he and the other riders personally knew Phil, I became fully convinced that Phil is gay or bisexual, and I'd think about how miserable he must be, encapsulated in a prison cell of machismo.

I FINALLY STARTED TO come down around ten the next morning. Sweat collected on the back of my neck and insides of my thighs. I felt filthy and exhausted, but my heart was still racing, so I couldn't fall asleep. I wanted to smoke a bowl but didn't have any weed, and I needed to be alone. I sat on the pile of clothes in Tyler's room, watching kaleidoscopic patterns in the ceiling plaster slowly fade away.

I had a shift at Jovita's at four, so I left the co-op around three. On my way to work, I got some KFC, feeling claustrophobic in my truck as I waited in the drive-thru line. My windows and windshield were covered in a thin scrim of smoke, and ash speckled the carpet and seats. When I got my food, the mashed potatoes and chicken grinned at me. As I ate, I could feel grease from this food seeping through my pores, and I knew that I shouldn't be eating this bullshit.

Jovita's was on the south side of town. I parked on a dead-end street behind the restaurant, got out of my truck, walked a few steps, and collapsed onto the asphalt. No one had told me about how much it sucks to come down from acid, and I remember thinking, *Oh shit, I must have OD'd.* I gagged and dry-heaved as the world spun, pressure accumulating behind my eyes.

When I walked into the restaurant lobby, the manager, Brad, a small guy with slicked-back hair and a goatee, took one look at me and said, "Why don't you work the parking lot tonight and direct cars?"

The restaurant didn't get busy, so I just stood outside until midnight or so, staring at the trees surrounding the parking lot and thinking about how much more beautiful the world seemed on acid.

DISTENSION

I STARTED DOSING A FEW times a week, usually just taking one or two hits at a time. I believed that acid would reveal my true life path, and I craved the same perception-altering experience I had my first time. During most of these nights, I'd see shifting patterns in walls, ceilings, carpet, and cement, but nothing as beautiful as the lizards in the puddle, the waving road, or the kaleidoscopic trees.

I sat in Matt's room in the co-op one night. He was an older, pudgy guy who wore vintage button-downs, polyester pants, and old lady glasses with clear frames and large, circular lenses. Along with a handful of other people, he'd been living in the co-op since it started. Landry and Tyler sat next to me on the floor. Matt played acoustic guitar on his bed, Paige sitting next to him. Matt's cheeks jiggled slightly as he sang, and I laughed hysterically. I'd taken two hits about an hour earlier.

"Play some Zeppelin," I said to him.

He chuckled and played a few refrains from "Black Dog," his voice raspy, tinged with years of whiskey and cigarettes. I slapped my thighs and stomped my right foot on the ground, pretending to play Bonham's drum parts. We all started talking about how much we loved classic rock.

"I've been listening to 'Shooting Star' like nonstop," I said. Landry told me that she loved the song, too, and I wondered if we were meant for each other.

I told everyone that I'd taken acid.

"You've been doing that a lot," Landry said. "Maybe you should take it easy with that stuff."

"I want some drugs," Matt said, his voice rising like he was getting turned on.

Paige said, "Yeah, maybe some ecstasy."

I became convinced that a wild orgy was about to erupt, and I had to leave. Ever since discovering the homoerotic underground of BMX, I'd started to believe that everyone in the co-op was fucking each other, which was partly true, but not sinister as I had imagined. Sexual freedom and experimentation had become attached to the malevolence I'd seen at the Ratty House, and then exaggerated into something terrifying by my drug-addled brain. But I was still curious about messing around with another guy.

I got up and went outside, feeling like I'd barely escaped. I smoked a cigarette and then went into the co-op's computer room to check Myspace. I also looked at the FBM Bikes website to see if there was anything about me on it, which I'd been doing since I started going to the Ratty House. Dave King, Maniac, and Yeagle all rode for FBM, which stands for 'Fire, Beer, Mayhem.' The company owner, Steve Crandall, often posted stories about team riders' partying on the FBM site. I hoped Dave had told Crandall about me, and that Crandall would put me on the website.

The text on the webpage congealed into word salad, except for one line: Dave King is a sick motherfucker.

AFTER TAKING TWO HITS another night, I convinced Garrett and Tyler to come with me to the Ratty House. Dave King ran up to me when I walked in, wrestling me to the ground. Holding my pant leg, he spun me around in circles on the beer-spattered concrete floor. A few minutes later, hanging out on the back porch, I asked Dave when I was going to be on the website.

"What the fuck are you talking about, Double Jay? What website?"

Inside, one of the riders smashed a metal chair on the floor. Roughly the size and age of Dave King, he wasn't wearing a shirt, and sweat glistened on his hairy chest and back. He picked up the folded chair, held it over his head, and slammed it onto the ground as hard as he could, repeating the process several times. I knew about the rush he felt while smashing the chair. Still, I felt unsettled and almost sick to my stomach as I looked at his empty eyes.

A few nights later, I invited Dave and some of the Ratty riders to the co-op. We sat on the floor in Tyler's room, smoking pot and drinking forties. The same guy who'd asked me about Floor on the night of my first trip said something about a kid Dave had hung out with and tormented a few years back.

"One night," Dave said, laughing, "I convinced him to suck my dick. He got on his knees, and when he moved toward my cock, I punched him in the face." He and the other riders burst into hyena laughter.

Steve Crandall and his team riders constantly fucked with each other. An FBM ad that ran in an internationally distributed BMX magazine featured a picture of Dave soaring over a dirt jump in the woods. Crandall put in "Dave King ain't shit!" at the bottom of the page. As an intro to his section in *Chapter 2*, a group of Dave's friends shout the epithet. After Dave passed me the pipe, I asked, "Are you familiar with the phrase 'Dave King ain't shit'?" knowing it would irritate him.

The other riders laughed and Dave forced a chuckle, although he was annoyed. He told us how, after the ad ran, random kids had started coming up to him at skate parks and telling him that he wasn't shit. "I never know what to say," he said. "So I usually just tell them that I'm going to come on their mom's tits or some shit like that."

Wanting to fuck with Steve Crandall, Dave gave me his cell number and told me to call him. I started leaving long, rambling messages for him, saying stuff like "Crandall, this is Double Jay. When are you coming to Austin you piece of shit? And when are you going to put me on the website?"

When I went to the Ratty House one night later in the week, Steve Crandall was there. On a road trip from Binghamton, he and a few buddies had stopped in Austin. Crandall looked exactly like he did in all the videos and pictures I'd seen of him, wearing jeans, a black T-shirt, and a backwards trucker hat. Without saying anything to me, he put me in a headlock and spit a mouthful of beer in my face. I remember thinking, *Holy shit, Steve Crandall just spit beer in my face.*

Garrett, Tyler, and I played every open mic at the co-op, but we only got two outside gigs, even though we'd been handing out demo CDs ever since arriving in Austin. One of these shows was at the Twenty-First Street Co-op, which consisted of a few wooden buildings surrounded by trees. Stairways and walkways intertwined with the two-story buildings, and the place reminded me of the lost boys' hideout in *Hook*.

We played in a large room on the second floor and had to load our equipment up a narrow flight of stairs. Band members got free drinks, so, before our set, I downed five rum and Cokes, although Tyler had told me not to get wasted before we played. Sitting across the room, I looked at him as I took hits from a fat joint with Landry.

I realized that I'd gotten way too fucked-up as soon as we started playing. There was a lag between the signals my brain sent and the movement of my arms and legs. I didn't have a drum rug, so I'd set up my kit on the smooth plywood of the stage. Within seconds, my floor tom and ride cymbal slid to the right, and my kick drum moved a few feet forward. I had to reach as far as I could with my leg and arms to hit the drums, and I'm a lanky guy. I'd move everything back after each song, only to have my drums immediately slide away again. During one song, I knocked both of my cymbal stands over. Tyler looked at me like he wanted to punch me in the face.

ONE NIGHT, SOMEONE NEAR the co-op threw a house party with seven kegs. I hung out at the house and drank with Garrett, Tyler, and my co-op friends for a while, but I was tired because I'd just gotten off work—seven hours of ridiculously hot waitresses yelling at me for not bussing fast enough. So I went home early.

Tyler hooked up with some girl and didn't come back to the co-op until the next morning. By noon, a few of us realized that we hadn't heard from Garrett since the night before. At about two, he called Tyler from a gas station downtown.

When I pulled into the gas station, Garrett got up from the curb in front of the convenience store and stumbled to my truck. The smells of body odor, piss, and beer emanated from him, and black dirt was engrained into his right cheek. He had a ratty, blue faux-fur coat wrapped around his neck, and he carried a filthy teddy bear in the crook of his arm like it was a kitten.

"Where the fuck have you been?" I asked, laughing.

"You assholes left me at the party, so I stayed until five this morning, when the beer ran out." He spoke in the wacky, high-pitched voice that only came out when he was completely shit-faced. He told us that he'd tried to walk home but got lost and decided to sleep in a gutter. I was never sure why he didn't find a bench, although it might've had something to do with his love for gutter punks. He needed something to sleep on, so he broke into a nearby car and stole the fur coat and teddy bear.

Driving back to the co-op and looking at Garrett in my rearview mirror, I knew that I'd be telling this story for years. He looked both cartoonish and heartbreakingly human. Tyler and I laughed at him, but I also saw a smart young guy who truly hated himself, and part of me was scared of Garrett.

A FEW NIGHTS LATER, I was hot boxing alone in my truck when James knocked on my window. I'd been listening to Sleep's *Holy Mountain* and feeling completely at home in Matt Pike's pillowy, weed-laden riffs.

"What are you listening to?" James asked.

"Sleep."

"I can see how this would put you to sleep."

When James and I first started hanging out, we'd talk about how underrated Sabbath's early material is among most musicians. But he quickly started mocking me, saying stuff like "Yeah, man, Black Sabbath," slowly, like one of the characters from *Detroit Rock City*.

On the morning after James made the joke about Sleep, I smoked a cigarette with Steve, the co-op's manager, sitting on a bench next to the front doors. Steve was a small guy with black hair that covered his ears, and he spoke with the slow drawl of an Austin stoner. When he asked me who some of my favorite bands were, I listed off doom and stoner metal bands, not expecting him to know any of them.

"Yeah, there's a big scene for that stuff, here," he said, picking a piece of tobacco off his lip. "You know that most of the guys that are into that stuff are really stupid, right?"

AFTER GARRETT'S FUR COAT escapade, I decided that I needed to turn him into a stoner, to show him how much better weed was than booze. Soon, Garrett and I started getting high together every night. We'd drive around the neighborhood, park in a random alley, and smoke ourselves silly.

When we were high, Garrett and I started talking to each other in a bizarre gibberish/baby talk that we'd invented. I'd say something like, "Cochuanocochimipo-opy?" and Garrett would answer with, "Ohbeenaponny-boonononny." We'd go on like this for a few minutes and then laugh our asses off.

Lindsay called during one of these nights, right after Garrett and I'd gotten back to the co-op. She was drunk and kept saying, "It's not metal enough for J. J." She'd been saying this to me since we started hanging out, poking fun at the fact that I only listened to metal. I knew that Lindsay's teasing stemmed from love, but, on this night, her words also evoked the self-hate that I'd been struggling with. She never left my thoughts for long, and I'd recently been thinking that we should just break off contact so we could both move on. I can't remember what I said, only that it was extremely hurtful.

After hanging up, I rolled down my window and waterfall-puked in the parking lot, having smoked myself sick.

ABOUT A MONTH AND a half after moving into the co-op, I woke up and found a note that someone had slid under my door. 'J. J.' was written on it in large letters, with little hearts instead of periods, and it said it was from Landry. I giddily read about how she had a crush on me and might be looking for a new boyfriend. Written in the same cutesy handwriting that hot girls used in high school, the note ended with, "Maybe we could have a rendezvous sometime. Whatever U R n2, U know?"

Reading it for the third, fourth, and fifth times, I convinced myself that someone in the co-op was trying to fuck with me. Several tenants—mostly serious musicians who didn't party much—hated me because I was constantly fucked-up, and I didn't do my chores. I also knew that several people had noticed me flirting with Landry. Rich was the co-op treasurer, and he'd lived there since it started. Everyone loved him, so trying to get me to overtly hit on Landry seemed like a good way to get me kicked out.

Not sure what to do, I showed the note to James. "I can't tell if someone is fucking with me or not."

"I don't think anyone is fucking with you, dude," he said after reading the note. "I didn't know Landry was down to cheat on Rich."

Today, I think James was probably right, although I'm still not sure. Looking back, it's hard to see how I could've been so certain that the note was part of someone's plan to get me kicked out of the co-op.

After my first LSD trip, people's facial expressions and body language had begun to seem much more significant than ever before. I started to believe that any backhanded comment or strange gesture signified some plot against me, or a desire to fuck me. I found hidden layers of meaning beneath even the most mundane interactions. Isolation was miserable, but I didn't have to worry about what someone wanted from me or how they saw me when I was alone. During this time, I started each day by finding an alley near the co-op and getting high alone.

It also became harder and harder for me to play music in the co-op. James had explained one of John Bonham's signature drum licks to me one night, and I learned the triplet pattern by playing it very slowly. After I'd been practicing one afternoon, Jarrell came up to me and said, "I really like what you were doing with those triplets." Coming from this amazing musician, I felt sure that he was fucking with me.

Along with James and a few other people, Jarrell had also directly criticized my drumming. Instead of using it as a way to get better, which would eventually become the case, I felt increasingly insecure, constantly arguing with myself about whether or not I really was destined to be a drummer. I thought everyone was constantly evaluating me, which was partly true, but didn't matter nearly as much as I thought it did.

In the co-op, I'd found a community that embraced me, but I had to destroy it, reading into it until it no longer made sense.

ONE EVENING, THREE WEEKS or so after my first trip, I went into James's room to buy more acid, but he told me that he'd run out. "I'll sell you the vial for ten bucks, though. You just cut it into pieces and put them in a glass of water for like fifteen minutes and then drink it. It's called The Wash." The acid stuck to the inside of the Clear Eyes dropper would seep into the water. He wasn't sure, but I'd probably get between ten and fifteen hits. "The last time I did The Wash, the visuals were fucking sick."

In the kitchen, I cut the plastic eyedropper into four or five pieces and put them in a glass of water. Greenish-blue residue clung to each piece. After stirring them around for about ten minutes, I drank the water and chewed on each piece like James had told me to, gnawing on them until they became mushy. When I bit onto the dropper nozzle, a burst of minty LSD squirted onto my tongue.

Forty-five minutes later, I watched a sapling outside my window rapidly grow into a massive live oak, which reminded me of those time-elapse videos of plants growing that teachers show in grade school. Garrett and Luke were hanging out in our room, playing a hockey game on Xbox. Luke spoke backwards, his already deep voice several octaves lower than usual. Homoerotic innuendo laced all of the videogame announcers' words. Garrett's crotch rose as he played, like he was softly humping his controller, and I knew that he wanted to fool around with me.

Sifting through acid trips for meaning is often confusing and pointless. In the midst of irrationality and absurd paranoia, kernels of truth sometimes arise, though. Earlier in the day, I'd bought a gram of skunk weed. When I took it out of my pocket to smoke with Garrett and Luke, the nugget mutated into a ball of writhing maggots. I dropped the weed on the ground, knowing that I shouldn't be a stoner. There was too much tension connected to weed from my past—tension that, when I smoked, would probably always transform into self-loathing.

Looking at the nugget on the ground, these thoughts dissipated as quickly as they'd surfaced. I stuffed half of it into my pipe, took a big hit, and passed it to Luke. Tendrils of scraggly hair rose from his head, as if he was touching an electrified orb. He reminded me of Benicio Del Toro in *Fear and Loathing in Las Vegas*. The hockey announcers' homoerotic banter made my chest tighten, so I went into Tyler's room, where he was sitting on his bed and playing guitar.

When I sat next to him, a sickly grin crawled across his face.

"Dude, I'm fucking tripping balls," I said.

He kept playing, making strangely childlike sounds with his guitar. "Look at that picture," he said, pointing to a whale he'd drawn on his wall with magic marker. "I bet that's pretty trippy, huh." His voice rose like he was about to come. The picture looked the same as it always did—like a whale a fourth grader might draw, filled in with messy circles.

This wasn't the first time I'd gotten weird sexual vibes from Tyler. One night about four weeks earlier, driving back to the co-op from McDonald's, Tyler blurted, "You know all gay people were molested as kids, right?" We were both sober, and there was no segue for his words, which didn't seem like his own—something he'd probably been told when he was a kid. I didn't know how to respond, so I just ate my burger.

A day or so later, we were sitting in a mall parking lot when Tyler suddenly said, "There's nothing wrong with getting jacked off by another guy. You know that, right?" He took a drag from his cigarette. "Everyone in the co-op is really open-minded about that stuff."

Tyler had said these things before my first trip. What he said about fucking around with other dudes was true, but I still needed to dismantle my misconception that real men were supposed to be perfectly straight. Sitting next to Tyler on the night I took The Wash, I thought about him saying these things, and I needed to get away.

Three or four community bikes were propped against a wall next to the co-op's front doors. I picked out a red mountain bike and started riding it around the neighborhood. The front wheel wobbled from side to side, and, as I pedaled, the cranks popped and the chain skipped. I thought about riding my BMX bike—how smooth and comfortable I'd feel doing bunny hops and sharp turns—and I wished that I'd brought it to Austin.

Before going through each cross street, I'd stop, look one way, the other, then back, repeatedly, convinced that, once I turned my head one way, a car would now be coming from the other direction.

The surrounding trees were waving globules of black ink. Looking at the gelatin sky, I wondered if I was in a Petri dish. I could hear wild, free form jazz coming from somewhere, and I wasn't sure if people were actually playing it, or if it was just in my head.

Back at the co-op, I stared at my tattoos in our bathroom mirror. The person that had needed to advertise his favorite bands on his body seemed like someone else, and I hated how I'd attempted to confine myself within a metalhead stereotype. At that moment, I wished that I could erase my tattoos. I thought about how I'd idolized each member of Black Sabbath, Pantera, and Metallica, seeing them as gods. I'd recently started to hear a hollowness in Pantera and Metallica's music—repetitive and predictable song structures, too many guitar solos, and too much double bass. With Pantera, I could feel Phil's battle with his sexuality, which he covered with a facade of toughness.

When I listened to Sabbath, I focused on the jazz flourish in Bill Ward's drumming, convinced that I'd never be that good. I loved Sabbath as much, if not more, than I ever had, but I still hated my Sabbath tattoos, especially the words around my left wrist: Killing Yourself to Live. I didn't think about the thing in me that needs to test limits, to experience life in extreme ways—something that will always be part of my personality. I thought I was becoming a completely new person. Now, I think I was examining myself in new ways, which breeds change, but I was also the same person I'd always been.

I'm not exactly sure what I did for the next couple of hours, although I do remember smoking pot with James and watching parts of *Dirty Harry* with Garrett. James silently criticized every word that came out of my mouth. Clint Eastwood's cragged cheeks bubbled like the clay pots in Yellowstone, and all of Garrett's words were laced with sex.

At about eight in the morning, I decided to go for a drive. The sun had just penetrated the gray blanket of sky, and the streets were mostly empty. I put the first disc of Zeppelin's *BBC Sessions* in my CD player. During Bonham's fills, I saw an infinite chain of energy that he tapped into and guided, just letting bits and pieces of it loose. Jimmy Page's riffs played forwards and backwards simultaneously, building upon the geometric chain of rhythm that Bonham and John Paul Jones explored. Robert Plant sang about a girl squeezing his lemon and making the juice run down his leg. Thinking about how badly I wanted to have sex with Landry, I drove fast, feeling like no one in the world could fuck with me.

And then I accidentally turned onto I-35, instantly getting engulfed in a sea of rush-hour traffic, which made me feel nauseated and claustrophobic. A flood of mirrors and bumpers stutter-stepped forward. Two cop cars were parked on the shoulder, their lights flashing. I became convinced that someone had told them about me. I made sure not to make eye contact with the police officers when I passed them.

It felt like an hour before I finally made it to the next exit. As I glided down the off-ramp, Jimmy Page began playing the ending riff of "What Is and What Should Never Be." When the rest of the band joined in, an array of kaleidoscopic patterns erupted in my brain, melting my anxiety.

I didn't start to come down until three or four in the afternoon, when I was at work. I showed up with comically large pupils and messy hair. Like he'd done before, the manager just told me to direct cars in the parking lot, where I wouldn't have to talk with customers. For the rest of the night, I stared at nearby trees, watching their otherworldly movements gradually subside.

In addition to Landry, I'd been falling in love with Shelley, who'd moved into the co-op a few weeks after us. She was twenty-five, voluptuous, an amazing singer and keyboardist, and had long black hair. Zeppelin's "The Girl I Love She Got Long Black Wavy Hair" played in my head whenever I saw her. She'd tell me stories about tripping and listening to Tool when she was in high school. She also loved Mastodon, Melvins, Queens of the Stone Age, and a bunch of other awesome bands. She talked about music like a musician, not paying much attention to lyrics, and I loved listening to her.

About a week after I did The Wash, Jarrell told me that he could hook me up with some mushrooms. When I told Shelley, she said that she wanted to trip with me.

Right after she got off work one night, we both ate about an eighth-ounce of the large, white mushrooms that I'd bought from Jarrell's buddy. We decided to leave the co-op and go to a nearby park. I rode the shitty red mountain bike, and Shelley skated on her longboard.

A translucent curtain of geometric patterns covered the streets, but I immediately knew that mushrooms wouldn't compare to LSD. I coasted down a long hill, Shelley cruising alongside me. She got going too fast, and, suddenly, her board began to wobble. I was sure that she'd smash her face on the concrete, but she somehow rode out the speed-wobbles, gliding to the bottom of the hill. Stepping off her board, Shelley looked at me, her mouth open in disbelief. We burst into laughter.

I followed her through the park. We sat next to a live oak, its limbs reaching toward the sky. A few nights earlier, when we were both shit-faced, Shelley had said, "Isn't that what everybody wants to do? Just get drunk and fuck?" I should've made a move then but couldn't, feeling trapped in that rut of inaction that I'd often floundered in when I was with Lindsay. At this point, all sex had begun to seem sinister, and I couldn't get myself to push through fear's surface tension. Sitting next to Shelley on this night, I thought about how we should be having sex.

We didn't talk much, just staring at the psychedelic blanket of grass and foliage.

THE NEXT DAY, I decided that I'd wait to eat the remaining mushrooms. In Rock Springs, Bryan had gone to my parents' house and packed my BMX bike into a box, and my mom was going to ship it to me within the next two weeks. I couldn't wait to feel my handlebar grips, worn and grooved in the centers. I thought about how fun it would be to eat mushrooms and then ride around Austin.

Throughout the day, I couldn't stop thinking about the shrooms. At about five that night, I finally decided that I'd just eat some of them. Of course I ended up eating the rest. Twenty minutes later, I was smoking a bowl in an alley when a sickly film started to crawl across my brain. I could faintly see patterns in the weeds and fences around me, but I felt filthy, like tar was enveloping my mind.

Back at the co-op, I went into James's room, where he was smoking pot with Jarrell, Pod, and Bird, an amazing guitarist who'd recently moved into the co-op. Bird beat out a polyrhythmic groove on James's djembe, laughing at me when I told him how amazing it sounded. I hadn't known that Bird could play percussion. He handed the drum to Pod, who started playing a fast, oddly timed rhythm. I realized that both of them knew more about drumming than I did. Listening to them talk about music with James and Jarrell, I felt sure that I'd never be on the same level as any of these guys.

I left the co-op and drove down Guadalupe. I stared at my massive pupils in the rearview mirror, hearing myself say *hmmm* over and over, as if I was a sleuth from an old noir movie caught in a repeating loop. With each repetition, there was a new me in my brain. Soon there was a room full of J. J.s, bumping into each other, all of us saying *hmmm, hmmm, hmmm.*

I saw a Jack in the Box and decided to get some food. Looking at signs for fast-food restaurants after my first acid trip, I saw a black scrim behind the letters, knowing in a vague but undeniable way that most corporations are evil. The other co-op tenants would scold Tyler, Garrett, and I when they caught us eating McDonald's and other fast-food, so these thoughts partly came from buying into the hippie ideals that permeated the co-op, as well as the rest of Austin. But I also knew that corporations like these controlled America, and that people, animals, and plants were simply currency to them. Although these thoughts had been bubbling in my head for a while, I still ate fast-food every day. Waiting behind a few other cars in the drive-thru line, I thought about how I was just another piece of shit consumer—just another American. I stared at oil splotches on the concrete, pulled forward, and ordered a Jumbo Jack combo.

Near the co-op, I suddenly started seeing two versions of everything—a faint, ghost-image that floated away from the object, as well as the object itself. A ghost street reached beyond the actual street.

Needing to get out of my truck, I pulled over and ran around a weed-filled empty lot with an irrigation ditch cutting through it. I collapsed near the ditch, covering my head with my arms and bawling like a child. Not knowing what else to do, I called my best friend Steve and my mom, telling them that I needed to come home.

WHEN I SAID THAT I was moving back to Wyoming, most of the co-op tenants told me not to leave.

"Don't go back to Rock Springs," Tyler said. "You'll regret it."

Sitting on the kitchen counter with Shelley, she put her head on my shoulder and said, "But you're my buddy. I don't want you to go."

Rich told me that I should get my own room, and Bird told me that I just needed a girlfriend. They were all right, but I also knew that I couldn't control myself in the co-op. My brain felt like a discarded typewriter ribbon.

We had a show booked for the following week at an art collective across town, and I decided it would be my last with The Scissorhands. I wanted the show to be special, so, a few days before, I cut off the sleeves of a white T-shirt and wrote "Let's Get Dirty!" on it in magic marker.

After we set up our equipment on the night of the show, I went into an ill-kept bathroom at the art collective and changed into my sleeveless shirt, also putting on my black-and-neon-green spandex—the ones I'd worn for my Hulk Hogan costume.

The stage and room were both pretty big. Only about fifteen people showed up, though. Tyler, Garrett, and I rocked out like there was no tomorrow, playing one of our best shows. Tyler and I headbanged while Garrett stomped his foot to my simple beats. When Tyler climbed on my bass drum and jumped off, I pictured hundreds of photographers fighting each other for a shot of The Scissorhands.

After our set, three or four people told us that they liked it.

ON A GRAY MORNING two days later, I rented a trailer. At the U-Haul office, a clerk told me that he was a guitarist and had just moved to Austin from a small town in Oklahoma. When he said that he loved Stevie Ray Vaughan, Jimi Hendrix, and Eric Clapton, I thought, *Yeah, you and every other guitarist in Austin.*

Back at the co-op, I hurriedly stuffed my things into the U-Haul. I'd been thinking that everyone would gather outside, waving and crying as I drove away. I saw James in the hall just before I left.

"Oh, you're leaving? Well I guess I'll see you later then," he said, shaking my hand before going into his room.

THE BIG TEXAN II

I DROVE NORTH, TOWING A jam-packed U-Haul behind my Tacoma. Outside the cultural Petri dish of Austin, most of Texas seemed desolate. Staring at flat, empty plains, I felt like I was approaching the edge of a square earth.

When I put Pantera's *The Great Southern Trendkill* in my CD player, I'd go back and forth from feeling energized by the band's Southern metal to hating its idiocy. In "Living Through Me," one of my favorite songs during high school, there's an industrial midsection with several layers of Phil speaking. His vocals swirl amidst percussive clanking, and it's hard to hear what he's saying most of the time, but a few words come through clearly, like "faggot." When I heard Phil say this, I pictured him getting fucked by Dave King—both of them at the front of a train with the other Ratty House riders, all of them laughing at me.

I tried to listen to *Leviathan* but couldn't make it through one song. Brann Dailor's complicated drumming, which is rife with odd timings and polyrhythms, made me feel anxious and insecure. I got similar feelings while listening to Zeppelin.

During the afternoon, I pulled off the interstate to get high. Trying to find an empty stretch of road, I passed decrepit farmhouses, each surrounded by large yards and barbed-wire fences. Paint curled up from the siding of these houses, and weeds covered the walkways.

After about ten minutes of driving, I parked on a grassy shoulder. Staring at a white house as I smoked, I felt like I'd wandered onto the set of *The Texas Chainsaw Massacre*. I thought about how people living in this house could do whatever they wanted without worrying about their neighbors hearing or seeing.

When I tried to drive away, my wheels just spun. I got out and realized that the ground was spongy and wet. The tires of my truck and U-Haul had sunk a few inches, and the trailer sat at an angle, keeping the truck in place when I tried to drive forward. I didn't have phone service, so I decided to wave down the next vehicle I saw. For fifteen minutes, I only heard grasshoppers and the quiet rustle of burning paper and tobacco when I took a drag from my cigarette.

I felt a mix of fear and relief when I saw a truck in the distance. I stood on the side of the highway, waving my arms. The driver was a skinny guy with a work-hardened, humorless face and cragged wrinkles around his eyes. He hooked his winch to my truck and pulled it out within minutes. When I thanked him, he said, "Don't worry about it. Happy to help. Nice to test out my new winch."

I GOT A MOTEL room in Lubbock that night. Before checking out the next morning, I smoked a fat joint in my truck, keeping the windows up to trap the smoke.

Hot boxing seemed like a good idea before I was high. And then I thought about driving through rural Texas in a truck that reeked of skunk weed. Trying to cover up the smell, I lit an air freshener that hung from my rearview mirror on fire and blew it out, hoping the acrid smoke would overpower the weed smell.

I checked out, and, when I came back, smoke flooded my truck, billowing out as I opened the door. Coughing from the noxious fumes, I realized that the air freshener had kept burning, melting the plastic on the back of my mirror. I was lucky that my entire truck hadn't caught fire.

I let the cab air out and then tried to start my truck, but I only heard an empty ticking when I turned the key. Although my starter had begun to go out right after we'd moved to Austin, I never got it fixed. At the motel in Lubbock, I couldn't push-start my truck with the U-Haul attached, so I had to get the starter fixed here.

I called a towing company, and a driver showed up twenty minutes later. He was huge—over 6'5" and at least 250 pounds. His gray hair was cut into a perfect flattop, and he wore oil-stained overalls. He looked at me—a frail, blond-haired stoner in a Black Sabbath T-shirt—as if I was a gob of shit on his shoe. When he tried to start my truck, I thought, *Fuck, he's going to smell weed and call the cops*, but he didn't seem to care. He attached my truck and U-Haul to his tow truck, and we drove to an auto shop on the outskirts of town.

The shop was an old, gray warehouse that stood in front of a thicket of trees. Dismantled cars and trucks were scattered in front of the corrugated metal building. Hank Williams' voice, scratchy and distorted, slithered from a radio in the garage. The driver went inside and came out with the shop manager, a guy in his late forties who wore a Carhartt hat, filthy jeans, and a gray T-shirt. He said something, and I didn't realize that he'd asked for my keys until he held out his hand.

He talked to me after trying to start my truck and checking under the hood. I could only pick out a few words, though. I'd always thought Boomhauer's speech in *King of the Hill* was a ridiculous exaggeration, but this guy sounded really similar, except that his voice was deeper and raspier. I heard "three hundred dollars," not sure what he was going to fix or why it was so expensive. He could've said, "I'm going to fuck your face and then smoke PCP out of your asshole," and I probably wouldn't have known the difference.

WITHIN A FEW HOURS after leaving the shop, signs for the Big Texan steak challenge sprouted up on the side of the road. Looking at them, I remembered the giddiness that pulsed in my chest when Garrett, Tyler, and I were on our way to Austin. I also thought about taking on the steak challenge and puking my brains out.

I could've made it to New Mexico before nightfall, but I decided to stay at the Big Texan motel, which seemed fitting for my last night in Texas. I hoped to recapture the excitement I'd felt while driving to Austin before returning to the dead-end boomtown that is Rock Springs. I'd also been constructing a fantasy in which I ordered room service at the Big Texan, and a waiter who'd want to suck me off delivered my food.

Driving through Amarillo toward the motel, a vague menace loomed. Barbed-wire-topped fences surrounded used car dealerships, and fast-food restaurants emitted filth into the air. At streetlights, I stared into oil splotches on the concrete. I'd been feeling increasingly cynical about humans, and, everywhere I looked, I saw evidence for my belief that people are parasites, and that society is a plague.

Still, pulling into the parking lot of the Big Texan, I felt tinges of the giddiness I'd experienced when Garrett, Tyler, and I stopped here. But this place also seemed gross and empty in a way that it hadn't two and a half months earlier.

I drove over to the motel, about one hundred yards from the restaurant. I recognized the tall metal cowboy that stood next to the motel, pointing to a sign that proclaimed "The Big Texan Steak Ranch." The motel was divided into sections by color—pink, yellow, gray, brown, and green—and the paint of each section was bright, making the building look like it was made out of neon lights. A wooden sign that said "Big Texan Lodge House" stood atop the building. Both the motel and restaurant looked like plywood facades from the set of a shitty Western movie.

I parked my truck and U-Haul horizontally across four or five spaces. Only a few other cars were parked in the lot, so I didn't think anyone would care. After getting a room, I ordered a regular-sized steak from room service. The waiter was a bald, middle-aged guy, and he left immediately after I gave him a tip.

I ate the steak, got high, fingered my asshole while bending over and looking through my legs in the mirror, and passed out.

I WOKE UP JUST after eleven the next day. Checkout was at ten, so I hurriedly packed my stuff and went downstairs. Walking to the front desk, I glanced at my truck and stopped. My U-Haul was gone. I searched the outside of my truck for a ticket, hoping the trailer had been towed. But I didn't find one, and no one had broken into my vehicle, so I went to the front desk to see if a motel employee had gotten my U-Haul towed.

"No, I don't think anyone here had your trailer towed," said the clerk, a tired-looking woman with thin hair and veiny arms. "You know, this type of thing happens all the time here, it being a tourist trap and everything." She told me that most people don't think of locking their trailer to the hitch—a mistake I'd made. I locked my truck and the door to the trailer, but didn't think about locking the trailer to the hitch. "That makes it real easy for the thieves." Her voice was flat. "All they have to do is come by with a truck with a hitch and just take the trailer." She paused, pointing to a phone on her desk. "You want me to call the cops?"

Waiting for the police, I sat in my truck, chain-smoking Marlboro 27s. I still hoped my U-Haul had been towed. Nearly everything I owned was in the trailer, possessions that, in a lot of ways, defined me: my drums, two acoustic guitars, one electric guitar, a guitar amp, computer, TV, DVD player, several DVDs, and most of my clothes.

I couldn't stop thinking about my metal and BMX T-shirts. Before living in Austin, I'd worn these shirts like badges of honor. My relationships with metal and BMX had become strained, but I also knew that these things were irrevocable parts of my psyche. For each band tattooed on my body, I had at least three shirts. I'd been collecting BMX T-shirts since junior high, and I can still list several that I'd never see again. I also kept thinking about my drums.

A policeman pulled into the lot after about fifteen minutes. He had a crew cut, and a fine line of sweat just below his hairline glistened. I told him that I'd woken up to discover that my trailer was gone.

"Yeah," he said, beginning to fill out his report. "This type of thing happens a lot here. A lot of people come through town with trailers full of stuff, and most of them don't think to lock their trailer to the hitch."

I listed off my belongings for him.

"I'm going to be honest with you." He tapped his pen on his clipboard. "We usually find the trailers somewhere outside town with nothing in them. But you had a lot of unique stuff, so you might be able to find some of it at the local pawn shops."

He got a call from dispatch just before he finished his report. "Looks like a tow truck driver found your trailer about ten miles outside town," he said, clipping his radio back onto his shirt. "I don't know if there's anything in it, though."

It seemed strange that a tow truck driver would be wandering around the empty plains outside Amarillo on a Tuesday morning. I also thought it was weird that dispatch would call so quickly, and just before the officer finished his report. Today, I realize that these coincidences don't necessarily lead to any answers about who stole my trailer, but I'm still confused and intrigued by the paranoid conspiracies my frazzled brain gravitated toward. The policeman gave me directions to the tow yard and left.

Sitting in my truck, I stared at the metal cowboy. He looked back at me with smiling, black eyes. The plastic steer in front of the restaurant also seemed to mock me. The idea that I'd been caught in a crime ring involving the Big Texan, a towing company, and the Amarillo police began to solidify in my brain. With the bizarre certainty that supported most of my conspiracy theories at the time, I thought that a clerk from the motel had called a driver at the towing company, who then came to take my trailer. I didn't think the thieves would randomly happen upon my trailer without already knowing it was there, and I was the only motel guest towing a U-Haul.

I recognize now that thieves probably checked the Big Texan for trailers regularly, especially considering how many people stop at this tourist trap every day—people often towing U-Hauls. Still, I can't completely discount the idea that someone at the motel called the thieves to let them know there was a U-Haul in the parking lot. At the time, I also thought someone at the Amarillo police department must've been connected to the U-Haul crime ring, and it still seems oddly convenient that the cop got a call from dispatch when he did—like something you'd read in a clunky mystery novel. But the link to the Amarillo police is the most tenuous in my crime ring theory. I'm not sure what to make of the situation now. Looking back, it's hard to see through the interference between my current perception and that of the LSD-addled metalhead who was running home to his parents.

Driving to the tow yard on the south side of Amarillo, fast-food restaurants, pawn shops, liquor stores, and used car dealerships morphed into a decayed industrial area. I decided to get high next to some warehouses near the yard, thinking weed would calm me.

Staring at corrugated warehouse roofs, I wished that I hadn't left Austin. I could hear Garrett, Tyler, and my co-op friends telling me that I shouldn't move back to Rock Springs. While I felt like I couldn't control myself in the co-op, and I'd started to doubt my musical skill, I also knew that nothing made me as happy as playing the drums. To me, music has always been a form of expression that's the product of human thought while also existing somewhere beyond consciousness.

A work truck rumbled past as I sat in my own, smoking pot and staring at rectangular waves in a warehouse roof. I left, afraid of getting busted.

The neighborhood surrounding the warehouses seemed like the setting of a post-apocalyptic movie. Cars and trucks in various states of disassembly sat in driveways and yellowed lawns of dilapidated, one-level houses. Children wearing dirt-encrusted shorts and T-shirts played on sidewalks and in the streets.

My feeling that I'd wandered into a scene from *Mad Max* intensified when I reached the tow yard. Tall, chain-link fencing surrounded rusted car parts, a dated yellow school bus, a few tow trucks, and other random vehicles. Three U-Haul trailers sat in the yard.

Inside the office, I told a clerk that one of their drivers had found my stolen trailer. "Come outside," the skeletal woman said, leading me to a metal door. She had frayed, bleached hair, and her brownish-gray teeth were eroded. "You can see which one's yours."

The Texas sun cast a queasy glare over the yard. Oil puddles and weeds speckled the dirt. I looked in the first trailer. As my eyes adjusted to the dark, I saw the shells of my drums and none of my other belongings. My stool, cymbals, and cymbal stands were all gone, but the drums themselves were still there. When I left Austin, my U-Haul had been stuffed, and I had a hard time closing the door. Now, the gray-floored trailer looked like a void.

Inside, the woman told me that I needed to pay 275 dollars to take the trailer, and she began writing a receipt. Not sure what to do, I called U-Haul. A customer service employee told me that, since the trailer was already reported as being stolen, it didn't matter if I returned it. I'd paid the extra money for insurance, and the situation was now out of my hands. After this phone call, I told the clerk that I just wanted to take my drums and leave. We argued for a few minutes, each of us becoming more agitated, before she went to get the manager.

The manager was a skinny man, probably in his mid-forties, wearing faded Wranglers and an old flannel shirt. Deep crags cut through his ashen cheeks. Like the clerk, his teeth were jagged and scum-ridden. Meth use is a scourge in Rock Springs, and I knew most of the signs, so I felt certain in my guess that the manager and clerk were both tweakers.

I told the man about my conversation with the U-Haul employee. "I just want to get my drums and leave."

He called U-Haul and got the same information. After hanging up, he said, "You can't just take the drums without paying, though." He took a cigarette from a pack in his shirt pocket and lit it, exhaling smoke through his nose. "It cost me money for my driver to pick up that trailer." At this point, I felt absolutely sure that I'd gotten caught in a crime ring. Someone with the towing company had stolen and gutted my trailer, and the manager of the same company was now trying to charge me a fee just so I could take my drums.

Barely restraining myself from cussing the guy out, I kept trying to convince him to let me take my drums without paying. He eventually reduced the fee but still demanded that I paid him. Tired, confused, and feeling like I needed to get the fuck out of Amarillo, I gave him 100 dollars, loaded the drums into my truck, and left.

It took me two more days to get back to Rock Springs. When I stayed at a motel in Colorado, I crammed my drum kit inside the cab for the night. Aside from that night, I tried to keep a constant watch on my drums, only letting them out of my sight when I had to use the bathroom.

I felt like my identity had been broken down, leaving only the barest functioning parts. I had that drum kit since I was twelve. My CDs were in my truck when the trailer was stolen. In addition to the clothes I was wearing, I had two T-shirts and a pair of jeans in my backpack.

*

AFTER ABOUT A MONTH of living back in Rock Springs, a detective from the Amarillo police department contacted me. He was investigating a series of U-Haul thefts at the Big Texan, but he never told me if anyone at the motel or towing company was involved. Because my belongings were easily identifiable, the detective was able to connect my recovered goods with other thefts at the Big Texan.

Throughout May, June, and July, he emailed me pictures of stolen goods, and I'd tell him if I saw any of my stuff. The pictures showed ratty motel rooms filled with stereo equipment, TVs, jewelry, CDs, DVDs, videogame consoles, bikes, snowboards, and other valuables. In one, my guitar amp, which my older cousin had given me years earlier, sat next to my drumstick bag on dingy, aquamarine carpet. Two of my BMX T-shirts and one Black Sabbath shirt were laid out in front of the amp and bag. The detective sent these things back to me.

I recently decided to wear the Sabbath shirt that was stolen and recovered, which I don't do very often. In purple letters, "Black Sabbath" sits atop a faded black-and-white picture of the band from 1972. On the back: "Listen to Black Sabbath" in white lettering. The black T-shirt still fits perfectly, but I also wonder if someone else has worn it.

INHERITANCE

A WEEK AFTER I MOVED back to Rock Springs, I started working for my second cousin, Paul Jr., again—the same vending job I'd done when I moved back from Aurora.

A typical day at Golden Opportunity Vending: I get to Paul's apartment, which is in Imperial Apartments, shortly after noon. Because Paul's dad is dead, his mom, Donna, owns and operates the apartment complex. I'm completely ripped.

Paul is in his living room, sitting on his La-Z-Boy in his tighty whities and talking to his bookie on the phone. He keeps his brown hair slicked back, and he has a thick handlebar mustache. He wears glasses that are supposed to get dark outdoors and clear indoors, but they never lose their tint.

"What's the line for LA and San Antonio?" Paul asks his bookie, glancing at me when I walk in and then turning back to the TV, fingering his mustache. I sit on the couch and pet Paul's dog, Chummy, a rotund black lab mix to whom Paul regularly feeds Big Macs. "Christ, alright," he says. "Give me LA with a teaser of six and an over of one hundred ninety-eight." He closes his phone after placing the bet.

"How you doing, Jay? You want to grab me a beer from the fridge? And grab one for yourself, too." Usually, only close friends or relatives call me Jay. It's also what most people call my dad.

Paul and I drink our beers and smoke a few cigarettes while we watch *Law And Order*. Commemorative NFL mugs line a shelf on the side of the room—a porcelain mug representing every team from 1992. A picture of Paul kneeling behind a dead elk, holding its head up by the horns, hangs on the wall above the mugs. Although the picture was taken fifteen years earlier, it shows Paul with the same glasses, mustache, and hairstyle that he has now.

A mounted coyote with murderous yellow eyes sits on top of the entertainment center. Paul's porcelain Precious Moments figurine collection is set up on a shelf under the coyote. Blond-haired children stare into the living room with their trademark Precious Moments eyes.

When *Law And Order* finishes, Paul tells me what arcade games and vending machines need to be collected and/or restocked. "After you do that," he says, "come back to the apartment and we'll eat." He gets up from his La-Z-Boy, scratches his hairy gut, and walks to the bathroom to take a shower.

I drive around Rock Springs and collect quarters from Paul's games and vending machines, also restocking the vending machines. After five or six hours, I go to American National Bank to cash in the coins. Like Imperial Apartments, the Holiday Inn, and Comfort Inn, Paul's mom now owns and operates the bank.

I carry in two or three canvas moneybags filled with quarters. The white marble floors in the lobby glisten. Each employee knows who I am and whom I work for. A teller runs the quarters through an electronic counting machine. Handing me the cash, she asks how my parents are doing.

"Hey, Jay," Paul says when I get back to his apartment. "Did we make any money today?" I give Paul the cash, and he licks his fingers before counting the bills. Then he calls in an order at a nearby restaurant and has me pick it up.

After eating, I smoke a bowl in Paul's bathroom. Knowing that I usually get stoned in my truck, Paul encourages me to smoke at his place, often saying, "You know the cops in this town would love to bust an Anselmi."

Paul asks me if I want to stay over after I get high. "You're always more than welcome," he says.

I often stay the night at Paul's apartment. Watching TV and talking shit about most of the Anselmi family, Paul and I drink stiff vodka and 7-Ups until we can't see straight. He also feeds me percocets and oxycontins. Paul swallows five percocets and three oxycontins every night, and I take one or two of each, which is more than enough. Seeing two distinct Pauls sitting in his dingy burgundy recliner, I laugh my ass off.

"You're all fucked-up, aren't you," Paul says, chuckling. "You remind me of your dad."

FAULT AND FRACTURE

SOME OF THE BIGGEST natural gas fields in the US—Pinedale Anticline and Jonah Field—lie just seventy miles north of Rock Springs. Together, these fields contain over fifty trillion cubic feet of methane.

People trickled into Rock Springs for the methane boom in Jonah and Anticline during my high school years, but it wasn't until I moved back from Austin that I started to notice any real changes. Work trucks with four rear wheels, dual exhaust, and an industrial toolbox in the flatbed suddenly seemed ubiquitous. While getting high alone on dirt roads stemming from highways, I'd watch Halliburton and Schlumberger trucks zoom in both directions. I noticed license plates from Louisiana, Mississippi, Arkansas, Texas, Florida, Alabama, Kentucky, and Georgia in parking lots of bars, restaurants, and stores like Walmart and Kmart.

This energy boom revolves around hydraulic fracturing, also called fracking. A wellbore drills into a rock formation, piercing a vein of shale. Workers then inject fracking fluid—a mixture of water, sand, diesel, methanol, formaldehyde, sulfuric acid, nitrilotriaceptic acid, phenol, benzene, copper, lead, and several other volatile chemicals—into the shale. The corrosive liquid fractures the surrounding rock formation, and methane rushes to the well.

Rock Springs is built upon the fleeting rush. When I interviewed the mayor in 2008, he said, "The Jonah Field is one of the largest gas providers in the nation, and we have to produce that." More than 1,100 wells are currently sucking gas from the Pinedale Anticline. In Jonah Field: more than 1,800. Trying to picture the wells, I imagine mechanized versions of Hieronymus Bosch's birds; swarms of them force their steel beaks into the ground, and they drone like massive tattoo guns.

Wyoming, Texas, California, Oklahoma, Ohio, Utah, New Mexico, Colorado, Louisiana, Pennsylvania, West Virginia, Montana, Arkansas, and New York have all gotten fucked-up by fracking. Among other things, this industry contaminates water wells, creates vegetation-destroying levels of soil salinity, and makes the surrounding air filthy.

There's a tiny town called Pavillion in Pinedale Anticline. EPA scientists found 2-butoxyethanol, another chemical in fracking fluid, in Pavillion's drinking water a few years ago. This chemical destroys red blood cells, as well as the spleen and liver.

A little over two thousand people live in Pinedale, which is just north of the Jonah Field. Emissions from the army of machines in Jonah loom over the tiny town. Each drilling rig relentlessly spews noxious smoke into the air, and trucks of every size constantly go in and out of the field. The Wyoming Department of Environmental Quality has issued several ozone alerts for Pinedale since the fracking boom took off. During these alerts, people in the small town are simply advised to stay indoors. Ozone levels in Pinedale have reached 124 parts per billion. On its worst days, ozone levels in LA only reach 114 parts per billion.

Three years ago, during my last trip to Rock Springs, I watched a wraith of white smoke, whose origin, I'm pretty sure, was Jonah Field, slither over the northern section of town, reaching toward the Outlaw. Like every other type of mining, fracking reinforces the mindset that leads people to destroy themselves, whether it be through drugs, booze, or suicide. Most people in Rock Springs know that fracking fucks everything up. But they also know that Rock Springs exists because of mining, and the town can't detach from its past. A lot of people here try not to think too far into the future. They just want to do what it takes to get through each day, even if that means destroying themselves and their surroundings. But this process creates a void of hopelessness.

Recently, I've learned about how fracking can also cause earthquakes. In 2011, earthquakes ranging from magnitudes of 2.7 to 4.0 shook areas just outside

Youngstown, Ohio. Seismologists believe that waste fluid from hydraulic fracturing caused the quakes.

When methane erupts from a well, it pushes fracking fluid back to the surface. Only a small part of the fluid can be reused, and most drilling companies just inject the liquid back into the ground to get rid of it.

Hydraulic fracturing is a process of producing controlled earthquakes, and even though most of the quakes are too small to notice, disposal sites have been causing them unintentionally. At these sites, fluid is pumped underground for longer amounts of time and at deeper levels than fracking wells. Injecting or extracting large amounts of fluid into the ground offsets the pore pressure in soil, which is largely what keeps faults from moving. Seismologists have known about the potential for waste wells to trigger earthquakes since the nineteen-sixties. The likelihood of a quake increases with the amount of waste that gets injected.

In Jonah Field alone, there are almost three times as many disposal wells as in Ohio—over 500 in Jonah versus 177 in Ohio. As a whole, there are over five thousand disposal wells in Wyoming, and each one could cause unplanned earthquakes. The faults in Pinedale Anticline and Jonah are much larger than the ones in Ohio.

*

LIVING BACK IN ROCK Springs, I mostly hung out with people from the party crowd I'd joined after high school. We all lived with our parents.

With Steve, I started going over to Mikey's house on the northern edge of town, where he lived with his mom and step-dad. I'd known Mikey since junior high but had only started hanging out with him at Garrett and Tyler's apartment. While he had an unspoken agreement with his mom—she knew that we got ridiculously stoned in Mikey's basement room—he still had to hide it from his younger brother and sister.

In my memory, it's hard to separate all the nights I went to Mikey's house with Steve, partly because of the weed, but mostly because every night was the same. Steve would pick me up at my parents' house in his Bronco, and we'd listen to Pantera on our way through town. We'd pass the Outlaw before taking a road that led to the northern edge of Rock Springs.

Hard-packed dirt roads snaked through Mikey's neighborhood. Stretches of dirt and sagebrush yawned between each house. At Mikey's tan, rectangular house, which looked like a mobile home but wasn't, Steve or I would call his cell and wait for him to come upstairs and let us in.

Inside, Mikey's mom would usually be smoking Marlboro Reds at the kitchen table. She had frazzled brown hair, and she always had dark circles beneath her eyes. Steve grew up across the street from Mikey and his mom. He'd shoot the shit with her while I stood behind him, not saying anything. Mikey's dad was a tweaker and ex-con, and I always saw a lifetime of pain in his mom's eyes.

Mikey's step-dad would usually be watching TV in the living room. A crew leader on a rig in Jonah Field, he had thick arms, short, graying hair, and he always wore dirty Wranglers. He'd look away from the TV and stare at Steve and me when we walked inside. I waved at him one night. He looked right through me, not acknowledging my presence.

Downstairs, we'd huddle in Mikey's closet and take bong rips. Matt, another guy who I'd started partying with after high school, also hung out here. I often went over to Mikey's house after I'd smoked all my own weed. Mikey would get me high, but I knew he always thought about how much longer his stash would last if he smoked it alone. After loading a bowl, he'd hold his bag up to the light, silently calculating how much he had left. I always felt unwelcome when he did this, like I was taking up too much space.

During the first few weeks after I moved back, I entertained Mikey, Matt, and Steve with my Texas stories. I'd tell them about the co-op, tripping on acid, the Ratty House, the night when Garrett slept in a gutter, and getting my U-Haul stolen at the Big Texan. But I quickly started repeating myself. Hanging out with someone I hadn't seen since moving back, I'd tell the same stories. It was almost as if I was trying to convince myself that I actually had those experiences, that I'd lived somewhere besides Rock Springs. I remember more than a few times when I lost my place in a story, and Mikey, Matt, or Steve reminded me where I'd left off, or what happened next.

After we got high, we usually played Halo on Mikey's Xbox. He always dominated all of us, laughing the entire time and calling us pussies. I tried to tell myself that I didn't care about losing to him, that there was nothing at stake, but I usually felt small when I left his house.

During one of the nights I went to Mikey's without Steve, Matt and Mikey told me that they'd just bought some coke. I'd tried cocaine in Austin but thought it was lame, immediately knowing that it would never compare to acid. Whereas coke just got you amped up, LSD revealed a new universe. I had no reason not to do it now though, so I sniffed a few lines.

A few days later, after getting stoned with Matt on a dirt road outside town, I said, "I'm never going to do cocaine again." I'm not exactly sure why I said this, but it probably had something to do with how closely related coke and meth are. To me, meth had become another word for filth. I'd started to see it as the worst possible manifestation of consumer culture—anyone can make it with products from Walmart. I didn't want to fuck with something that might lead to meth, although I also couldn't understand why anyone would get addicted to cocaine. It didn't even get you that high.

Later, during the same day I told Matt that I was never going to do coke again, he and I hung out with Mikey, who told us that he still had some blow left. Not wanting to look like a pansy, I railed a few lines. Afterward, Matt laughed and said, "I thought you said you were never going to do coke again."

"Remember how J. J. used to be straight edge?" Mikey said.

When I first started hanging out with Mikey and Matt, I wanted them to see me as a crazy party animal. Now, I realized that this was how they'd always see me, no matter what I did.

GETTING WEED IN ROCK Springs was a pain in the ass, and I often wished that I hadn't left Austin, where I could get pot whenever I wanted, and where no one cared about my last name.

A lot of Rock Springs stoners didn't like me. I was loud and obnoxious when I'd get fucked-up, and, throughout junior high and high school, I'd routinely told kids who partied that they were dumbasses. To top it all off, I was an Anselmi. Most of the stoners in town that I knew came from lower-middle class, blue-collar families. Hanging out in their dingy apartments, I'd brag about how much acid I'd done in Austin, trying to prove to them and myself that I wasn't a poser.

I only knew one dealer I could buy from regularly, and the stuff he sold was dry, crumbly, and overpriced. When I had my own weed, I'd smoke most of it alone, driving on dirt roads and staring into the unchanging sea of prairie surrounding me.

PLAYING DRUMS WAS MY favorite thing to do when I was high. My parents' insurance covered a portion of my possessions that were stolen at the Big Texan, and I used the money to buy new cymbals, cymbal stands, and a drum throne. Stoned out of my gourd and playing sloppy beats and fills, I'd periodically imagine thousands of people watching and cheering. But I also knew that my drumming was a joke.

When Dad was home, the racket coming from the basement usually grated on his nerves. Throughout high school and junior high, he'd always encouraged me to play. But now my drumming mostly seemed to irritate him, and we'd frequently get into fights after I came upstairs from the basement. I think he was worried about the person I'd become—a worthless stoner who'd just moved back into his parents' house. I only worked for my second cousin Paul part-time, and I wasn't making much money. Dad would tell me that, instead of playing the drums, I should be looking for a real job.

I also loved to hang out with my cat, Ozena, when I was stoned. My parents had taken care of her while I was in Austin, and she'd gained a lot of weight during those two and a half months. Mom would feed her a can of tuna every day, in addition to her regular food. With Ozena purring in my lap, I'd speak gibberish to her, using the bizarre baby talk that Garrett and I'd invented, and laugh hysterically. I'd put my head next to her when she cleaned herself, and she'd lick my hair with her sandpaper tongue.

At some point, I started looking at gay porn on my parents' computer while I was high. Ever since that night when, tripping on acid, I'd first fantasized about fucking around with Josh from the Ratty House, I really wanted to know what it would feel like to have another guy suck my cock. But my curiosity made me feel filthy. I mostly tried to find video clips of dudes sucking or jacking each other off, although I was also weirdly repulsed and fascinated by watching two men fuck. Jacking off to these clips, scenes from the Ratty House would flash in my mind. Terror and pleasure swirled in my stomach, and I'd come hard, immediately feeling numb with shame.

After masturbating one day, I found an old prescription of mine for oxycodone, which I'd gotten after separating my shoulder in a bike wreck two years earlier. In my room, I crushed a pill with the handle of a screwdriver and railed it, not feeling anything afterward.

WHEN THE SNOW STARTED to melt, I'd get high and ride my bike. I'd cruise down the hill leading from my parents' house, feeling completely at one with the machine. Stoned and on my bike, the harsh edges of Rock Springs were temporarily dulled. I could see geometric patterns in the asphalt, and the colors of grass and trees became more pronounced. But my bike had also started to seem like a children's toy, and I couldn't detach BMX from the sadistic Ratty riders.

Sometimes I'd ride with Steve, and occasionally with Bryan. Living in Austin, I'd called Bryan and Jared a few times to tell them about acid, even though I knew drugs made them both uneasy. Jared was still going to school in Thornton, but Bryan had one more year of high school to finish in Rock Springs.

Hanging out with Bryan during this time, I usually felt awkward. Noticeable silences replaced the brotherly banter that had defined our interaction throughout the past six years. He didn't sympathize with my decision to destroy myself, and I knew he was right to feel this way. Our friendship was originally built on the attempt to define ourselves in different ways than our dads, but I'd become what Bryan, Jared, Steve and I had so often criticized.

Although Steve would get fucked-up with me, he also worked full-time, saving up for his own place. He was mostly just having fun with weed and booze, but he knew that I was intentionally destroying myself. One night, after we'd gotten stoned on a dirt road, Steve suddenly said, "You'd have to be a true coward to kill yourself." I was surprised when he said this, and I didn't know how to respond. Thoughts about suicide had been latching onto my brain, but I hadn't told anyone.

Getting high alone, I'd listen to Pantera's "Suicide Note Pt. I" over and over. As Phil sang, "Would you look at me now? / Can you tell I'm a man?" I could feel his tar-soaked voice in my bones, and I'd picture him, Dave King, and the Ratty riders fucking each other. I also listened to Down's "Stone the Crow" on repeat. The line "I've never died before" constantly reverberated in my brain. Listening to these songs, I'd also feel trapped, wanting to hear other types of music. But my CD case only contained heavy rock and metal albums.

Like Jim Morrison and dozens of other rockers before me, I began to see death as the ultimate escape. My life revolved around getting high, and it had become static. I was constantly making up excuses to my parents about why I needed to leave the house, even though they both knew I was just leaving to get high; and I never had enough weed. Even when I had a new bag, getting stoned just wasn't that great anymore. I wanted to find escape through perception-shattering drug experiences, but smoking weed had become mundane—not to mention that I couldn't even get good shit in Wyoming. I was also beginning to recognize that, after LSD, you can't really get much higher. I wanted to permanently live in the padded psychedelic world I'd discovered on acid. In the back of my mind, I knew that dying was the best I could do.

I'd also become really curious about the moment right before death. I'd been in a few car wrecks throughout the years, experiencing the slowing of time that everyone talks about. Something told me that, right before dying, the present moment would expand, making me feel like I was swimming in a tank of clear molasses. I wanted to harness that moment, knowing it would be the greatest high of all.

WHILE I WAS IN Austin, Arielle, my seventeen-year-old little sister, had started dating John, who I knew as one of the redneck kids from school. Like several of my other classmates, he'd dropped out of high school and started working in the coalmines.

As I was about to leave my parents' house one afternoon, John pulled into the driveway in his lifted Chevy. I hadn't talked to him since tenth grade, when we took a welding class together. He was scrawny in school, but he'd grown a lot, getting taller and burlier. He'd just gotten off work, and coal dust covered his face, T-shirt, and jeans. I asked him how he'd been doing.

"Shit, I made forty-five grand the first year I dropped out of school. Best decision I ever made."

The fact that John had dropped out of high school disgusted me, even though I'd recently dropped out of college. After nineteen years in Wyoming, I knew about the violence that ignorance breeds, but I didn't understand how skewed and narrow my own worldview was. In Rock Springs, John's outlook was actually more practical than mine. I still believed that art was the only thing in life that mattered. But, living in a place where the land and weather constantly tell you that nature has no sympathy for humans, abstractions like music, literature, and visual art can easily seem unnecessary. The need to ensure physical survival dominates the Rock Springs consciousness, and physical survival is ensured by money.

Of course, I wouldn't have hated John as much if he wasn't dating Arielle. She was a straight A student through junior high and high school, constantly obsessing about her grades and studying late into the night. She also played piano, practicing until she could glide through her weekly lessons. When I stopped giving a shit about my grades, my parents would often tell me that I should study more, like Arielle.

While I was in Austin, Arielle told me that she'd been drinking a lot, probably wanting to connect with an older brother who, for most of our childhood and adolescence, was selfish and removed. Within the past few years, she's often told me that she's always looked up to me. After I moved back from Austin, I didn't see how anyone could admire a piece of shit like me. Arielle drank with John and his friends, most of whom had also dropped out of high school to work in the coalmines or gas fields. I worried that she'd marry John and stay in Rock Springs, because I knew she was way too smart for that bullshit. To me, a life in Rock Springs had become synonymous with death.

I still believed that pot and psychedelics opened the true realm of reality—a perspective everyone needed to have. Although it sounds strange to me now, I decided that turning Arielle into a pothead would help her realize that she needed to stay away from John and his redneck friends. Weed was a way to numb myself, but drugs had also shown me new layers of my mind. At the time, I thought that, if Arielle saw these layers of her psyche, she'd realize how scary John and his redneck friends truly were. They all hated weed, so I hoped that turning her into a stoner would create a distance between her and those assholes. She'd smoked pot once or twice before, but I knew that she hadn't really gotten high from the way she talked about it.

After buying a bag of weed one night, I drove east on Highway 430 with Arielle, eventually pulling off and parking on a dirt road. The Wyoming night surrounded us, wind quietly droning. Before I stuffed a nugget into my pipe, I put on Sabbath's "Sweet Leaf," feeling like an old friend was patting me on the shoulder as Ozzy sang, "You introduced me to my mind."

I took a huge hit, showing Arielle how to cover the carb on the side of the bowl with her finger and then let go, releasing the smoke. Awkwardly holding the lighter to the bowl, she inhaled smoke and immediately blew it out.

"No," I said, laughing, "you have to hold it in your lungs." I took another hit, holding it in for about five seconds. She tried to do the same but started coughing and gagging. We repeated this process until the bowl was cashed. I made sure to keep the windows rolled up to trap the smoke.

As we drove back to Rock Springs, Arielle said, "Shit, be careful, J. J. Look out for all the animals on the side of the road."

"What?" There was nothing around us but sagebrush and prairie grass.

"Can't you see all the animals? Look at the animals."

Proud that I'd gotten her completely ripped, I laughed my ass off. The next day, Arielle told me that I was right: she'd smoked pot before but hadn't experienced anything like the night before. During the upcoming weeks, I'd watch her develop a craving for weed that rivaled my own. Like me, Arielle would always connect weed with Dad's pot smoking, the reasons for it, and our embarrassment when kids at school asked us about his drug use. But being a stoner also gave me a place in the world, and I wanted to show her this place, even though it was a void.

Now, I refuse to forgive myself for getting my little sister high for the first time. Within a year after this night, the Rock Springs drug culture would devour her, and she would experience horrors during this time that I'll never comprehend.

Even though she's told me not to blame myself for anything that's happened to her, I'll probably always hate myself for introducing Arielle to weed. It's easy to say that she would've eventually gotten into drugs anyway—we're Anselmis, our dad gets high, and we're from Rock Springs. But I'm her older brother, and she's always admired me, often finding more value in my words and actions than I do. During this time, I liked to believe in the bullshit idea that my self-destruction began and ended with me.

A FEW NIGHTS AFTER getting Arielle high, I went to a party with a few of my female friends, Brittany, Jessie, and Elysa. After the party, we drove to a gas station just past the Outlaw to get potato logs and chicken strips.

As I drunkenly ordered my food, Jason and Philip, two rednecks that Arielle's boyfriend hung out with, walked inside. Jason was short and stout, with a shaved head, thick arms, and pudgy cheeks. He stared at me, hate emanating from his eyes. Philip was skinny and a bit taller than Jason, with ears that stuck straight out. Raised in torrents of neglect, hate, and abuse, they were both high school dropouts. They wore dirty Wranglers and camouflage hunting caps. I was wearing a yellow Jimi Hendrix shirt and a knitted beanie that Sarah, my friend from the co-op, had given me before I left Austin.

I heard one of them mutter, "Fucking faggot." During this time, the ratio of men to women in Rock Springs was something like eight or nine to one, because most of the people who'd moved to town for the fracking boom were men. Brittany, Jessie, and Elysa were all cute, so I'm sure it irritated Jason and Philip to see me, an Anselmi, with three girls and no other dudes.

Sitting in my truck, my friends and I ate our food. When I pulled onto the main drag, Philip's lifted Dodge with dual exhaust shot out from the parking lot. Philip tailgated me, revving his engine and flashing his brights. Scared shitless and not sure what to do, I just kept driving.

About ten minutes later, near East Junior High, Philip pulled up next to me, driving in the wrong lane on a narrow street. Jason leaned out the window, screaming, "Pull over and fight you little faggot!"

"Don't do it, J. J." Elysa said.

"Yeah, fuck these assholes," Brittany said. "Just keep driving."

I wanted to kill Jason and Philip, but knew that either one could easily kick my ass. I took a sudden left turn and floored it. Philip followed closely behind, still flashing his brights on and off, on and off.

Finally, after about five minutes of driving around this neighborhood, Philip blasted past us and drove away. Brittany, Jessie, and Elysa all told me that I'd done the right thing, but I felt like a pitiful excuse for a man.

I'D BEEN TRYING TO get acid in Rock Springs but couldn't find any, so I was excited when Elysa told me that she could hook me up with some mushrooms. She ended up getting them on 4/20—a stoner holiday. When I picked Elysa up at her mom's house, she held up two bags of mushrooms.

"Look at those caps, dude," she said, exaggerating her stoner drawl. "They're like pure blue. We're going to have such a badass 4/20." The off-white mushrooms were long with curled stems, looking like pictures of shrooms I'd seen in *High Times*. Elysa told me that her chemist friend had grown them.

After we each ate an eighth, I headed east on Highway 430. Wind pushed hard against my truck, making me veer to the right. We drove to a park in Arrowhead Springs, the small community where Bryan still lived with his mom and dad. I started to feel giddy, but, as soon as I got out of my truck, frigid, metallic wind wrapped around my brain, and I had to get back inside. I wished we had somewhere to go where we could trip in peace.

On our way back to Rock Springs, we passed SF Phosphates, a large chemical plant. It looked like a dystopian city—spectral, blinking lights, wormlike piping, and large metal cylinders. Plumes of smoke rose from concrete pillars and coagulated into a massive, diseased snake that coiled above the plant.

I pulled off the road and puked my brains out, Elysa watching from the passenger seat. Afterward, geometric patterns in the road and dirt became more defined. Elysa told me that she wanted to go home.

When I dropped her off at her mom's house, she said that she'd see me later, although I'd been hoping she'd ask me to stay. I didn't want to go to my parents' house, but I also didn't want to drive around anymore, wasting gas and feeling claustrophobic in my truck.

I parked in my parents' driveway and stared at my BMX ramp, which still sat next to the retaining wall. My tags on the quarter pipe—"Six Six Six," "Destroy," and "Hate"—which were still visible, seemed idiotic. I couldn't believe that, just one year earlier, I'd thought I was a badass for spray-painting those things.

I walked into the living room, where Mom was reading. Her lips concretized into a frown. In that moment, she seemed like a deteriorating statue. On her face, I think I was seeing the pain and disappointment she felt while watching her son destroy himself—the same pain and disappointment that swirled beneath her relationship with my dad.

"Are you okay, baby?"

"Yeah, I'm fine," I said, quickly. "I'm just really drunk." As I turned to go upstairs, I looked at Dad's world-record fish. Its tail swished back and forth, and its yellow eyes stared through me.

Upstairs, I lay down on my bed, staring at a glow-in-the-dark star sticker that I'd put on my ceiling when I was a kid, hoping it would expand into a psychedelic constellation. But it looked the same as it always did.

When I closed my eyes, a movie of myself played in my head: after waking up the next morning, I'd go downstairs to Dad's hunting room and take his .44 magnum. Twenty or thirty miles out of town, kneeling in the dirt, I'd put the gun to my temple and pull the trigger. A stunning wraith of white energy would finally be released from my body. *Of course,* I thought. *You're supposed to kill yourself.*

The same scene repeated in my head for the next five hours.

HANGING OUT AT MIKEY'S step-dad's house a few nights later, Mikey told me that he had some shrooms left over from his birthday two months earlier. "You can eat them if you want," he said, handing me a bag of crushed stems and caps.

I ate the mushrooms, partly because I wanted to show Matt and Mikey how badass I was. But I also held out hope that psychedelics would reveal my true life path, refusing to admit how quickly tripping had become a dead end. At the same time, I knew exactly where another trip would lead, and I needed a catalyst. I ate the eighth, washing the stale taste away with gulps of cheap wine.

After we smoked a bowl in Mikey's closet, Matt drove us to a nearby gas station, where we stocked up on chips, candy, and soda. On our way back, I watched a dead tree in front of someone's trailer multiply into several versions of the same tree, and I thought about how endlessly repetitive life was, especially in Rock Springs. When we got back to Mikey's house, I told him and Matt that I needed to leave.

I remember being relieved that my parents weren't home when I pulled into the driveway. Now, I wouldn't have to try to sneak a gun out of the house while they were home. I went down to the basement and tried to get into Dad's gunroom, but the door was locked, which was unusual. Irritated, I decided to try something else.

Upstairs, I popped the remaining ten or so pills of my old oxycodone prescription.

An image of the large cliffs near my family's cabin in Bondurant flashed in my head. I thought about how beautiful it would be to jump from one of them, my body getting pummeled by the rocks below. Before I left my parents' house, I grabbed a pen and notepad. I also took a fifth of Jack Daniels from the liquor cabinet.

I filled up at a gas station next to the Outlaw. Inside, the clerk talked and laughed with her friend, who was sitting on the counter. Their eyes latched onto me when I walked in, and I could feel that they were tweakers. The clerk, a girl I knew from school, and her friend, a middle-aged man with a skeevy beard, both had meth-eroded teeth.

Meth has been a plague in Rock Springs for as long as I can remember, but I didn't start to see it as being inherently evil until I moved back from Austin, where I'd constantly been lectured about the malevolence of corporate America. Although I was destroying myself with weed and psychedelics, I also saw these drugs as tools for expanding my consciousness. Meth seemed like the opposite: a way to narrow one's consciousness and focus on the day-to-day. Killing myself seemed like a better idea than smoking meth, and I thought everyone should feel the same way. Because the people at the towing company in Amarillo were tweakers, meth had also become attached to theft in my mind.

I became convinced that meth was a conspiracy: corporations were producing the ingredients—allergy medication, pipe cleaner, paint thinner, rat poison, and several others—and then disseminating information on how to make the drug. I also started to believe that oil and gas companies were funneling meth into Rock Springs because it creates the ideal worker. I can't remember how many stories I've heard about tweakers working in Jonah or Anticline for over twenty-four hours straight. Someone once told me that a guy who'd been up for three days on crystal got his arm caught in some machinery on a rig. The machine ripped a sheet of skin from his arm, but the guy wanted to keep working.

I paid for my gas and left, not making eye contact with the clerk or her friend. I stared at the sign for the Outlaw when I passed it. Wind pressed on my truck from every direction, like an invisible vise.

A few miles outside town, an ocean of prairie sprawled. I thought about how, at any moment, I could smash my truck into a guardrail, or drive off a cliff. The possibility of killing myself became a room in my brain. Inside this room, my fingers tingled with power. I think this night was the first time I truly understood—in a way I could feel in my bones—that I could always kill myself, that existing is a choice.

I put *The Great Southern Trendkill* in my CD player, wanting to hear "Suicide Note Pt. I." Eerie synths and acoustic guitar notes swirled. As Phil sang, "Would you look at me now? / Can you tell I'm a man?" I started screaming at him, calling him a coward for glorifying his suicidal thoughts but never actually killing himself. Dying seemed like the easiest thing I could do. I orchestrated my notes—one to Phil Anselmo, and one to my family—by screaming them.

I remember the rest of the drive in snippets. I tried to listen to Tool, but Danny Carey's complex drumming coiled around my chest, making me think about how badly I sucked. The same thing happened when I put in a Sabbath CD.

The Wyoming night yawned.

Three hours north of Rock Springs, I drove into the one-hundred-person town of Bondurant, a place I'd been visiting since I was a kid. Suddenly, I was jolted out of my trance. I thought about Lindsay and my cat. I thought about Steve, Jared, and Bryan. I thought about my mom, sister, and dad. I thought about my mom reading my notes and looking at my splattered gore at the bottom of a cliff, trying to identify my body.

I decided to turn around.

*

EXCISION

THE SURGEON DRAWS AN ellipse on my forearm with black marker, injecting anesthetic at several different points. When my skin is numb, she delicately traces the marker plan with her scalpel. Each cut loosens taut forearm flesh that, throughout the past eight years, has been stretching and regenerating to compensate for over twenty square inches of removed, tattooed skin.

Six inches down from the beginning point, she cuts out the remaining scar tissue, formed during the seven months since I've last gone through an excision. A burning sting pulses through my arm.

I see a reflection of gray muscle in the glass cover of the surgical lamp. Small whorls of skin dot a strip of gauze on the surgeon's tray. Slowly, she works up my forearm, stretching skin and suturing.

While she threads, I remind myself that this scarification process has kept me sober, which has, in turn, kept me from dropping out of school. During the upcoming months, my body will build a protective barrier around this wound, only to be excised after my skin has once again stretched enough for another procedure. Although the surgeon initially told me that I'd be done in two years, it's been eight since I started, and at least two or three more years of excisions loom.

*

IN SEPTEMBER OF 2006, a few months after my dad's motorcycle-riding friend, Joey Hay, committed suicide, and a year and five months after I drove to Bondurant to kill myself, I stopped drinking and getting high.

About nine months earlier, I'd found out that some of my BMX buddies from Denver were looking for a roommate, at which point I was partying as hard as ever. That spring, I had moved out of Rock Springs and enrolled at Denver Community College, knowing that I needed to get out of Wyoming.

During the spring semester, I worked at a shitty pizza place, smoked and drank constantly, and half-assed my classes. When I was honest with myself, I knew that, if I was ever going to finish school, I had to get sober. I also knew this wouldn't happen in a party house where I was known as the resident stoner. In June, I moved into an apartment downtown, alone. Joey shot himself a few weeks later.

I tried to quit getting fucked-up a few times throughout the summer, but the longest I made it was three weeks. Searching for the rigid stability I was able to find throughout high school and junior high, I'd tell myself that I was meant to be straight edge. I'd rant to my friends about how society revolves around getting fucked-up, and how I wanted no part in this.

Then, a few days or a week later, I'd convince myself that I could control my pot smoking and drinking. Most of my favorite musicians smoked and drank, and I somehow still believed that I was destined to be a famous drummer. I remember waking up after ruining my brief stints of sobriety—which happened several times—and feeling empty, erased. In the back of my mind, I knew that I needed something extreme to keep me sober, that I needed to destroy parts of myself in order to create a new sense of personal identity.

In September, I went to a kegger and forced myself to only have one beer. After I drank it, though, I couldn't stop thinking, "You can have one more." I didn't have another drink, but the phrase constantly repeated in my head, and I thought about how much more fun this otherwise boring party would be if I got completely shit-faced. Throughout the past two years, my reaction to these situations had been to ask myself what Dimebag Darrel would do, and act accordingly. But Joey's death and my own drug-fueled thoughts of killing myself made partying inseparable from suicide in my brain.

Some of my mental cobwebs cleared during the following month. For me, weed made all the daily bullshit a lot harder to get through. I was constantly forgetting something important, like paying a bill or turning in some form for school, which only created new problems. After my short-term memory came back, I started to see society as a maze of inconvenience and irritation rather than a sea of grinding cogs. I also began to realize how much space weed and booze had occupied in my brain. Now, instead of worrying about my next bag or how to get booze, I could focus on other things. But new levels of anxiety also crept into this mental space.

Although I was clean, I woke up every day for the next two years seeing psychedelic patterns writhe on ceilings and walls.

I'D NEVER STOPPED HATING my tattoos after living in Austin. Each one reminded me of who I was and where I was from. In Wyoming, my tattoos were badass. In Austin and Denver, they made me feel like a white trash jerk.

On one level, Wyoming and heavy metal had become attached to idiocy in my mind, ideas that were reinforced by my smart-ass roommates in Denver and their hipster friends. We often hung out in the living room of our rental house, getting twisted and listening to underground metal. Although I knew these guys were assholes, they also showed me bands like Torche, Big Business, and

Saviours—bands that understand what it means to be heavy while also conveying a sense of irony.

Like the Ratty House riders, my roommates and their friends often asked about my tattoos, never hiding their laughter as I explained each one. Four or five guys would huddle around me, saying stuff like, "Fuck yeah, J. J., that's badass," when I showed them my Pantera tattoo, or Tony Iommi's guitar on my left wrist. Laughing, they'd talk about getting tattoos of metal bands, too.

A few of these guys loved to ironically watch Pantera's *Home Videos*. Just one year earlier, I'd watched this same footage of Dime, Phil, Vinnie, and Rex, laughing at their antics while also idolizing them. Now, I couldn't help but think about what dumbasses these guys were, constantly saying and doing incredibly stupid shit. My roommates and their friends would laugh hysterically throughout the *Home Videos*, constantly mocking my metal heroes.

Hanging out with these guys at first, I felt like I'd found a new, improved version of my crew from Garrett and Tyler's apartment. But, unlike Garrett, Tyler, Nate, and Steve, when these dudes told me I was a badass, it was always with a smirk.

While this teasing made me insecure, it also helped me see how I'd tried to stifle my mental evolution by inhabiting a metalhead caricature. Soon though, I also started to oversimplify what metal meant for me, not realizing that my attraction to destruction, which is deeply tied to metal, is both my tragic flaw and saving grace.

My ink also reminded me of John, Philip, and Jason, the scary rednecks from Rock Springs. They all thought tattoos were badass, and I'd heard John talk about the tattoos he and Jason planned to get. A lot of roughnecks and coalminers in Wyoming spend their extra money on shitty ink. I hated Wyoming and often wished that I'd grown up somewhere else, but my tattoos constantly reminded me that I'll always be from Rock Springs.

I STARTED RESEARCHING TATTOO removal in October, after a month of staying clean—my longest stretch at that point. I wanted to completely erase my tattoos, but I found out that laser removal leaves a faint shadow of the original. One technician told me that, in the best-case scenario, a laser could only remove ninety-five percent of a tattoo. Even though other people probably wouldn't notice the shadows, I wanted to completely disconnect from my past, not seeing the violence in this ideal. In my case, this violence became physical as well as mental.

I found a plastic surgeon who removed tattoos via excision—a process of cutting out pieces of tattooed flesh and suturing the skin back together. Each excision creates a new scar, which, until the tattoo is gone, the surgeon also cuts out during the procedures. When the process is done, I'll be left with large, gnarly scars instead of tattoos. The surgeon warned me that, while going through this process, my tattoos would look worse than they originally did, with scars cutting through the black ink.

That fall, I don't think anyone could've talked me out of getting my tattoos excised. I've always been a hardheaded motherfucker, and when I decide to do something, there's usually no turning back. But I did decide to keep the effeminate Sabbath demon on my right shoulder, both because I wanted and had to. I knew Black Sabbath's music would always be part of who I am, and also that removing this tattoo, which covers several square inches of skin on my shoulder, wouldn't be possible via excision. If the tattoo was smaller and in a place on my body that would make it easier to remove, I think I still would've kept it, although I'm also not sure if this is true.

I started to picture myself with scars instead of tattoos, deciding that the scars would represent my return to straight edge.

I HAD TO KEEP going after the first excision.

During that first procedure, the surgeon cut out 'Killing Yourself to Live' from my left wrist, and the center portion of the CFH tattoo from my right. Just before she began, I felt the same uncertainty lodge in my throat that I'd felt before getting each of my tattoos. But I told myself that, if I was going to stay sober, I *had* to go through with this. Reclining in the surgeon's chair, I stared at the gray tissue beneath my skin before she sutured me back together.

As scar tissue formed on my wrists during the upcoming weeks—red wounds slowly transforming into white skin—I realized how grotesque my arms were going to look until I finished the excision process. After the next session, my tattoos became unintelligible. Scars cut through my ink, and you couldn't tell what the tattoos were originally unless you'd seen them before. I immediately regretted my decision to have them removed. At the same time, I knew that, once the ink was gone, my scars would be beautiful in a weird and fucked-up way.

Looking at the jagged scar on my forearm, as well as scars crawling up both of my wrists, I see my mental progression. If I'd never started this process, I'm not sure if I'd have my MFA, if I'd ever have become a teacher and writer.

But this scarification has fucked me up in ways that I never expected. Although getting tattoos of metal bands was a way to conform to a metalhead stereotype, my tattoos also gave me access to a sense of community that I haven't been able to find again. And they didn't prevent me from interacting with people. My scarification has introduced me to completely new levels of social isolation.

When I wear short sleeves, the first thing people typically notice about me is the massive scar on my right forearm, which prompts questions about what happened. I've lied a few times, telling people that the scar is from a gnarly wreck on my road bike. Usually though, if someone asks about my scars, I tell them that I'm going through an intense and bizarre tattoo removal process, which leads to questions about why I'm doing this, and what the tattoos were originally. It's hard to pick up casual conversation after you tell someone that you're having pieces of yourself surgically removed. When my scars are exposed, I can only find intermittent comfort in social situations, which is worsened by the fact that I won't allow myself to drink—even though I think I could control it if I really wanted to now. Even with close friends, I neurotically fold my arms or position myself in ways so they won't be able to see my scars.

At metal shows, I feel disconnected from other fans in ways I never foresaw. I used to see myself as inhabiting the center of the metal world. Now, I feel like I'm always on the periphery, even when playing shows.

A typical conversation at a metal show:

Me: "Have you heard that new Converge album, dude? It's so good."

Metal dude: "Fuck yeah, man. I love that shit."

The guy has shoulder length hair and tattoos covering his arms. I started talking to him because he's wearing a shirt of one of my favorite bands.

We feel at ease with each other, bonded by our enthusiasm. But then the guy notices my scars, and I can tell that he suddenly feels uncomfortable. As we keep talking, he glances at my arms. He's curious but feels like he shouldn't ask about my scars, not wanting to offend me. I can't count how many times this scenario has played out.

Routinely getting asked about my scars, as well as the looks of confusion, fascination, and disgust that I get on a daily basis—if I saw someone with massive scars snaking through their tattoos, I'd stare, too—eventually made me feel physically repulsive. It took me four years after I started this scarification to finally get myself to kiss a girl I'd been dating, although I'd had a few opportunities—times when it was more awkward *not* to kiss a girl. Nevertheless, my self-imposed isolation led me to focus on school, which helped me realize that I'm a writer.

For two to three weeks after an excision, I can't play the drums. Before I started this process, and ever since I began playing, I'd never gone more than a few days without practicing. During that first two-week period, I needed a creative outlet, and I gravitated toward writing, beginning a very early and shitty draft of this book. I fell in love with the space writing opened in my brain, which, I think, is the same space I've often found through BMX, vandalism, and acts of self-destruction.

On one level, I'm ashamed of my scars, knowing that they're products of the same extremist thinking I used to define myself in high school, which, in large part, led to my destructive use of drugs and booze in the first place. My scars are also a different kind of tattoo, symbols I'll have on my body for the rest of my life.

At the same time, I can't deny that the need to make my scarification mean something has kept me from getting high or drunk, which has made me more productive. I constantly scold myself for not doing enough, and I can only rarely shut off that critical voice. Without finding meaning in my scars, I'm not sure that I'd want to keep living, even though I also know this meaning is fundamentally fucked up.

WHEN I LOOK AT my arms, I see how violent it was to believe that I could become a completely different person. But this scarification process has also permanently changed who I am.

Newly sober and just beginning my tattoo removal, I started to view Metallica, Slayer, Pantera, and Sabbath through a more thoughtful lens, which eventually became part of me. Now, I see Black Sabbath as a husk of itself, each member knowing that they can get away with half-assed musicianship while still playing packed stadiums. The band's legacy is undeniable—they fucking *invented* metal. But, when they play now, the jazz flourish in Geezer, Ward, and Iommi's playing that made the early albums so heavy is gone, even though, if they really wanted to, I think they could be tight again. Throughout the years, I've watched countless underground bands that will never make a living on their music, but who refuse to settle for anything less than their best, and I now hold most musicians, including myself, to this standard.

I've also come to understand what should've been clear about Pantera a long time ago: they're ignorant rednecks, sporting the Confederate flag on instruments and banners, also printing it on their merch. Throughout junior high and high school, I didn't think about how fucked up this actually is. I bought into the bullshit idea that the band was just proud of their Southern roots—that flying the rebel flag isn't racist. After living in a mostly-black neighborhood in Denver and taking a few eye-opening sociology classes about race, I've learned that, in order to attempt to understand the current picture of racial inequality in America, you can't disconnect our country's history with racism from the present, which means that the Confederate flag will always represent a pro-slavery South. Phil also used to give speeches at packed Pantera shows about blacks hating whites, as if reverse racism was actually oppressive.

Despite their punk and anarchist roots, James and Lars of Metallica have become greedy, Republican assholes, and they haven't released a decent record since the early nineties. While their first four albums are all classics, Metallica is also largely responsible for what I like to call mall metal—bands like Godsmack, Creed, and countless others that regurgitate the generic rock that Metallica popularized with *The Black Album*.

Throughout the years, I've also thought a lot about Metallica's lawsuit against Napster. While I agree with the idea that artists should be able to earn a living with their craft, I think Metallica's lawsuit stemmed from their own shortsightedness about what the Internet is and the changes it would inevitably bring. They were also millionaires when they sued Napster. Downloading and streaming makes it virtually impossible for most bands to earn a living on album sales, but the Internet has also placed new levels of power in musicians' hands in terms of distribution, as well as information about recording.

In examining my idol worship throughout my late teens and early twenties, I've realized that Slayer's uncomplicated disavowal of religion has become a form of religion for a lot of fans. Also, the hatred in Slayer's music often seems scary to me now. I'm still an angry guy that dislikes most forms of organized religion, but I try to be smarter about it than I once was. The last time I saw Slayer, I remember feeling uneasy as I listened to people in the crowd rabidly chanting, "Slayer! Slayer! Slayer!" Just a few years earlier, I would've been chanting right along with these fans.

But these thoughts have never been able to overshadow the fact that, when I listen to Sabbath, Pantera, Metallica, or Slayer, I still feel compelled to headbang. Although criticism creeps in, listening to metal is still an electric experience for me. Jamming to any of these bands at home or in my car, I can stop thinking for a few moments and just rock the fuck out. I still love the raw energy in metal, and heavy music is easily the most fun to play. I get to completely let loose, beating the shit out of my drums. I've played in multiple heavy bands throughout the years, and I'm currently jamming with a doom band, as well as a blackened post-metal project.

MY PANTERA TATTOO HAS been replaced by a fat, two-inch-long scar. Only a sliver of Tony Iommi's guitar remains on my left wrist. An asymmetrical white scar slices through the splotch of black ink that was once the guitar body. A massive shard of pearly scar tissue is consuming the skull on my right forearm, and the bats that went through the skull jut from my scar.

With a queasy sense of regret, I often wonder who I'd be if I had never begun this excision process. At the same time, I think it was weirdly inevitable that I'd become this neurotic, isolated, self-loathing, awkward and bespectacled man with short blond hair, a red beard, and scars.

ACKNOWLEDGMENTS

I CAN'T THANK MY MOM and sister enough for their undying support and encouragement. You're both my main sources of inspiration—always. Also for their amazingly kind support throughout the years (even when I was acting like a shit head), thanks to everyone in the Wessel clan. Grandpa, thanks for teaching me, at an early age, about the importance of storytelling.

Jared, Bryan, Steve, and Paul, you guys are family. Thank you for believing in me and being who you are. TBC will never die.

John Hales put an insane amount of work into giving me much needed feedback throughout the drafting process, and he's been nothing short of an editor of this book. For this, I can't thank you enough, John.

For all of the amazing conversations and brilliant feedback, heartfelt thanks to Rusty Birdwell, Shane Velez, Xai Lee, Michael Flatt, and Jeffery Gleaves.

Also for invaluable feedback and support, thank you to Steven Church (your idea on how to open the book saved my ass) and my amazing colleagues at CSU Fresno: Jamie Barker, Carole Firstman, Yinka Reed Nolan, Nicole Lassen, Erin Alvarez, Rachanan Anunnub, Belén Lopez, Gavin McCall, Sally Vogel, Phyllis Brotherton, Melanie Weger Kachadoorian, Ashley Wells, Jackie Heffron Williams, and Christina Hayes. Huge thanks also to Christopher Merkner, my first creative writing teacher. You taught me about the ongoing process of literary self-awareness via the gospel of Barry Hannah and Dennis Johnson.

Also for much-appreciated encouragement and inspiration, thanks to Remy Mason, Lindsay Bauer, Jason Andrade, Randa Jarrar, Brandi Spaethe, Grant and Melissa Netzorg, Ronald Dzerigian, Sean Kinneen, Carleigh Takemoto, Stacey Balkun, Marcus Allen, Andrew Thompson, Andre Yang, Jared Mitchell, Justin Stubbert, Brian Donald Duncan, Connie Hales, Ryan Tallman, Tim Skeen, Jason Heller, John King, Janna Marlies Maron, Philip Joseph, Mike McClane, and Amy Vidali.

Rare Bird is precisely that in the context of the publishing world. You all picked this motherfucker from the slush pile, which is about as punk rock as it gets. Tyson Cornell and Julia Callahan, thanks for everything. Alice Marsh-Elmer, you're a complete badass, and I can't thank you enough for the massive amount of work that you've put into this book. Hearty thanks also to Samantha Allen for her thoughtful edits and suggestions.

Finally, I'd like to offer gratitude to Robert Clark Young of *Connotation Press*, Christian Lukather of *The Writing Disorder*, and the late Jake Adam York of *Copper Nickel*, all of whom not only published parts of this manuscript but also expressed encouragement at early stages of the drafting process. Thanks also to the editors of *Under The Gum Tree*, *Flyway*, *Entropy*, *Slab*, *The Jackson Hole Review*, and *The Dr. T. J. Eckleburg Review* for publishing parts of this manuscript—typically in different forms.